Interdisciplinary Perspectives on Shame

Interdisciplinary Perspectives on Shame

Methods, Theories, Norms, Cultures, and Politics

Edited by
Cecilea Mun

LEXINGTON BOOKS
Lanham • Boulder • New York • London

Published by Lexington Books
An imprint of The Rowman & Littlefield Publishing Group, Inc.
4501 Forbes Boulevard, Suite 200, Lanham, Maryland 20706
www.rowman.com

6 Tinworth Street, London SE11 5AL, United Kingdom

British Library Cataloguing in Publication Information Available

Library of Congress Control Number:2019950359

ISBN 978-1-4985-6136-5 (cloth)
ISBN 978-1-4985-6137-2 (electronic)

Contents

Acknowledgments

The editor of and the contributors to this edited collection would like to thank everyone who helped us in our endeavor to bring about this edited collection, especially Lexington Book's anonymous referees, and our colleagues, friends, and family who provided us with their constructive comments, support, and/or care. Thank you!

Introduction

Each chapter in this edited collection represents an *interdisciplinary* perspective on shame rather than a *disciplinary*, *multidisciplinary*, or *transdisciplinary* perspective. Unlike a disciplinary perspective, which is circumscribed within the boundaries of a single discipline, each chapter is written from a perspective that reaches beyond these boundaries and into the wells of knowledge of other disciplines, while also remaining squarely rooted within the author's primary discipline. It is a perspective that explicitly accepts the value of the knowledge offered by other disciplines, not only in their own right but also as contributions toward the creation of new knowledge, and the distribution of both old and new knowledge. Given the fact that each chapter is authored by at least one author of a single discipline rather than multiple authors of various distinct disciplines, each chapter represents a perspective that is not multidisciplinary. Furthermore, no chapter represents a transdisciplinary perspective, which aims to reconceive both interdisciplinary and multidisciplinary perspectives so as to erase all boundaries between the relevant disciplines.

This edited collection, as a whole, approaches shame as a richly layered experience, and focuses on the following three themes: questions about theory and methods for studying shame, normative considerations regarding shame and its import to understanding ourselves as individuals and in relation to our communities, and how the context of culture and politics, broadly construed, affects our understanding of what shame is and who we are in the face of shame. More specifically, it aims to weave together the various threads in the scholarly discourse on shame into an intricate and deep understanding of what shame is, and its implications on our lives. It does so by collecting and organizing the contributions contained herein into two parts: The first part addresses questions about (1) how the science of shame ought to be pursued, (2) how it ought to identify its object of study, (3) what methods are appropriate for a rigorous scientific study of shame, and (4) how a method of study can determine or influence a theory of shame. The second part addresses questions of (5) how shame is related to a normative understanding of ourselves as individual persons, which includes an understanding of ourselves as epistemic and moral agents within a community, (6) how culture and politics affect the value and import of shame, and (7) what the relationship between culture and politics is in the construction of shamed identities. These questions are intended to address a broad range of concerns—from questions about appropriate methods for research and theorizing about shame to questions about how such theories, along with one's normative, cultural, and political background, can inform the way in which one understands (i.e., makes sense of) one's self, one's community, and one's lived experiences.

Pedagogically, it aims to both introduce the reader to the scholarly discourse on shame, and to address questions and concerns that any rigorous, scholarly study of shame ought to consider. It seeks to help inspire both novice and experts—from diverse disciplines and at various levels of expertise, including (under)graduates, (post)graduates, and professional scholars—who are interested in the rigorous study of shame, and emotions in general, to engage the past, present, and future discourse on shame by providing them with an accessible opportunity to engage the scholarly discourse on shame. It addresses preexisting concerns within the discourse on shame and emotion, including the problems that have persisted throughout the scholarly discourse, and gives voice to alternative perspectives that are often ignored yet ought to be recognized. Each chapter, and the edited collection as a whole, therefore adds new insights that move the preexisting discourse beyond its persistent problems or makes these problems more tractable for the project of understanding shame and its import to our self, others, and our community. It thereby bridges past scholarly research with future research, and each chapter is both timely and on the cutting-edge of research on shame.

Past scholarly research on shame has addressed a broad range of concerns on the topic, including concerns regarding the appropriate methods for research, the concept of shame, the interpersonal aspects of shame, the psychopathological aspects of shame, and the cultural aspects of shame. Many of these contributions take a distinctly white, cis-male, heteronormative, biological, evolutionary, psychological approach or perspective to understanding the phenomenon of shame. Although these contributions are still significant to the current and future discourse on shame, they do not address marginalized or emerging interests, concerns, or perspectives. For example, as illustrated by at least some of the chapters in this edited collection, prototypical, standard accounts of shame in the past literature have characterized shame as a self-conscious emotion of global, negative self-assessment, which can be understood as presupposing a white, cis-male, heteronormative perspective that can both establish and reinforce the stigmatization and marginalization of women and minorities. Although such contributions are valuable to the discourse on shame, they do not directly or explicitly engage all the questions and concerns about shame that are of interest to contemporary and future researchers. They also do not offer insights into how the approaches, methods, or works from the humanities and arts (e.g., philosophy and literature) can be employed in the science of shame.

CHAPTER SUMMARIES

Part I: Methods and Theories

In chapter 1, "Shame is a Folk Term Unsuitable as a Technical Term in Science," Dolichan Kollerath, Mariko Kikutani, and James A. Russell also draw primarily from the disciplines of linguistics, history, sociology, and philosophy in order to argue from a psychological perspective for the claim that the ordinary English word "shame" is not an object of scientific inquiry insofar as it refers to some kind of fundamental phenomenon of study. They therefor propose a bifurcated approach for the science of shame: the *descriptive program*, which takes the meaning of the everyday English word "shame," including its associated concept(s), as its object of study, and the *prescriptive program*, which takes the fundamental psychological aspects of shame to be its objects of study. Kollerath, Kikutani, and Russell also propose a prescriptive project in favor of a standard account of shame, and regards a global negative self-evaluation to be a significant aspect of many experiences of shame.

In chapter 2, "Unification through the Rationalities and Intentionalities of Shame," Cecilea Mun also draws primarily from the disciplines of psychology and sociology in order to argue from a philosophical perspective for a unified approach to the scientific study of shame that is grounded in the experience—what some might call the phenomenology—of shame. In contrast with Kollerath, Kikutani, and Russell's proposal, Mun's unified approach maintains the significance of the intimate relationship between the ordinary language, English word "shame," its equivalent translations in other languages, and the phenomenon of shame to scientific enquiry, broadly construed. This is evident in her reliance on the *ontological rationality of shame*, which necessarily reflects ordinary language judgments about the appropriateness of shame on given occasions. She concludes with a proposal for a non-standard account of shame, which does not regard a global, negative self-evaluation to be an essential, necessary aspect of all experiences of shame.

In chapter 3, "Oppression and Liberation via the Rationalities of Shame," Cecilea Mun argues again from her interdisciplinary philosophical perspective, which also draws primarily on the disciplines of psychology and sociology, in support of her phenomenologically inspired, non-standard account of shame. She takes a distinctively feminist approach to theorizing shame and stresses the oft-ignored concern of how choices made at the level of theorizing about shame can have significant implications on lived experiences of shame. She deconstructs standard, ordinary English-language experiences of shame and shaming, primarily in the United States, in order to uncover the specific ways in which standard accounts of shame can function as mechanisms for epistemic injustice, not only to one's self-understanding but also to community understandings of individuals and their experiences.

In chapter 4, "The Virtues of Epistemic Shame in Critical Dialogue," Laura Candiotto explicates a phenomenologically inspired, functionalist, embodied approach to theorizing shame. Also drawing on the disciplines of psychology and education, she looks to the works of Plato, as well as Aristotle, in order to inform the reader of the positive transformative function that shame can have as an epistemic emotion, especially within the context of cooperative group learning. In doing so, she challenges the common, contemporary, Western notion that shame is necessarily associated with negative consequences and negative community interactions by calling our attention to the epistemically inclusive nature of some experiences of shame—*"lovely shame."*

In chapter 5, "Being In and Excluded from the Sociotechnical World," Matthew Rukgaber argues from an interdisciplinary philosophical perspective that also draws from the disciplines of anthropology and disability studies. He also highlights a specific kind of experience of shame—*"prepersonal shame"*—in order to demonstrate the possibilities of a *phenomenological approach* to theorizing shame. Through his account, one not only gains an understanding of shame as, ultimately, an exclusion from a community, but also an appreciation of both the taken-for-granted way of experiencing the world and the difficulties this causes people who are labeled with a disability. By relying on the works of phenomenologist Maurice Merleau-Ponty and Martin Heidegger, he introduces a non-standard account that theorizes shame as an existential feeling and affective attunement, which is experienced as a pre-reflective, bodily engagement with the world that does not require a fine-grained cognitive component, as with beliefs or image-like perceptions.

Part II: Norms, Cultures, and Politics

In chapter 6, "Nietzsche, Shame, and the Seal of Liberation," Daniel R. Herbert writes from the interdisciplinary perspective of the history of philosophy in order to argue for a particular interpretation of the controversially regarded existentialist and phenomenologist Friedrich Nietzsche's account of shame. He does so by first identifying the two forces that, for Nietzsche, mediate shame—the *Dionysian* and the *Apollonian*—and then by placing Nietzsche's account in opposition to Arthur Schopenhauer's modern, Christian-inspired account of shame. In doing so, Herbert brings light to a perspective that has been mostly ignored in both the literature on shame and Nietzsche scholarship, which often regards Nietzsche's works to be both philosophical and literary. By revealing the differential effects that the pagan cultures of ancient Greece and modern Christianity can have on one's understanding of what shame is, Herbert also addresses the question of how the normative values and import of shame can be influenced by a community's culture and politics.

In chapter 7, "Shame and Moral Learning in Coetzee's *Disgrace*," Alba Montes Sánchez writes from an interdisciplinary philosophical perspective that takes an interpretative, literary approach to theorizing shame. Through her interpretation of John Maxwell Coetzee's (1999) novel *Disgrace*, Sánchez argues that the widely acknowledged negative aspects of shame, for which it has often been criticized as a dysfunctional emotion (such as its self-consciousness and its challenge to one's ego), can play a morally positive function while still being an affectively negative experience. According to Sánchez, in *Disgrace*, Coetzee presents an argument for the deeply personal nature of shame, in which acts of public shaming may never be appropriate and which interprets the main character of *Disgrace* as a person struggling with the experiences of shame that are imposed on him not only by his own psychology, but also by the culture and politics of a post-apartheid South Africa.

In chapter 8, "Body Shaming in the Era of Social Media," Lisa Cassidy writes from an interdisciplinary, feminist, philosophical perspective that utilizes the approaches of communication and new media studies, women studies, and critical race studies to reveal an understanding of ourselves as individual members of a contemporary, possibly global, cultural, and political community. Through her examples, which emphasize the racist and sexists uses of shame in U.S. social media, she calls our attention to the fact that one of the most significant social, normative, cultural, and political functions of shame is to mediate the negotiation of norms and values within a society. Cassidy begins her theorizing from a more traditional, standard conception of shame, which entails the acceptance of a global, negative, self-evaluation. Yet by depicting the ethical relations involved in online body shaming and body shame, she illuminates how, in contemporary times, our relationships with others can operate beyond the modes of occurrent, physically embodied interactions.

In chapter 9, "Shame and Its Political Consequences in the Age of Neoliberalism," Mikko Salmela also draws from the disciplines of sociology, psychology, political science, and economics to highlight the social-political function of shame as a mechanism through which the norms and values of a society are negotiated. Salmela writes from an interdisciplinary philosophical perspective in order to extend sociologist Thomas Scheff's (1994) observation that a contributing cause to the two world wars was the experience of shame among members of French and German communities. He argues that the rise of populist political parties, especially of the political right in contemporary neoliberal societies (such as in Europe and the United States), are rooted in the history of the shame that fueled the hatred that sparked the fires of the first two world wars. Salmela adds to Scheff's observation by identifying the mechanism of *ressentiment*, through which repressed shame operates, in order to untangle the dynamics of populist political movements as consequences of *societal shame*.

In chapter 10, "Queering Shame," Julian Honkasalo introduces reflections and insights from a perspective within a social-political movement that aims to address the concerns of the oppressed and the marginalized. By also drawing from the disciplines of transgender and queer studies, disability studies, critical race studies, and feminist studies, Honkasalo writes from an interdisciplinary, gender studies, and political science perspective to critique liberatory anti-futurist movements within the queer community that have attempted to overturn the shaming values of heteronormativity. In contrast to such arguments, Honkasalo proposes an understanding of shame as being a practically significant aspect of marginalized lives that ought to be acknowledged rather than displaced in order to gain a more in-depth understanding of queer and transgender experiences, as well as the experiences of people labeled with a disability, as experiences that are shared by an even greater community of marginalized people.

Part I

METHODS AND THEORIES

Chapter 1

Shame is a Folk Term Unsuitable as a Technical Term in Science

Dolichan Kollareth, Mariko Kikutani, and James A. Russell

What is shame? Definitions of "shame" can take one of two forms: descriptive and prescriptive. Both are scientific projects, and not unrelated, but about different topics. The descriptive project is in the general domain of understanding natural language. What do English speakers mean by "shame"? What do people understand by the term, what are the term's properties, how did that term come about historically, how and when is the term used, how do children acquire it, and the like? Into what broader conceptualization is the term embedded? How does "shame" differ from "guilt," "embarrassment," and so on? English contains a set of related terms and phrases—"shame," "ashamed," "shameless," "shame on you," "shameful," "shaming"—that need such a descriptive analysis. To anticipate, we believe that "shame" refers to a heterogeneous set of events with an internal structure, with blurry borders, and embedded in a dubious folk theory of emotion.

The descriptive project for "shame" is a branch of cognitive science in which the English folk word "shame," and similar words in other languages, is the object of study. Similar words in other languages ("xiuchi," "vergüenza," "honte," "haji," "lajja," etc.) (and "shame" in other historical eras of the English language) require systematic analyses. What do Japanese speakers mean by "haji"? We doubt that "xiuchi," "shame," "vergüenza," "honte," "haji," "lajja," etc., are exact synonyms. More generally, what do people understand by any everyday term? What do English speakers mean by "dog," "red," "ghost," and "zombie"? A general descriptive project includes the scientific study of folk biology, folk physics, and so on.

The prescriptive project is to the descriptive project as physics is to the study of folk physics. The prescriptive project for shame is a scientific analysis of the events referred to as "shame," without being too bound by just that term, since the term is pre-scientific. The word "shame" refers to real events, and the prescriptive project is to develop a scientific theory about, roughly, those important events. The main aim of our chapter is to challenge the implicit assumption that the everyday folk term "shame" can be co-opted as a scientific term for an analysis of those events. Sometimes, everyday folk concepts prove themselves fit for scientific duty, but sometimes not. "Air" was once considered a fundamental element in the chemistry of the day, but the folk term "air" is no longer used as a technical term in chemistry. (See Russell (1991), and Widen and Russell (2010), for more on the distinction between descriptive and prescriptive projects in the study of emotion. Similarly, Wierzbicka (2009), Scarantino (2012), and Scherer (2005) distinguish everyday from scientific concepts of emotion.)

We believe that using "shame" as if it were a scientific term has been the main obstacle to progress in the prescriptive project. An article in the *New York Times* argued that experiencing shame causes behaviors that might help someone overcome an addiction (Satel and Lilienfeld 2016). A letter commenting on that article argued the opposite: shame causes further harmful effects on those addicted and can also cause relapse for those treated for addiction (Szalavitz 2016). Science has no consensual theory of shame to resolve this debate, and we suspect that it never will if it continues to borrow the folk concept of shame with its implicit assumptions. As assumed by both sides of the debate in the *NY Times*, much of psychology treats shame as a distinct entity with causal powers. Indeed, emotions in general are treated as distinct entities (much like stars and planets) that can be clearly distinguished from each other by their fixed features (such as shame's causes and causal powers, and hence consequences). Different societies (or individuals) may have different ideas about shame or different labels ("shame," "vergüenza," "honte," "haji," "lajja," etc.) for shame, but the emotion itself is a distinct and universal part of human nature—or so it is assumed.

We diverge from a traditional approach in emotion research in psychology that assumes emotions, in general, to be distinct entities with essential features and with names provided by the English language (Ekman and Cordaro 2011; Izard 2011; Scarantino 2017; Tomkins 1960). In that tradition, echoing a folk theory, an emotion is presupposed to be a mechanism within the person that can be identified by and assessed in terms of its causes and consequences. That is, the emotion cannot be observed but is inferred from the specific kind of situations or appraisals that trigger it, from its underlying brain circuitry, and from its manifestations in conscious subjective experience, peripheral physiological changes, expressive signals, and behavioral effects. A coherent and predictable pattern of manifestations is predicted for each occurrence of a particular emotion because they stem from a single cause: the emotion. Thus, for example, every instance of the emotion "shame" would be invariably associated with a coherent set of features, unless deliberately inhibited. The generic account of shame would be that it is triggered by exposure to a specifiable type of event, and that it leads to a specifiable conscious subjective experience, nonverbal signal, and instrumental behavior.

As it happens, no such pattern has been found, but theorists continue to believe that it must exist, since the word exists. As a consequence, theorists then try to save the theory. They might add that the features are only probabilistic—thus distancing the theory from any empirical test: shame has a certain feature except when it doesn't. The problem is that even this loosened scientific agenda has not faired well empirically. Instead, in an emerging alternative research program, allegedly discrete emotions (such as fear, anger, and shame) are viewed as overlapping vaguely defined clusters (Barrett 2006; 2017; Clore and Ortony 2013; Lindquist 2013; Russell 2003; 2015).

In this chapter, before suggesting future directions for research on shame, we briefly look at current psychological thinking about shame and argue that insufficient progress is being made. Our diagnosis is that the fault lies in the underlying presupposition that shame is a discrete entity with essential features that make it distinct from other emotions. On this presupposition, one scientific task is to describe the features of shame episodes, and to use the everyday, ordinary language folk concept, which is labeled as "shame," as a scientific concept when accounting for behavior and other psychological processes. We have no *a priori* argument that "shame" is not a viable scientific concept; the issue is an empirical one. We find that "shame" has not yet yielded a successful scientific project, and that it is time to move on to an alternative research program. Based on a review of the literature on shame, mainly from psychology, we propose that "shame" is a cluster concept—"shame" does not refer to a single and discrete class of events with common features, but refers to a loose cluster of heterogeneous events. We propose abandoning it as a scientific term and finding a different way to account for all episodes referred to as "shame."

In our proposal to eliminate "shame" as a scientific term, we side with Bickle (2012), who described his position as "eliminative materialism with a small e"—a position on epistemology rather than ontology. The same stance was advocated on emotion in general by Meyer (1933) and Duffy (1934). Duffy (1934, 103) stated, "abandonment of a term does not imply abandonment of the study of the phenomena loosely referred to by that term." Shame events exist, and people within the English-speaking world interpret themselves and others in terms of shame—an interpretation that must be studied. All the same, a scientific account of those events needs to be formulated in more basic terms.

Our suggestion is to abandon "shame" as the hypothesized scientific concept and then to develop a theory that explains the events that are now called "shame" with a different set of concepts. We would abandon the criterion that the theory explains all and only events now called "shame." To illustrate the direction of a possible alternative approach with different basic concepts, we specifically discuss the fundamental concepts of self, cognitive evaluation, and core affect that might provide an explanation for many (not all) of the events now referred to as "shame" and likely some not called "shame." In other words, we propose that future progress will be best achieved by abandoning the requirement that a scientific theory of shame be as faithful as possible to the everyday word "shame." In their prescriptive analysis, scientists need not require that it coincide with how everyday folk label events, any more than chemists would worry if everyday folk occasionally referred to oxygen as "air."

CURRENT PSYCHOLOGICAL RESEARCH ON SHAME

Of course, a valid prescriptive theory of shame events based on the everyday concept of shame might be just around the corner; we cannot prove it is not. All the same, progress toward that goal has so far been elusive. Here we suggest that current theories and empirical findings based on the concept of shame are not encouraging, but are consistent with the idea that "shame" is a cluster concept not suitable as a scientific term.

Theoretical Viewpoints

For centuries, astute observers have attempted to articulate the features of shame. If shame is indeed a distinct entity, then one might expect a convergence on a clear conceptualization of shame in terms of singly necessary and jointly sufficient features. However, theoretical views have not converged but differ markedly from each other. (For reviews, see Elision 2003; Blum 2008; Pattison 2000; Teroni and Deonna 2008.) In one theory, shame is caused by public exposure (Ausubel 1955); whereas, in another, shame is caused by violating internal private standards rather than by public exposure (Edelmann 1981); and, in yet another theory, shame is caused not by any external event per se, but by a focus on the self as flawed (Tangney and Dearing 2002). One theory assumes a unique combination of bodily and behavioral display associated with shame (Kemeny, Gruenewald and Dickerson 2004); another theory has no expressive signal that is unique to shame (Tracy and Robins 2004). In one theory, shame leads to maladaptive and pathological reactions (Tangney and Dearing 2002), whereas, in another, shame leads to adaptive reactions (Gilbert 1998). It might seem surprising that theorists can offer such different accounts of supposedly the same type of emotion.

On the one hand, different theorists may have in mind different subsets of shame. If shame is a cluster concept, then it would be understandable if different theorists emphasized different subsets of events called "shame." Our review of competing theories is therefore consistent with the view that shame is a heterogeneous cluster: Different events called "shame" consist of different subsets of those features found in the full set of all shame events: no set of features is both necessary and sufficient. Thus, one subset of events called "shame" may be caused by mere public exposure, but a different subset may be caused by violation of an internal standard. These theories are in competition only if one assumes that they are all characterizing the same type of event. If, as we propose, each theory characterizes a different set of events, then they are not in competition and each may have merit.

On the other hand, it might be argued that theoretical differences are of little importance. After all, perhaps one of the theories is correct and the others wrong, or perhaps we have not yet developed the correct theory. Alternatively, perhaps theorists meant to use a modified version of the folk concept "shame" but have not been sufficiently explicit on their definition and the implications of the modification. Presumably, empirical studies can point to the correct theory. We therefore next turn to empirical studies on shame.

Empirical Research on Shame

Psychology's empirical literature on shame consists of studies of events labeled, directly or indirectly, with the everyday language term "shame." Again, the empirical literature is consistent with our claim that each event called "shame" consists of a subset of a cluster of features but that different shame events need not have the same features. Thus, different studies will tend to include different subsets. Therefore, different conclusions arise.

Causes of Shame

Empirical studies have been reported as support for each of the conflicting theoretical views on what causes shame—whether shame was caused by public exposure or by violation of internal private standards. Much of this work took the form of distinguishing shame from guilt or embarrassment. In support of the view that shame is caused by public exposure, participants reported more shame for transgressions discovered by another person than when the same transgressions were done in private (Smith, Webster, Parrott, and Eyre 2002; see also Fontaine et al. 2006). In other studies, participants reported more shame than embarrassment for violation of important personal standards, whereas they reported more embarrassment than shame for flaws exposed to the public (Babcock and Sabini 1990; see also Sabini, Garvey, and Hall 2001). In still other studies, shame was caused by both public exposure and private events, a finding hardly helpful in isolating shame: 22 percent of the participants recalled an event as eliciting shame in which they failed to meet others' expectations; however, 20 percent of the participants recalled an event as eliciting shame in which they felt disappointed with the self (Keltner and Buswell 1996). Participants recalled rather an equal number of public exposure events for both shame and guilt; they also recalled, again, an equal number of solitary events for both shame and guilt (Tangney 1993; Tangney, Miller, Flicker, and Barlow 1996). The view that shame is caused by a general negative evaluation of self rather than a specific behavior also did not have unanimous support: Some studies found that the shamed participants tended to change their flawed qualities of self more often than their specific behavior (Niedenthal, Tangney, and Gavanski 1994). However, in other studies, shamed participants attempted to alter specific behaviors more often than the whole self (Andrews, Qian, and Valentine 2002; De Hooge, Zeelenberg, and Breugelmans 2010; Frijda, Kuipers, and Schure 1989). In these summaries, phrases such as "more often" or "tend" were used, showing that the shame events sampled did not reveal necessary features.

Non-Verbal Expressions of Shame

Researchers sought support for the hypothesis of a distinct nonverbal signal of shame. One such signal—head and gaze down—was labeled as shame more than any other emotion, including embarrassment (Haidt and Keltner 1999; Keltner 1995; Keltner and Buswell 1996). However, these studies employed a forced-choice response format—participants chose the one word from a short list that was the best available match for the emotion displayed in the face. As such, the response format limited participant choice and is known to channel a variety of responses into one category (Russell 1993). By contrast, when participants freely label facial expressions, they indicate a variety of emotions. When free-labeling the emotion seen in the alleged shame face (head and gaze down), 38 percent of people labeled it as sad, whereas only 16 percent of people labeled it as shame (Haidt and Keltner 1999); and in another study, 35 percent of people labeled it as sad, whereas 22 percent of people labeled it as shame (Widen, Christy, Hewett, and Russell 2011). Such results challenge the claim that shame is linked to a distinct nonverbal signal. And even these studies provide only a constrained task to respondents who are asked about emotions and given no contextual information. Surely there are contexts in which a person gazes down and drops the head that have nothing to do with emotion.

Consequences of Shame

Studies support opposing conclusions on the consequences of shame. Some studies reported that shame leads to aggression, but the actual results were that aggression occurred in a majority of, but not in all, cases. Similarly, shame proneness—tendency to experience shame—was only moderately (0.35) correlated with anger reaction (Harper, Austin, Cercone, and Arias 2005; see also Tangney, Wagner, Fletcher, and Gramzow 1992; Tangney 1995; Tangney, Wagner, Hill-Barlow, Marschall, and Gramzow 1996; Tangney, Stuewig, and Mashek 2007). In other studies, when participants were induced to experience shame, they showed, not aggression but avoidance behavior. However, again, the actual results were that avoidance occurred in a majority of cases, but not in all: 73 percent of the participants who were induced to feel shame chose to work alone in a task (Chao, Cheng, and Chiou 2011; see also Gilligan 2003; Lindsay-Hartz, de Rivera, and Mascolo 1995). If aggression is taken as different from, or even the opposite of, avoidance, then it seems no one consequence of shame has been established.

Further, in support of shame being a heterogeneous set of events, studies showed support for the mutually opposing views that shame leads to maladaptive and adaptive consequences. Some studies supported the view that shame often leads to maladaptive consequences such as depression and anxiety: Participants' vivid shame memories were moderately correlated with depression (0.31) and stress (0.23) (Pinto-Gouveia and Matos 2011; see also Andrews et al. 2002; Andrews, Brewin, Rose, and Kirk 2000; Cunha, Matos, Faria, and Zagalo 2012; Fedewa, Burns, and Gomez 2005; Murray, Waller, and Legg 2000). Other studies supported the view that shame leads to adaptive consequences such as prosocial behavior and protection of the self from devaluation: Across 29 scenarios describing various behaviors of a hypothetical person, there was a strong correlation (0.69) between participant rating of the negative evaluation of the person in the scenarios and participant rating of the shame they would feel in the scenarios (Sznycer et al. 2016; De Hooge, Breugelmans, and Zeelenberg 2008; Miller and Tangney 1994).

CULTURAL AND LEXICAL DIFFERENCES RELATED TO SHAME

We have emphasized that "shame" is a concept of the English language. Other languages lack an exact equivalent, although some languages have similar (albeit not identical) concepts. What we just said might surprise some readers because "shame" is often translated into other languages, and the method of translation-back-translation seems to confirm the adequacy of the translation. However, translation-back-translation yields the most similar term, not necessarily an equivalent term. Commonly used translations, such as "haji" for "shame," are not exact. For example, English allows "shame" to be used for a misfortune beyond anyone's control ("What a shame that the earthquake came when it did!" "What a shame it's raining today"), whereas Japanese speakers do not allow "haji" for such an event. Nor would Chinese speakers use "xiuchi" in this context of an event for which no one is to blame. "Vergüenza" is used in contexts in which English speakers would not use "shame." For example, a Spanish speaker might say "Me da vergüenza hablar en público," whereas an English speaker, to express that thought would say "I feel shy speaking in public." Hindi speakers use "lajja" to describe the state of someone exposed to unsolicited positive evaluation. Similar contexts might not be appropriate for English speakers to use "shame" or Japanese speakers to use "haji."

Studies with more demanding standards than translation-back-translation indicate that lexical terms in other languages for shame often did not have the exact meaning of "shame." There were cross-cultural variations in the typical causes, consequences, and nonverbal expressions associated with the emotion experiences denoted by shame or its translations (Edelstein and Shaver 2007). Table 1.1, in the appendix, summarizes lexical studies on shame not reported by Edelstein and Shaver.

Even when language is the same, cultural differences have been found. Although both groups speak French, when asked to display expressions for "honte" (assumed to be a translation of "shame"), those from Quebec and those from Gabon displayed different expressions (Elfenbein, Beaupre, Levesque, and Hess 2007). Although both groups speak English, European Americans remembered shame events as mostly ones experienced by themselves, whereas first-generation Asian Americans remembered them as experienced equally by self, parents, or other family members (Liem 1997).

Language differences in the concepts related to shame do not prove that the English version is flawed (Scarantino 2012), but then no argument has been advanced as to why the English "shame" is the correct one, whereas "haji," "honte," "lajja," and all others are incorrect. A theorist who suggests that shame is due to noticing a flaw in oneself likely comes from an individualistic culture, whereas a theorist from a collectivist culture might suggest that "haji" is due to comparing oneself to others. Cultural differences in causes and consequences of shame do not prove that events named "shame" are culturally variable, but then no evidence has been advanced on just what the universal features are in all and only shame events.

HISTORICAL LINGUISTICS OF "SHAME"

So far, we have written of "shame" as an English language concept, as if its meaning were fixed in time. The view that shame is a distinct biologically founded emotion would favor a constant meaning of the word over its history. However, the word "shame" did not have a fixed meaning over the history of English. Research in the historical linguistics of the English word "shame" showed change in the meaning and frequency of the word use. The meaning of "shame" depended on historical time periods and the kind of texts in which the word was used. The word was used more frequently and in increasingly diverse contexts in later periods. The meaning of "shame" changed from being an event defined by the social situation to being more of an experience in the individual, often with a moral connotation. Thus, in Old English (before 950 CE to 1150 CE), "shame" referred to an event that resulted in a change in social status. "Shame" then gradually took on the meaning of the experience of dishonor or a general internal negative evaluation of oneself (Diaz-Vera 2014).

"Shame" had diverse meanings depending on the context of the word use. In Early Modern to the present-day English writings (from a period of 1418 CE to 1991 CE), there is a shift of emphasis in the meaning of "shame" from being an experience in the religious and social duties context to an experience in the individual and moral context (Tissari 2006). Shame words in the English translation of the Psalms—translated from Latin to English from the eighth to the eleventh centuries—communicated conversion and repentance in a religious context (Birnbaum 2015). In the late Medieval English texts (fourteenth and fifteenth centuries), "shame" meant evil in religious texts; in texts describing chivalry, it meant failure; in texts describing romantic love, it was a desirable quality; and in advisory text, it meant a restraint on undesirable behavior (Flannery 2012).

The frequency of the word use varied over historical periods. The word was used in increasingly diverse contexts. There was very little use of "shame" before 850 CE. Between 850 CE and 950 CE, "shame" occurred only in religious and philosophical texts. Between 950 CE and 1050 CE, the word also occurred in fiction and private letters. Between 1050 CE and 1150 CE, the word also occurred in legal texts. Over these periods, there was also an increase in the use of shame-specific metaphors (Fabiszak and Hebda 2006). Similarly, there was an increase in the number of metaphors for shame from 1150 CE to the present-day English, such that some of the present-day shame-specific metaphors of shame—such as having no clothes on, shame as a decrease in size, an ashamed person being small, and to be ashamed is to block out the world—were not observed in Old English.

THE DESCRIPTIVE PROJECT ON "SHAME"

In descriptive definitions, as mentioned, the goal is to characterize the meaning of a word, and the concept it names, as used in everyday language. A word, such as "shame," may have different meanings in different subcultures and historical periods and even in different individuals in the same culture. Descriptive definitions, as explanations of everyday word use, can also be context dependent. This variation is legitimate, because the goal is descriptive, just as descriptions of vehicles must vary with place and historical period. The descriptive enterprise makes no assumptions about the ontology of the referents of the word. It is equally legitimate to articulate descriptive definitions for "elf" and "demon," as it is for "moon" and "planet" or for "chariot" and "rickshaw."

We take much of the research cited above as relevant to the descriptive task. We therefore often differ from the original researchers in how we would interpret their results. Still, everyday use of "shame" is likely broader than any one of these theories on shame seems to imply. For example, a common use of "shame" is simply to mark some misfortune: "Oh, what a shame!" In some cases, "Oh, what a shame!" seems to imply that the victim is not to blame. "Shame" is used widely by English speakers in their everyday discussions, but we know of no catalog of all its uses.

Unlike figures in geometry, a descriptive analysis of "shame" suggests that it is not well defined, and instead refers to a cluster of events that share overlapping features, but none are defining. The idea of cluster concepts is similar to Wittgenstein's (1967) notion of family resemblance, illustrated by the category "game." There is no precise definition of game; instead, there are different kinds of games, which vary from one another in fundamental ways (cf. soccer vs. chess vs. poker vs. solitaire vs. tag). These different activities may be called a "game" because they share a family resemblance—each contains some subset of the features that games have. Along similar lines, Averill (1980) employed the notion of a *"syndrome"* to indicate that each emotion type (such as fear, anger, or embarrassment) covers a variety of elements. A syndrome is a collection of all of the components of a particular emotion, any one or more of which may at certain times constitute the emotion, but none of which are essential or necessary for that emotion syndrome. In a similar way, different events may be called "shame" because they share a family resemblance—each contains some subset of the features that shame has, but different exemplars have different subsets of these features. Because of this conceptual structure, a specific event can resemble both shame and guilt (and other) concepts. Put more formally, a traditional assumption is that a concept is well defined because it has individually necessary and jointly sufficient features (as in geometry), but family resemblance concepts lack this structure. Well defined concepts are achieved through careful analysis and honing over time (as in geometry and other sciences) rather than borrowed directly from everyday language. Achieving well defined concepts is a prescriptive project.

PRESCRIPTIVE PROJECT

The prescriptive project for shame is the development of a scientific account of the phenomena now loosely referred to as "shame" or at least some of the phenomena. A prescriptive account does *not* define the everyday word, in this case "shame." Indeed, we must be open to the possibility of a qualitatively, even radically different, conceptualization of events now referred to as "shame." Instead, at least some of the events referred to as "shame" (as well as others referred to perhaps as other emotions) can be explained in scientific terms. There will be different proposals on the prescriptive side, and each such proposal will need to be under scientific scrutiny. Earlier, we listed various theories of shame, and each can be taken as a prescriptive analysis provided the claim that the theory accounts for all and only events called "shame" is dropped. So, theories of the consequences of public exposure (Ausubel 1955), of the violation of an internal private standard (Edelmann 1981), and of the experience of the self as flawed (Tangney and Dearing 2002) can be taken to be about psychological effects of different types of antecedent events. Construed in this way, the accounts have merit and complement rather than compete with one another.

We do not have our own prescriptive account to offer, but we do want to suggest a direction we think is promising. To that end, we propose "negative core affect caused by negative cognitive evaluation of oneself" as the starting concept to help understand many (but not necessarily all) of those events referred to as "shame" (as well perhaps as many referred to by other emotion labels). "Negative core affect caused by negative cognitive evaluation of oneself" needs a set of prescriptive definitions based on the concepts of self, cognitive evaluation, and core affect as understood in science, not in everyday language. None of these three concepts is language or culture dependent. As with any scientific concept, each can be honed and improved, but we do not anticipate their elimination.

No consensual theory of self exists, but we anticipate that self, as a knowledge schema for oneself (Markus 1983), will remain a fundamental concept in psychology. Humans of different ages as well as different species often perform the mirror test successfully—a performance that signifies the existence of the concept of self. Thus, the self as an object of knowledge is a basic process in a range of species. Analyses of the self date from the beginning of scientific psychology (e.g., James 1884/1950) and continue today (Higgins 1996; Showers and Zeigler-Hill 2007). A rudimentary sense of self may be rooted in our biology (Feinberg and Keenan, 2005; LeDoux, 2002). Theories differ in details, but these differences do not refute a basic sense of self. In Higgins's (1987; 1996) theory, self is complex; what we are calling the self he calls the "actual self" as distinct from ideal and ought selves; the latter two are perhaps part of the process of cognitive evaluation.

We propose a simple concept of self, but acknowledge that a more complex analysis might be warranted. Sedikides and Skowronski (Sedikides and Skowronski 1997; 2000; Skowronski and Sedikides 1999), in their proposal of a symbolic self, highlighted the complexity of the human self. Symbolic self is not unitary but a dynamic system of multiple self-relevant representation of information such as one's attributes, personal history, goals and values, social roles, social relations, ideas about the future, etc. In light of this theory, our initial proposal might need to evolve into separate accounts for different aspects of self, but that is an empirical question.

Cognitive evaluation too is a fundamental concept in psychology. Again, we are not advocating any one account of cognitive evaluation, but one will be needed. Traditional work by Osgood (1969) suggested that evaluation is a fundamental feature of information processing, as evidenced by its ubiquity in semantics. Prominent theories of emotion similarly point to evaluation as a prominent feature of the appraisal of emotion-eliciting events (Scherer 1999). An evaluative response is basic in the formation of mental representations (Ye and Gawronski 2018). The brain basis of a cognitive evaluation process is a current topic in psychology (Paniukov, Dmitrii, Davis, and Tyler 2018).

One of the objects we cognitively evaluate is the self. There is a set of evolved evaluation motives that promote the adaptive value of the self (Sedikides and Skowronski 2000). On one theory, self-evaluation aims at self-protection and self-enhancement by handling information that is not favorable to the self, and magnifies information that is favorable to self (Brown and Dutton 1995; Tesser 1988). Self-evaluation is ultimately geared toward an adaptive level of social relationships (Leary, Terdal, Tambor, and Downs 1995). Self-evaluations are not simple introspections but embedded in social relationships, in social experience, and in attachment histories (Srivastava and Beer 2005). The specific context may be telling of the aspect of the self that is under evaluation, whether it is a public self, private self, global self, or a specific aspect of the self. Empirical studies could examine whether a specific aspect of the self under scrutiny is linked to a specific nonverbal expression or a specific behavioral consequence.

Above we used the term "cognitive evaluation" to imply a distinction between cognitive evaluation and one's affective state (roughly a cold vs. hot distinction). There is no current consensus on affect, but we anticipate that it too will remain a fundamental concept. Our specific hypothesis is the concept of core affect (Russell 2003). A negative cognitive evaluation of oneself is often associated with an unpleasant affective state (Duval and Wicklund 1972; Shrauger and Lund 1975)—often, but not always: For example, religiously, some may experience positive affect when cognitively evaluating oneself as inferior before God. There are likely cultural and individual differences in which some people welcome a negative evaluation of self as a means to future improvements. The causal arrow between cognitive evaluation and affect might well go in both directions: evaluating oneself negatively is unpleasant, but being in an unpleasant state may lead to evaluations of self being more negative than they would be in a more pleasant state. The process is of course more complicated than just described, as demonstrated in Schwarz and Clore's (1983) study of affect as information. Positive affect (good mood caused by good weather) led to a positive global evaluation of the self, unless the good weather was made salient so that the positive affect was attributed to the weather. In other words, the link between affect and self-evaluation is an attribution process.

Because, on the prescriptive project, we are not seeking to characterize the everyday word "shame," we need not be troubled if some negative self-evaluations fail to cause negative affect; our definition would include only those that do. Nor need we be troubled if some negative self-evaluations are not labeled "shame;" our definition would not mention shame. The significant question, we suggest, would be what the consequences are of the negative core affects that are caused by a negative cognitive self-evaluation. So, roughly, we would ask, when does negative core affect caused by negative self-evaluation lead to various consequences, such as those studied by shame researchers: aggression, avoidance, maladaptive behavior, adaptive behavior, or the self-ascription of shame, guilt, or embarrassment. These are tractable empirical questions rather than matters of definition.

In addition, other dimensions will be relevant to characterizing specific episodes including all those called "shame." Those dimensions include features offered by theorists as definitions of "shame." Even though we find that definitional approach lacking, the dimensions are obviously relevant. So, a person might experience negative core affect caused by a negative self-evaluation focused on the entire global self, on a specific action, or on an outcome. By our proposed account, it does not matter whether one, two, or all of these alternatives occur, but the alternative itself does matter in characterizing the specific token episode. Similar considerations apply to the other features previously discussed as features of shame: public versus private precipitating events, unique versus no specific expressions, and maladaptive versus adaptive behavioral consequences. Thus, the specific behaviors (approach, avoidance, or more specific actions), expressive gestures and signs, and physiological changes) all need to be characterized. These are matters to be worked out empirically as the usefulness of our account is explored.

How does the concept of "shame" fit into our analysis? To avoid misunderstanding, let us state explicitly that we are *not* proposing that negative core affect caused by negative cognitive evaluation of oneself is necessary or sufficient for shame. *Some* cases of negative core affect caused by negative cognitive evaluation of oneself will give rise to the subjective experience of shame (by which we mean a self-perception under the everyday folk concept of "shame"). But some might not. The question is: What is the process and consequence of interpreting—or not—one's own state specifically as "shame" (for English speakers, of course)? Note that in this case, "shame" is being used in the descriptive, folk-project sense. Or, for Spanish speakers, what is the process and consequence of interpreting—or not—one's own state as "vergüenza"? Japanese speakers as "haji"? Hindi speakers as "lajja"? (A parallel question would be: What is the process and consequence of interpreting oneself as a witch or as bewitched?) We anticipate individual differences here such that two persons both feel bad because they have failed miserably, and one experiences the episode as shameful but another as prideful because it was better to have tried and failed than never to have tried at all.

Folk psychology, as seen in the pages of the *New York Times*, offers the hypothesis that interpreting oneself as feeling shame causes specific behaviors. Current psychological accounts offer many such hypotheses, but what we propose is different. Here, the conscious experience of shame, vergüenza, haji, lajja, etc., is limited to a self-ascription in terms of "shame," "vergüenza," "haji," "lajja," etc., and nothing else. This self-ascription may or may not accompany the negative core affect caused by a negative cognitive evaluation of the self. This theoretical separation raises a series of questions. What is the process that leads to the self-ascription of "shame," and what are the consequences of that self-ascription? For example, does the self-ascription per se influence specific behaviors, nonverbal signals, or physiological changes—that is, beyond what is already accounted for by the negative self-evaluation with negative core affect? What are the consequences of self-ascribing in terms of "shame" as opposed to "vergüenza," "haji," "honte," "lajja," or another concept? Current evidence has not, to our knowledge, been designed to address such questions. Setting aside "shame" as a scientific concept and recognizing it as the folk concept opens the door to a large set of important and empirically tractable questions.

APPENDIX

Table 1.1   Lexical Studies on Shame

Publication	Language	Word/s for shame	The way the word differs (in meaning or its similarity to other emotions) from English shame
Abu-Lughod 1999	Bedouin of western Egypt	Hasham	An emotion used to pay deference to people of higher status.
Al Jallad 2002	Arabic Javanese	xajal, fadiHa, 9ar, isin, isan-isin, ngisin-isini	Can be translated as shame, embarrassment, and humiliation.
Alonso-Arbiol et al. 2006	Basque	Lotsa	When categorizing emotions, *lotsa* falls within the realm of fear and anxiety.
Bedford and Hwang 2003; Bedford 2004	Mandarin from Taiwanese	can kui, xiu kui; and diu lian, xiu chi	Two types of shame: *can kui, xiu kui*—internal private shame; and *diu lian, xiu chi*—external public shame.
Castelfranchi and Poggi 1990	Italian	Vergogna	Can be translated as shame and embarrassment.
Crozier 2014	Welsh	cywilydd and gwarth	*Cywilydd* can be translated as shame and embarrassment; *gwarth*, as shame, reproach, and disgrace.
De Mendoza, Fernandez-Dols, Parrot and Carrera 2010	Spanish	Vergüenza	*Shame* (United States) and *vergüenza* do not share the cluster of central features.
Dineen 1990	Shame/embarrassment words in Danish	flov, forlegen, ilde berort, pinlig, skamfuld	The use of these words is more restricted than the English words. Example, unlike English speakers, they do not use it to refer to anything connected with body or body functions.
Fessler 2004	Begkulu	Malu	*Shame* (United States) is more guilt-like compared to *malu*.
Fischer, Manstead and Rodriguez Mosquera 1999	Dutch and Spanish	schaamte and verguenza	The prototypical cause of *schaamte* is loss of self-esteem, whereas *verguenza* is being the focus of others' attention.
Fontaine, Poortinga, Setiadi and Markam 2002	Dutch and Indonesian	schaamte and Malu	*Schaamte* is more like anger, and *malu* is more like fear.

(Continued)

Table 1.1 Lexical Studies on Shame (Continued)

Publication	Language	Word/s for shame	The way the word differs (in meaning or its similarity to other emotions) from English shame
Geertz C. 1973	Balinese	Lek	*Lek* is more like stage fright.
Keeler 1983; Geertz H. 1961,1974	Javanese	Isin	Can be translated as shame, shyness, embarrassment, guilt. It is a value praised by parents in their children.
Kollareth, Fernandez-Dols and Russell, 2018	Spanish and Malayalam	Verguenza and nanakedu	In comparison with Spanish and Malayalam speakers' ratings of their translations, American English speakers rated shame and guilt to be more similar to each other.
Li, Wang and Fischer 2004	Chinese speakers in US identified 113 Chinese terms		These terms indicate two broad categories of shame: self-focused shame and the shame when being the focus of others' attention.
Menon and Shweder 1994, 2003; Parish 1991; Levy 1984	Many South Asian languages	lajya/lajja	Can be translated as shame, shyness, embarrassment, modesty. It is a desirable quality that people display in their interactions with significant others.
Myers 1979	Pintupi	Kunta	Can be translated as shame, embarrassment, shyness, and respect.
Ogarkova, Soriano and Lehr 2012	Russian	Styd	Can be translated as shame, guilt, and embarrassment.
Rosaldo 1980	Illongot	Betang	Can be translated as shame, humility, respect, and sometimes even fear.
Rusch 2004	Japanese	Hazukashii	Can be translated as shame and embarrassment.
Scheff 2000	Greek Latin French German Italian	Asichyne—aidos foedus—pudor honte—pudeur schande—scham vergogna—pudore	Two types of shame: The first word of each pair means shame as disgrace, and the second, shame as modesty.
Scheff 2015; Ogarkova et al. 2012	Spanish	Vergüenza	Can be translated as shame and embarrassment.
Williams and Long 1993	Ancient Greek	Aidos	Can be translated as shame and guilt.

ACKNOWLEDGMENT

We thank Fernando Aguiar for helpful comments on the previous drafts of this article.

REFERENCES

Abu-Lughod, L. 1999. *Veiled Sentiments: Honor and Poetry in a Bedouin Society.* Berkeley, CA: University of California Press.

Al Jallad, N. T. 2001. *Shame in English, Arabic, and Javanese: A Comparative Lexical Study.* Ph.D. diss., University of Delaware. Accessed July 2018. PsycINFO: 619950666; 2002-95013-146.

Alonso-Arbiol, I., P. R. Shaver, R. C. Fraley, B. Oronoz, E. Unzurrunzaga, and R. Urizar. 2006. "Structure of the Basque Emotion Lexicon." *Cognition and Emotion* 20, no. 6: 836–65. http://dx.doi.org.proxy.bc.edu/10.1080/02699930500405469.

Andrews, B., C. R. Brewin, S. Rose, and M. Kirk. 2000. "Predicting PTSD Symptoms in Victims of Violent Crime: The Role of Shame, Anger, and Childhood Abuse." *Journal of Abnormal Psychology* 109, no. 1: 69–73. http://dx.doi.org.proxy.bc.edu/10.1037/0021-843X.109.1.69.

Andrews, B., M. Qian, and J. D. Valentine. 2002. "Predicting Depressive Symptoms with a New Measure of Shame: The Experience of Shame Scale." *British Journal of Clinical Psychology* 62, no. 1: 29–42. http://dx.doi.org.proxy.bc.edu/10.1348/014466502163778.

Ausubel, D. P. 1955. "Relationships Between Shame and Guilt in the Socializing Process." *Psychological Review* 62, no. 5: 378–90. http://dx.doi.org.proxy.bc.edu/10.1037/h0042534.

Averill, J. R. 1980. "A Constructivist View of Emotion." In *Emotion: Theories, Research, and Experience*, edited by R. Plutchik and H. Kellerman, 305–39. Orlando, FL: Academic Press.

Babcock, M. K. and J. Sabini. 1990. "On Differentiating Embarrassment from Shame." *European Journal of Social Psychology* 20, no. 2: 151–69. http://dx.doi.org.proxy.bc.edu/10.1002/ejsp.2420200206.

Barrett, L. F. 2006. "Solving the Emotion Paradox: Categorization and the Experience of Emotion." *Personality and Social Psychology Review* 10, no. 1: 20–46. http://dx.doi.org.proxy.bc.edu/10.1207/s15327957pspr1001_2.

———. 2017. *How Emotions are Made: The Secret Life of the Brain.* Boston, MA: Houghton Mifflin Harcourt.

Bedford, O. A. 2004. "The Individual Experience of Guilt and Shame in Chinese Culture." *Culture and Psychology* 10, no. 1: 29–52. http://dx.doi.org.proxy.bc.edu/10.1177/1354067X04040929.

Bedford, O. and K. Hwang. 2003. "Guilt and Shame in Chinese Culture: A Cross-cultural Framework from the Perspective of Morality and Identity." *Journal for the Theory of Social Behaviour* 33, no. 2: 127–44. http://dx.doi.org.proxy.bc.edu/10.1111/1468-5914.00210.

Bickle, J. 2012. "Lessons for Affective Science from a Metascience of Molecular and Cellular Cognition." In *Categorical versus Dimensional Models of Affect: A Seminar on the Theories of Panksepp and Russell*, edited by P. Zachar and R. D. Ellis, 175–88. Amsterdam, Netherlands: John Benjamins Publishing Company.

Birnbaum, T. 2015. "Naming Shame: Translating Emotion in the Old English Psalter Glosses. In *Anglo-Saxon Emotions*, edited by A. Jorgensen, F. McCormack, and J. Wilcox, 109–26. Burlington, VT: Ashgate Publishing Company.

Blum, A. 2008. "Shame and Guilt, Misconceptions and Controversies: A Critical Review of the Literature." *Traumatology* 14, no. 3: 91–102. http://dx.doi.org.proxy.bc.edu/10.1177/1534765608321070.

Brown, J. D. and K. A. Dutton. 1995. "Truth and Consequences: The Costs and Benefits of Accurate Self-knowledge." *Personality and Social Psychology Bulletin* 21, no. 12: 1288–96.

Castelfranchi, C. and I. Poggi. 1990. "Blushing as a Discourse: Was Darwin Wrong?" In *Shyness and Embarrassment: Perspectives from Social Psychology*, edited by R. Crozier, 230–51. New York, NY: Cambridge University Press. http://dx.doi.org.proxy.bc.edu/10.1017/CBO9780511571183.009.

Chao, Y., Y. Cheng, and W. Chiou. 2011. "The Psychological Consequence of Experiencing Shame: Self-sufficiency and Mood-repair." *Motivation and Emotion* 35, no. 2: 202–10. http://dx.doi.org.proxy.bc.edu/10.1007/s11031-011-9208-y.

Clore, G. L. and A. Ortony. 2013. "Psychological Construction in the OCC Model of Emotion." *Emotion Review* 5, no. 4: 335–43. http://dx.doi.org.proxy.bc.edu/10.1177/1754073913489751.

Crozier, W. R. 2014. "Differentiating Shame from Embarrassment." *Emotion Review* 6, no. 3: 269–76. http://dx.doi.org.proxy.bc.edu/10.1177/1754073914523800.

Cunha, M., M. Matos, D. Faria, and S. Zagalo. 2012. "Shame Memories and Psychopathology in Adolescence: The Mediator Effect of Shame." *International Journal of Psychology and Psychological Therapy* 12, no. 2: 203–18.

De Hooge, I. E., S. M. Breugelman, and M. Zeelenberg. 2008. "Not So Ugly After All: When Shame Acts as a Commitment Device." *Journal of Personality and Social Psychology* 95, no. 4: 933–43.

De Hooge, I. E., M. Zeelenberg, and S. M. Breugelmans. 2010. "Restore and Protect Motivations Following Shame." *Cognition and Emotion* 24, no. 1: 111–27. http://dx.doi.org.proxy.bc.edu/10.1080/02699930802584466.

De Mendoza, A. H., J. M. Fernández-Dols, W. G. Parrott, and P. Carrera. 2010. "Emotion Terms, Category Structure, and the Problem of Translation: The Case of Shame and Vergüenza." *Cognition and Emotion* 24, no. 4: 661–80. http://dx.doi.org.proxy.bc.edu/10.1080/02699930902958255.

Díaz-Vera, J. 2014. "From Cognitive Linguistics to Historical Sociolinguistics: The Evolution of Old English Expressions of Shame and Guilt." *Cognitive Linguistic Studies* 1, no. 1: 55–83.

Dineen, A. 1990. "Shame/Embarrassment in English and Danish." *Australian Journal of Linguistics* 10, no. 2: 217–29.

Duffy, E. 1934. "Emotion: An Example of the Need for Reorientation in Psychology." *Psychological Review* 41, no. 2: 184–98. http://dx.doi.org.proxy.bc.edu/10.1037/h0074603.

Duval, S. and R. A. Wicklund. 1972. *A Theory of Objective Self-Awareness.* Oxford, England: Academic Press.

Edelmann, R. J. 1981. "Embarrassment: The State of Research." *Current Psychological Reviews* 1, no. 2: 125–37. http://dx.doi.org.proxy.bc.edu/10.1007/B F02979260.

Edelstein, R. S. and P. R. Shaver. 2007. "A Cross-cultural Examination of Lexical Studies of Self-conscious Emotions." In *The Self-Conscious Emotions: Theory and Research*, edited by J. L. Tracy, R. W. Robins, and J. P. Tangney, 194–208. New York, NY: Guilford Press.

Ekman, P. and D. Cordaro. 2011. "What is Meant by Calling Emotions Basic." *Emotion Review* 3, no. 4: 364–70. http://dx.doi.org.proxy.bc.edu/10.1177/17540739114 10740.

Elfenbein, H. A., M. Beaupré, M. Lévesque, and U. Hess. 2007. "Toward a Dialect Theory: Cultural Differences in the Expression and Recognition of Posed Facial Expressions." *Emotion* 7, no. 1: 131–46. http://dx.doi.org.proxy.bc.edu/10.1037/1 528-3542.7.1.131.

Elison, J. 2003. *Definitions of, and Distinctions Between, Shame and Guilt: A Facet Theory Analysis.* Ph.D. diss., University of Northern Colorado.

Fabiszak, M. and A. Hebda. 2006. "Emotions of Control in Old English: Shame and Guilt." *Poetica: An International Journal of Linguistic-Literary Studies* 66: 1–35.

Fedewa, B. A., L. R. Burns, and A. A. Gomez. 2005. "Positive and Negative Perfectionism and the Shame/Guilt Distinction: Adaptive and Maladaptive Characteristics." *Personality and Individual Differences* 38, no. 7: 1609–19. http://dx.doi.o rg.proxy.bc.edu/10.1016/j.paid.2004.09.026.

Feinberg, T. E. and J. P. Keenan. 2005. *The Lost Self: Pathologies of the Brain and Identity.* New York, NY: Oxford University Press.

Fessler, D. M. T. 2004. "Shame in Two Cultures: Implications for Evolutionary Approaches." *Journal of Cognition and Culture* 4, no. 2: 207–62. http://dx.doi.o rg.proxy.bc.edu/10.1163/1568537041725097.

Fischer, A. H., A. S. R. Manstead, and P. M. Rodriguez Mosquera. 1999. "The Role of Honour-Related vs. Individualistic Values in Conceptualising Pride, Shame, and Anger: Spanish and Dutch Cultural Prototypes." *Cognition and Emotion* 13, no. 2: 149–79. http://dx.doi.org.proxy.bc.edu/10.1080/026999399379311.

Flannery, M. C. 2012. "The Concept of Shame in Late-Medieval English Literature." *Literature Compass* 9, no. 2: 166–82.

Fontaine, J. R., P. Luyten, P. De Boeck, J. Corveleyn, M. Fernandez, D. Herrera, and T. Tomcsányi. 2006. "Untying the Gordian Knot of Guilt and Shame: The Structure of Guilt and Shame Reactions Based on Situation and Person Variation in Belgium, Hungary, and Peru." *Journal of Cross-cultural Psychology* 37, no. 3: 273–92.

Fontaine, J. R. J., Y. H. Poortinga, B. Setiadi, and S. Markam. 2002. "Cognitive Structure of Emotion Terms in Indonesia and the Netherlands." *Cognition and Emotion* 16, no. 1: 61–86. http://dx.doi.org.proxy.bc.edu/10.1080/02699933014 000130.

Frijda, N. H., P. Kuipers, and E. T. Schure. 1989. "Relations Among Emotion, Appraisal, and Emotional Action Readiness." *Journal of Personality and Social Psychology* 57, no. 2: 212.

Geertz, C. 1973. *The Interpretation of Cultures: Selected Essays.* New York, NY: Basic Books.

Geertz, H. 1961. *The Javanese Family: A Study of Kinship and Socialization.* New York, NY: The Free Press of Glencoe.

————. 1974. "The Vocabulary of Emotion: A Study of Javanese Socialization Processes. In *Culture and Personality,* edited by R. Levine, 249–64. Chicago, IL: Aldine.

Gilbert, P. 1998. "What is Shame? Some Core Issues and Controversies." In *Shame: Interpersonal Behavior, Psychopathology, and Culture,* edited by P. Gilbert and B. Andrews, 3–38. New York, NY: Oxford University Press.

Gilligan, J. 2003. "Shame, Guilt, and Violence." *Social Research* 70: 1149–80.

Haidt, J. and D. Keltner. 1999. "Culture and Facial Expression: Open-ended Methods Find More Expressions and a Gradient of Recognition." *Cognition and Emotion* 13, no. 3: 225–66. http://dx.doi.org.proxy.bc.edu/10.1080/026999399379168.

Harper, F. W. K., A. G. Austin, J. J. Cercone, and I. Arias. 2005. "The Role of Shame, Anger, and Affect Regulation in Men's Perpetration of Psychological Abuse in Dating Relationships." *Journal of Interpersonal Violence* 20, no. 12: 1648–62. http://dx.doi.org.proxy.bc.edu/10.1177/0886260505278717.

Higgins, E. T. 1987. "Self-discrepancy: A Theory Relating Self and Affect." *Psychological Review* 94, no. 3: 319–40. http://dx.doi.org.proxy.bc.edu/10.1037/0033-295X.94.3.319.

————. 1996. "The 'Self Digest': Self-knowledge Serving Self-Regulatory Functions." *Journal of Personality and Social Psychology* 71, no. 6: 1062–83.

Izard, C. E. 2011. "Forms and Functions of Emotions: Matters of Emotion–Cognition Interactions." *Emotion Review* 3, no. 4: 371–78. http://dx.doi.org.proxy.bc.edu/10.1177/1754073911410737.

James, W. 1950. *The Principles of Psychology.* Oxford, England: Dover Publications.

Keeler, W. 1983. "Shame and Stage Fright in Java." *Ethos* 11, no. 3: 152–65. http://dx.doi.org.proxy.bc.edu/10.1525/eth.1983.11.3.02a00040.

Keltner, D. 1995. "Signs of Appeasement: Evidence for the Distinct Displays of Embarrassment, Amusement, and Shame." *Journal of Personality and Social Psychology* 68, no. 3: 441–54. http://dx.doi.org.proxy.bc.edu/10.1037/0022-3514.68.3.441.

Keltner, D. and B. N. Buswell. 1996. "Evidence for the Distinctness of Embarrassment, Shame, and Guilt: A Study of Recalled Antecedents and Facial Expressions of Emotion." *Cognition and Emotion* 10, no. 2: 155–71. http://dx.doi.org.proxy.bc.edu/10.1080/026999396380312.

Kemeny, M. E., T. L. Gruenewald, and S. S. Dickerson. 2004. "Shame as the Emotional Response to Threat to the Social Self: Implications for Behavior, Physiology, and Health." *Psychological Inquiry* 15, no. 2: 153–60.

Kollareth, D., J. M. Fernandez-Dols, and J. A. Russell. 2018. "Shame as a Culture-Specific Emotion Concept." *Journal of Cognition and Culture* 18, no. 3–4: 274–92.

Leary, M. R., S. K. Terdal, E. S. Tambor, and D. L. Downs. 1995. "Self-esteem as an Interpersonal Monitor: The Sociometer Hypothesis." *Journal of Personality and Social Psychology* 68, no. 3: 518–30.

LeDoux, J. E. 2002. *Synaptic Self: How Our Brains Become Who We Are.* New York, NY: Penguin.

Levy, R. I. 1984. "Emotion, Knowing and Culture." In *Culture Theory: Essays on Mind, Self, and Emotion*, edited by R. A. Shweder and R. A. LeVince, 214–37. Cambridge, England: Cambridge University Press.

Li, J., L. Wang, and K. W. Fischer. 2004. "The Organisation of Chinese Shame Concepts." *Cognition and Emotion* 18, no. 6: 767–97. http://dx.doi.org.proxy.bc.edu /10.1080/02699930341000202.

Liem, R. 1997. "Shame and Guilt Among First- and Second-Generation Asian Americans and European Americans." *Journal of Cross-Cultural Psychology* 28, no. 4: 365–92. http://dx.doi.org.proxy.bc.edu/10.1177/0022022197284001.

Lindquist, K. A. 2013. "Emotions Emerge from More Basic Psychological Ingredients: A Modern Psychological Constructionist Model." *Emotion Review* 5, no. 4: 356–68.

Lindsay-Hartz, J., J. de Rivera, and M. F. Mascolo. 1995. "Differentiating Guilt and Shame and their Effects on Motivation." In *Self-Conscious Emotions: The Psychology of Shame, Guilt, Embarrassment, and Pride*, edited by J. P. Tangney and K. W. Fischer, 274–300. New York, NY: Guilford Press.

Markus, H. 1983. "Self-Knowledge: An Expanded View." *Journal of Personality* 51, no. 3: 543–65.

Menon, U. and R. A. Shweder. 1994. "Kali's Tongue: Cultural Psychology and the Power of Shame in Orissa, India." In *Emotion and Culture: Empirical Studies of Mutual Influence*, edited by S. Kitayama and H. R. Markus, 241–84. Washington, DC: American Psychological Association Press.

———. 2003. "Dominating Kali: Hindu Family Values and Tantric Power." In *Encountering Kali: In the Margins, at the Center, in the West*, edited by R. F. McDermott and J. J. Kripal, 80–99. Berkeley, CA: University of California Press.

Meyer, M. 1933. "That Whale Among the Fishes—the Theory of Emotions." *Psychological Review* 40, no. 3: 292–300. http://dx.doi.org.proxy.bc.edu/10.1037/h 0071608.

Miller, R. S. and J. P. Tangney. 1994. "Differentiating Embarrassment and Shame." *Journal of Social and Clinical Psychology* 13, no. 3: 273–87. http://dx.doi.org.pr oxy.bc.edu/10.1521/jscp.1994.13.3.273.

Murray, C., G. Waller, and C. Legg. 2000. "Family Dysfunction and Bulimic Psychopathology: The Mediating Role of Shame." *International Journal of Eating Disorders* 28, no. 1: 84–89. http://dx.doi.org.proxy.bc.edu/10.1002/(SICI)1098-108X(200007)28:1<84::AID-EAT10>3.0.CO;2-R.

Myers, F. R. 1979. "Emotions and the Self: A Theory of Personhood and Political Order Among Pintupi Aborigines." *Ethos* 7, no. 4: 343–70.

Niedenthal, P. M., J. P. Tangney, and I. Gavanski. 1994. "'If Only I weren't' versus 'If Only I hadn't': Distinguishing Shame and Guilt in Conterfactual Thinking." *Journal of Personality and Social Psychology* 67, no. 4: 585–95. http://dx.doi.o rg.proxy.bc.edu/10.1037/0022-3514.67.4.585.

Ogarkova, A., C. Soriano, and C. Lehr. 2012. "Naming Feeling: Exploring the Equivalence of Emotion Terms in Five European Languages." In *Dynamicity in Emotion Concepts*, edited by P. A. Wilson, 247–333. New York, NY: Peter Lang.

Osgood, C. E. 1969. "On the Whys and Wherefores of E, P, and A." *Journal of Personality and Social Psychology* 12, no. 3: 194–99.

Paniukov, D. and T. Davis. 2018. "The Evaluative Role of Rostrolateral Prefrontal Cortex in Rule-based Category Learning." *NeuroImage* 166: 19–31.

Parish, S. M. 1991. "The Sacred Mind: Newar Cultural Representations of Mental Life and the Production of Moral Consciousness." *Ethos* 19, no. 3: 313–51.

Pattison, S. 2000. *Shame: Theory, Therapy, Theology.* New York, NY: Cambridge University Press.

Pinto-Gouveia, J. and M. Matos. 2011. "Can Shame Memories Become a Key to Identity? The Centrality of Shame Memories Predicts Psychopathology." *Applied Cognitive Psychology* 25, no. 2: 281–90. http://dx.doi.org.proxy.bc.edu/10.1002/a cp.1689.

Rosaldo, R. 1980. *Ilongot Headhunting, 1883–1974: A Study in Society and History.* Stanford, CA: Stanford University Press.

Rusch, C. D. 2004. "Cross-cultural Variability of the Semantic Domain of Emotion Terms: An Examination of English Shame and Embarrass with Japanese Hazu-kashii." *Cross-cultural Research* 38, no. 3: 236–48.

Russell, J. A. 1991. "Natural Language Concepts of Emotion." In *Perspectives in Personality: Self and Emotion*, edited by D. J. Ozer, J. M. Healy, Jr., and A. J. Stewart, 119–37. London, England: Jessica Kingsley Publishers.

———. 1993. "Forced-choice Response Format in the Study of Facial Expression." *Motivation and Emotion* 17, no. 1: 41–51.

———. 2003. "Core Affect and the Psychological Construction of Emotion." *Psychological Review* 110, no. 1: 145–72. http://dx.doi.org.proxy.bc.edu/10.1037/0 033-295X.110.1.145.

———. 2015. "The Greater Constructionist Project for Emotion." In *The Psychological Construction of Emotion*, edited by L. F. Barrett and J. A. Russell, 429–47. New York, NY: Guilford Press.

Sabini, J., B. Garvey, and A. L. Hall. 2001. "Shame and Embarrassment Revisited." *Personality and Social Psychology Bulletin* 27, no. 1: 104–17. http://dx.doi.org.pr oxy.bc.edu/10.1177/0146167201271009.

Satel, S. L. and S. O. Lilienfeld. 2016. "Can Shame Be Useful?" *The New York Times.* Accessed January 23, 2018. http://www.nytimes.com.

Scarantino, A. 2012. "How to Define Emotions Scientifically." *Emotion Review* 4, no. 4: 358–68. http://dx.doi.org.proxy.bc.edu/10.1177/1754073912445810.

———. 2017. "Do Emotions Cause Actions, and If So How?" *Emotion Review* 9, no. 4: 326–34.

Scheff, T. J. 2000. "Shame and the Social Bond: A Sociological Theory." *Sociological Theory* 18, no. 1: 84–99.

———. 2015. "Toward Defining Basic Emotions." *Qualitative Inquiry* 21, no. 2: 111–21.

Scherer, K. R. 1999. "Appraisal Theory." In *Handbook of Cognition and Emotion*, edited by T. Dalgleish and M. J. Power, 637–63. New York, NY: John Wiley and Sons, Ltd. http://dx.doi.org.proxy.bc.edu/10.1002/0470013494.ch30.

———. 2005. "What are Emotions? And how can they be Measured?" *Social Science Information* 44, no. 4: 695–729.

Schwarz, N. and G. L. Clore. 1983. "Mood, Misattribution, and Judgments of Well-being: Informative and Directive Functions of Affective States." *Journal of Personality and Social Psychology* 45, no. 3: 513–23. http://dx.doi.org.proxy.bc.edu /10.1037/0022-3514.45.3.513.

Sedikides, C. and J. J. Skowronski. 1997. "The Symbolic Self in Evolutionary Context." *Personality and Social Psychology Review* 1, no. 1: 80–102. http://dx.doi.o rg.proxy.bc.edu/10.1207/s15327957pspr0101_6.

———. 2000. "On the Evolutionary Functions of the Symbolic Self: The Emergence of Self-Evaluation Motives." In *Psychological Perspectives on Self and Identity*, edited by A. Tesser, R. B. Felson, and J. M. Suls, 91–117. Washington, DC: American Psychological Association.

Showers, C. J. and V. Zeigler-Hill. 2007. "Compartmentalization and Integration: The Evaluative Organization of Contextualized Selves." *Journal of Personality* 75, no. 6: 1181–204. http://dx.doi.org/10.1111/j.1467-6494.2007.00472.x.

Shrauger, J. S. and A. K. Lund. 1975. "Self-Evaluation and Reactions to Evaluations from Others." *Journal of Personality* 43, no. 1: 94–108. http://dx.doi.org/10.1111 /j.1467-6494.1975.tb00574.x.

Skowronski, J. J. and C. Sedikides. 1999. "Evolution of the Symbolic Self." In *Evolution of the Psyche*, edited by D. H. Rosen and M. C. Luebbert, 78–94. Westport, CT: Praeger Publishers.

Smith, R. H., J. M. Webster, W. G. Parrott, and H. L. Eyre. 2002. "The Role of Public Exposure in Moral and Nonmoral Shame and Guilt." *Journal of Personality and Social Psychology* 83, no. 1: 138–59.

Srivastava, S. and J. S. Beer. 2005. "How Self-Evaluations Relate to being Liked by Others: Integrating Sociometer and Attachment Perspectives." *Journal of Personality and Social Psychology* 89, no. 6: 966–77. http://dx.doi.org/10.1037/0022 -3514.89.6.966.

Szalavitz, M. 2016. Letter to the Editor. *The New York Times*. Accessed February 4, 2018. http://www.nytimes.com.

Sznycer, D., J. Tooby, L. Cosmides, R. Porat, S. Shalvi, and E. Halperin. 2016. "Shame Closely Tracks the Threat of Devaluation by Others, Even Across Cultures." *PNAS Proceedings of the National Academy of Sciences of the United States of America* 113, no. 10: 2625–30. http://dx.doi.org.proxy.bc.edu/10.1073/pnas.1 514699113.

Tangney, J. P. 1993. *Shame and Guilt*. Oxford, England: John Wiley and Sons.

———. 1995. "Shame and Guilt in Interpersonal Relationships." In *Self-Conscious Emotions: The Psychology of Shame, Guilt, Embarrassment, and Pride*, edited by J. P. Tangney and K. W. Fischer, 114–39. New York, NY: Guilford Press.

Tangney, J. P. and R. L. Dearing. 2002. *Shame and Guilt*. New York, NY: Guilford Press.

Tangney, J. P., R. S. Miller, L. Flicker, and D. H. Barlow. 1996. "Are Shame, Guilt, and Embarrassment Distinct Emotions?" *Journal of Personality and Social Psychology* 70, no. 6: 1256–69. http://dx.doi.org.proxy.bc.edu/10.1037/0022-3514.7 0.6.1256.

Tangney, J. P., J. Stuewig, and D. J. Mashek. 2007. "Moral Emotions and Moral Behavior." *Annual Review of Psychology* 58: 345–72. http://dx.doi.org.proxy.bc.edu/10.1146/annurev.psych.56.091103.070145.

Tangney, J. P., P. Wagner, C. Fletcher, and R. Gramzow. 1992. "Shamed into Anger? The Relation of Shame and Guilt to Anger and Self-reported Aggression." *Journal of Personality and Social Psychology* 62, no. 4: 669–75.

Tangney, J. P., P. Wagner, D. Hill-Barlow, D. Marschall, and R. Gramzow. 1996. "Relation of Shame and Guilt to Constructive versus Destructive Responses to Anger across the Lifespan." *Journal of Personality and Social Psychology* 70, no. 4: 469–78.

Teroni, F. and J. A. Deonna. 2008. "Differentiating Shame from Guilt." *Consciousness and Cognition: An International Journal* 17, no. 3: 725–40. http://dx.doi.org.proxy.bc.edu/10.1016/j.concog.2008.02.002.

Tesser, A. 1988. "Toward a Self-Evaluation Maintenance Model of Social Behavior." In *Social Psychological Studies of the Self: Perspectives and Programs. Advances in Experimental Social Psychology*, Vol. 21, edited by L. Berkowitz, 181–227. San Diego, CA: Academic Press.

Tissari, H. 2006. "Conceptualizing shame: Investigating Uses of the English Word Shame, 1418–1991." In *Selected Proceedings of the 2005 Symposium on New Approaches in English Historical Lexis*, Vol. 143, 154. Somerville, MA: Cascadilla Proceedings Project.

Tomkins, S. 1962. *Affect, Imagery, Consciousness: The Positive Affects*, Vol. 1. New York, NY: Springer.

Tracy, J. L. and R. W. Robins. 2004. "Putting the Self into Self-Conscious Emotions: A Theoretical Model." *Psychological Inquiry* 15, no. 2: 103–25. http://dx.doi.org.proxy.bc.edu/10.1207/s15327965pli1502_01.

Widen, S. C. and J. A. Russell. 2010. "Descriptive and Prescriptive Definitions of Emotion." *Emotion Review* 2, no. 4: 377–78. http://dx.doi.org.proxy.bc.edu/10.1177/1754073910374667.

Widen, S. C., A. M. Christy, K. Hewett, and J. A. Russell. 2011. "Do Proposed Facial Expressions of Contempt, Shame, Embarrassment, and Compassion Communicate the Predicted Emotion?" *Cognition and Emotion* 25, no. 5: 898–906. http://dx.doi.org.proxy.bc.edu/10.1080/02699931.2010.508270.

Wierzbicka, A. 2009. "Language and Metalanguage: Key Issues in Emotion Research." *Emotion Review* 1, no. 1: 3–14. http://dx.doi.org.proxy.bc.edu/10.1177/1754073908097175.

Williams, B. A. O. and A. A. Long. 1993. *Shame and Necessity*. Vol. 135. Berkeley, CA: University of California Press.

Wittgenstein, L. (1953) 1967. *Philosophical Investigations*. Translated by G. E. M. Anscombe. Oxford, England: Blackwell. Citations refer to the reprint edition.

Ye, Y. and B. Gawronski. 2018. "Contextualization of Mental Representations and Evaluative Responses: A Theory-based Analysis of Cultural Differences." In *The Psychological and Cultural Foundations of East Asian cognition: Contradiction, Change, and Holism*, edited by J. Spencer-Rodgers and K. Peng, 243–65. New York, NY: Oxford University Press.

Chapter 2

Unification through the Rationalities and Intentionalities of Shame

Cecilea Mun

One of the central points of contention within the philosophical discourse on shame has been between proponents of *standard accounts of shame* and those of *non-standard accounts of shame.* According to standard accounts of shame, a rational experience of shame necessarily entails that the subject holds a global, negative self-evaluation whereas non-standard accounts of shame deny the necessity of this criterion for a rational experience of shame. Both standard accounts and non-standard accounts of shame can also be identified within the psychological discourse on shame,[1] although conceptual and experimental difficulties in general—including issues regarding shame's cognitive content, physiological underpinnings, behavioral expressions, as well as its relationship with other emotions (such as embarrassment, humiliation, anger, guilt, disgust, and anxiety)—have been the central focus of such concerns.[2] Regardless of the differences between the philosophical and psychological discourse on shame, however, which are primarily due to the differences in the interests and approaches that are given by each discipline, it is clear that the problem of identifying shame's core—the feature or features that are thought to make shame the kind of emotion that it is[3]—has been the overarching aim of both the philosophical and psychological discourse on shame.[4]

I offer in response an alternative, non-standard, unified account of shame that is rooted in an interdisciplinary, unified, philosophical approach to the scientific study of shame, broadly construed. Accordingly, I propose that shame is an emotionally epistemic response that begins with (a) the sudden realization (of which the subject may be unaware) that one is being seen (by the self or at least one other) as an aberrant member of one's epistemic community, and this experience may lead to at least one of the following

27

epistemic conditions: (b) the recognition that one is taken to be an aberrant member of one's epistemic community, (c) the acceptance that one is an aberrant member of one's epistemic community, (d) the rejection that one is taken to be an aberrant member of one's epistemic community, or (e) the rejection of the (real or imagined) other as a legitimate authority on shared social or moral knowledge (such as knowledge pertaining to shared hermeneutic resources),[5] that is, ostracism, self-isolation, or revolution, all of which can include a breakdown in epistemic trust.[6]

My unified account of shame illuminates the logic of shame, its relation to our rationality, and how attending to the rationality of those who are oppressed and/or marginalized can help move research on shame forward, toward a unifying account. I begin, however, with a discussion of the ontological rationality of shame and the necessity of explicating the ontological rationality of shame, before offering my proposal for the ontological rationality of shame as constituting the unifying core of shame.

THE ONTOLOGICAL RATIONALITY OF SHAME

In *The Rationalities of Emotion* (2016a), I argued for the "rationality of emotions *qua* emotion" or "*qua* an emotion-type," which are both distinct from understanding the rationality of emotions in terms of their "instrumental rationality," "epistemic rationality," and their "evaluative rationality." To understand emotions as being *instrumentally rational* is to understand them as playing a prudential role in rational decision-making; it is to take one's emotional responses to be, at the least, to a certain extent, a significant factor in one's rational decision-making (52). To understand emotions as being *epistemically rational* is to understand them as being warranted or justified in accordance with an ideal of epistemic objectivity, which typically involves notions of truth and evidence (53). To understand emotions as being *evaluatively rational* is to understand them as being warranted or justified in accordance with our personal values, which are given to us by our biographical histories (53).

In contrast with these three ways of understanding the rationality of emotions, understanding emotions to be *rational qua emotion*, or *qua an emotion-type*, is to understand emotions as fulfilling what I referred to as the *criterion for the ontological rationality of emotions* (COR^e):[7]

COR^e: For *emotion* or *an emotion* there exists some normative standard that is given by what emotion or [that] emotion is against which our emotional responses can be judged or evaluated in virtue of the fact that our emotions manifest our rationality, i.e., the capacity for being both rational and irrational. (Mun 2016a, 51)

Given the above criterion for the ontological rationality of emotion, I described the understanding of emotions as being at times rational and at times irrational—*qua* emotion—in terms of "a category of rational operations that implement a more general category-level superordinate inference rule (at the level of emotion as a genus)," and I described emotions to be at times rational and at times irrational *qua* an emotion-type, in terms of token experiences of a type of emotion being either rational or irrational, in virtue of the reliable operation of a type-level superordinate inference rule (54).[8] In this chapter, I will primarily be concerned with the notion of a "type-level superordinate inference rule," specifically, the notion of shame as a type-level superordinate inference rule—the *superordinate inference rule of shame* (SUR^{SHAME}).

In regard to shame, the foregoing entails that an understanding of the rationality of emotions *qua* shame presupposes the existence of a criterion for the ontological rationality of shame. Furthermore, given the criterion for the ontological rationality of emotion (COR^e), we can derive the following as the criterion for the *ontological rationality of shame* (COR^{SHAME}) by narrowing the scope of the criterion to the context of experiences of shame:

COR^{SHAME}: For shame there exists some normative standard that is given by what shame is against which our emotional responses can be judged or evaluated in virtue of the fact that our shame manifests our rationality, i.e., the capacity for being both rational and irrational.

Thus, to understand the rationality of emotions *qua* shame is to understand both our rational and irrational experiences of shame as being judged against a normative standard, the fulfillment of which (by token experiences of shame) constitutes our experiences of shame *as experiences of shame*, and in virtue of which we make judgments about the rationality of our token experiences of shame. The rationality of our experiences of shame—that our experiences of shame can be at times rational and at times irrational—therefore *grounds* the superordinate inference rule of shame,[9] which *is* the normative standard that fulfills the criterion for the ontological rationality of shame.

Also in accordance with my understanding of what superordinate inference rules are (Mun 2016a), I suggest that the superordinate inference rule of shame *can* be defined by humanity's collective, phylogenetic experiences of shame and the reliable operations to which these collective experiences *give rise*, the respective sum and function of which are reflected in the intended, shared meaning(s) of the ordinary language use of the English word "shame" and its linguistic equivalents in other languages.[10] In other words, I suggest that the intended meaning(s) of the ordinary language use of the English word "shame," and its linguistic equivalents in other languages, refer to or describe our experiences of shame, which include an understanding of our experiences of shame as being products of an evolutionary history.[11] Yet, also consistent with my understanding of what superordinate inference rules are, the superordinate inference rule of shame does not entail or presuppose any particular type of view, approach, or theory besides (of course) what I have already introduced,[12] which includes the fundamental principles that the rationality and the intentionality of shame are indispensable to any adequate account of shame.

THE INTENTIONALITY AND RATIONALITY OF SHAME ACCORDING TO A STANDARD ACCOUNT

Our knowledge of the fact that there is at least one kind of intentionality— what philosophers might refer to as "aboutness" or what shame is about[13]—in our experiences of shame is a consequence of the intentionality of shame being intimately intertwined with its ontological rationality (i.e., its rationality *qua* shame). Without getting into an extensive discussion on the relationship between language, meaning, and intentionality, which is beyond the scope of this chapter, one can understand the relationship between the intentionality and rationality of shame by considering the everyday practices in which we judge the rationality of a token experience of shame. For example, consider a case of shame that is similar to the one experienced by Philip Carey, in W. Somerset Maugham's *Of Human Bondage* (1915).[14]

In Maugham's story, Philip, who was born with a club foot, experienced shame when one of his teachers, not realizing at the time that Philip had a club foot, asked Philip why he had not changed his clothes in order to play football:

> The boys went in charge of Mr. Rice, who glanced at Philip and seeing he had not changed, asked why he was not going to play.
> "Mr. Watson said I needn't, sir," said Philip.
> "Why?"
> There were boys all round him, looking at him curiously, and a feeling of shame came over Philip. He looked down without answering. Others gave the reply.
> "He's got a club-foot, sir."
> "Oh, I see." (40)

Based on earlier passages, which are not quoted above, one might conclude that Philip also experienced shame when the other boys at his school ridiculed him during the game of Pig-in-the-Middle, when he tucked his feet under the bench, or when Mr. Watson supposed that he could not play football. Yet,

Maugham only explicitly mentioned that Philip experienced shame when Mr. Rice questioned him while the other boys stared curiously. About those other occasions, Maugham noted that Philip was "completely scared," "could not make out why they were laughing," "his heart beat so that he could hardly breathe," "he was more frightened than he had ever been in his life," "he stood still stupidly," "he was using all his strength to prevent himself from crying," or he "blushed self-consciously" (40). Thus, I propose that a more accurate reading would be to interpret Maugham as differentiating, in these passages, the experiences of fear, bewilderment, anxiety, stupefaction, annoyance, and general self-consciousness or embarrassment from experiences of shame.

Furthermore, for my current purpose, I suggest that we can understand the rationality and intentionality of Philip's shame in terms of Gabriele Taylor's (1985) *cognitivist approach* in the philosophy of emotion[15]—which seeks to provide an analysis of emotions within a framework that regards beliefs to be the primary *unit of explanation.*[16] Besides using a cognitivist approach to shame, Taylor also provides a standard account of shame, which I will presuppose for my present purpose in this section, but I will offer an alternative non-standard account of shame later on in this chapter.

According to Taylor's standard account of shame, the intentionality of shame can be taken to be a belief that expresses a global, negative self-assessment that one is "defective and degraded" (66). This belief constitutes shame's *identificatory belief*, which is a belief that is constitutive of an emotional experience in the sense that it is the belief (or set of beliefs) that defines an emotional experience as the type of emotional experience that it is, and therefore conveys shame's intentionality (2). It is regarded to be the belief that articulates the intentionality of that emotion (i.e., what the emotion is about). The identificatory belief is also typically regarded as containing information about what de Sousa (1987) referred to as an emotion's "proper target" (116). In Taylor's, and many other accounts of shame, the proper target (*vs.* a mere "target") of shame is taken to be the self; it is the actual, particular object to which a successful experience of shame is related or directed.[17] This is why Taylor regards shame, along with the emotions of embarrassment, humiliation, guilt, and pride, to be an *emotion of self-assessment* (1).

What explains the rationality of a particular experience of shame, according to Taylor's standard account, is that it is logically entailed by a set of beliefs that are both the causes of and the reasons for the holding of an identificatory belief. I refer to these beliefs as "beliefs of rational intelligibility."[18] We can therefore suggest that, according to Maugham, Philip's belief that [*he-has-a-club-foot*][19] may be regarded as Philip's identificatory belief for his experience of shame, and his belief that [*he-is-unable-to-play-football*] may be identified as (at least) one of his beliefs of rational intelligibility: Philip's belief that [*he-has-a-club-foot*] would therefore be the belief that articulates the intentionality of his token emotion of shame—that his shame is about him being defective and degraded—and it would identify his experience of shame *as an experience of shame*.[20] It would also be the belief that suggests that the target or object of Philip's experience of shame—his belief that [*he-has-a-club-foot*]—is himself, in virtue of a synecdochic relation between himself and his club foot. The belief that [*Philip-is-unable-to-play-football*],[21] as his belief of rational intelligibility, would be the belief that would have caused Philip to consciously hold, at the time of his experience of shame, the identificatory belief that [*he-has-a-club-foot*], as well as the belief that would have been Philip's reason for consciously believing at the time that [*he-has-a-club-foot*].[22]

For Taylor, the logical relation between Philip's identificatory belief and his belief of rational intelligibility secures the rationality of Philip's experience of shame—that his identificatory belief is justified by his beliefs of rational intelligibility. The rationality of Philip's experience of shame, which is *determined* by the logical relationship between Philip's identificatory belief and his belief of rational intelligibility, however, is an epistemic rationality rather than an ontological rationality, since the notion of rational intelligibility is primarily concerned with logical rather than causal relations. It therefore cannot fulfill the criterion for the ontological rationality of shame, and consequently it cannot constitute the superordinate inference rule of shame.

In other words, given what Taylor identifies as the intentional content of shame—that *one-is-defective-and-degraded*—one could claim that the normative standard entailed by the criterion for the ontological rationality of shame is positively put, in accordance with Taylor's account, the standard that *one ought to believe that one is defective and degraded*, or the negative formulation that *one ought not believe that one is non-defective and non-degraded*. Yet, this account of the superordinate inference rule of shame, and therefore the ontological rationality of shame is problematic, primarily because it fails to explain how and why Philip's token experience of shame (the identificatory belief that [*he-has-a-club-foot*]) would express the intentional content that *one-is-defective-and-degraded*. The root of this problem is that it is derived from Taylor's standard account of shame, which regards the content that *one-is-defective-and-degraded* to define shame's intentionality (i.e., to define what experiences of shame are about). We are, therefore, left wanting a criterion for the ontological rationality of shame, which ought to be able to explain why and how Philip's token experience of shame (the identificatory belief that [*he-has-a-club-foot*]) expresses the intentional content that *one-is-defective-and-degraded*.

The epistemic rationality of shame, however, as described by Taylor's standard account, can ground the ontological rationality of shame. The epistemic rationality at work here presupposes the ontological rationality of shame, which entails the superordinate inference rule of shame, along with the standard rules of logical inference. For, in order to judge Philip's shame as being epistemically rational—that his belief of rational intelligibility appropriately justify his identificatory belief—we must not only presuppose certain logical rules in order to determine the appropriateness of his justification between his identificatory belief and his belief of rational intelligibility, we must also presuppose a rule or normative standard that at least warrants Philip's token belief that [*he-has-a-club-foot*] as being a belief that expresses the intentional content that *one-is-defective-and-degraded.*[23]

In other words, we must presuppose that there is some normative standard that would establish Philip's token experience of shame as an experience of *shame*, regardless of whether or not it is regarded as being rational or irrational.[24] Philip's experience of shame can rationally be an experience of rational or irrational shame only if there exists some standard that defines what it means for his experience to be either a rational or irrational experience of shame, that is, only if there exists some standard that defines what it means for his experience to be an experience of *shame*. Therefore, given the above interpretation of Maugham's story, we can appreciate how the epistemic rationality of token experiences of shame can, in accordance with Taylor's standard account of shame, entail, and thereby ground, their ontological rationality.

STANDARD VERSUS NON-STANDARD ACCOUNTS, AND THE GENUS OF SHAME

In this section, I consider some standard accounts of shame to address what one might consider to be a major point of contention between standard and non-standard accounts of shame: the significance of others in experiences of shame. In doing so, I identify the point of contention between standard accounts of shame and non-standard accounts of shame as not having to do with the question of whether shame is a social emotion but instead the question of whether shame necessarily entails a global, negative self-assessment. I also argue that the experience of "alterity,"[25] which Dan Zahavi ([2012] 2013) rightly highlighted as an essential feature of shame, is in fact a feature that is accounted for in both standard and non-standard accounts of shame, as well as in what he referred to as "non-social" accounts of shame. It is, as I shall argue, a unifying feature not only of standard and non-standard accounts of shame, but also of social and non-social accounts of shame, and perhaps accounts of shame across the disciplines.

Furthermore, I argue that, although the experience of alterity is an essential feature of shame, it does not constitute the *differentia* of shame. It is instead that which unifies all experiences of shame, along with experiences of emotions such as embarrassment, humiliation, humility, and guilt, as "self-conscious experiences," since all self-conscious experiences require a double perspective: the *first-person subjective perspective* and the *first-person subjective perspective as an "other."* Yet, as the essential feature that unites shame with other self-conscious emotions, it provides us with a window to an understanding of shame's intentionality by allowing us to isolate the genus of shame in order to derive its differentia, which will then allow us to identify the superordinate inference rule that constitutes the ontological rationality of shame.

One might suggest that one major source of contention between proponents of standard accounts of shame and proponents of non-standard accounts of shame is the question of what kind of significance others play in experiences of shame. Dan Zahavi ([2012] 2013) can be understood as framing this debate between accounts of, what Zahavi refers to as, "non-social shame" (312–13) and what he might refer to as "social shame." I will, respectively, refer to these accounts of shame as *non-social accounts of shame* and *social accounts of shame*,[26] although, as I will demonstrate later on, the categories of standard and non-standard accounts of shame do not neatly map on to the respective categories of non-social and social accounts of shame.

According to Zahavi, non-social accounts of shame (e.g., Taylor 1985; Nussbaum 2004; Deonna, Rodogno, and Teroni 2012) are accounts of shame that explicitly reject the claim that shame is essentially a social emotion, and instead, consistently with standard accounts of shame, hold that shame essentially involves a global, negative self-assessment. As such, according to Zahavi, non-social accounts of shame take shame to be an "essentially self-involving emotion." Furthermore, Zahavi notes several possible ways of understanding what one might mean by calling shame a "social" emotion, and he suggests that non-social accounts of shame reject all of these ways of understanding shame as a "social" emotion:

> That (1) the object of shame is specifically social—its object being either some-body else or our own social standing . . . (2) that the values involved in shame are acquired through contact with others, or (3) that shame always requires tak-ing an outside perspective on ourselves, or (4) that shame always takes place in a social context. (Zahavi [2012] 2013, 312)

Thus, it seems that for Zahavi, the categories of standard accounts of shame and non-standard accounts of shame neatly map on to the respective categories of non-social accounts of shame and social accounts of shame. He also argues throughout his paper that a notable problem with non-social accounts of shame is that they fail to appropriately recognize and appreciate the fact that the experience of *alterity*—"(3) that shame always requires taking an outside perspective on ourselves" (312)—is an essential feature of shame.

Zahavi speaks of this experience of alterity as involving a kind of "self-distancing and doubling of perspectives" and the influence of others on the "development and formation of our standards" (321). I argue in the following that as such, the experience of alterity can be found to be an essential element in both standard and non-standard accounts of shame, and the distinction between non-social and social accounts of shame may simply be a matter of interpretation.

For example, Taylor's (1985) standard account of shame accepts that such an alterity is an essential aspect of shame, especially in the fact that it acknowledges the necessity of what Deonna, Rodogno, and Teroni refer to as a "reflexive stance upon what one does or is" (2012, 149). Taylor speaks of this kind of reflexive stance as a "sophisticated type of self-consciousness":

Shame requires a sophisticated type of self-consciousness. A person feeling shame will exercise her capacity for self-awareness, and she will do so dramatically: from being just an actor absorbed in what she is doing she will suddenly become self-aware and self-critical. It is plainly a state of self-consciousness which centrally relies on the concept of another, for the thought of being seen as one might be seen by another is the catalyst for the emotion. (67)

Deonna, Rodogno, and Teroni (2012) have criticized Taylor's account for being too "social," in the sense that her account, as indicated in the above passage, relies on the concept of ANOTHER.[27] Yet, her observation about the reliance on the concept of ANOTHER is not, as Deonna, Rodogno, and Teroni suggested, that the concept of ANOTHER is always "deployed" in an experience of shame (Deonna, Rodogno, and Teroni 2012, 149, footnote 10).

Taylor's suggestion that the self-conscious state of shame relies on the concept of ANOTHER, is her way of conveying the structure of the self-consciousness—that of the self-conscious awareness of oneself—that is necessarily involved in shame, which Zahavi has, in opposition to Deonna, Rodogno, and Teroni, criticized Taylor's account for lacking (Zahavi [2012] 2013, 315). As Taylor observed:

There is, then, this point to the metaphor of an audience and of being seen: they reflect the structural features of the agent's becoming aware of the discrepancy between her own assumption about her state or action and a possible detached observer-description of this state or action, and of her further being aware that she ought not to be in a position where she could be so seen, where such a description at least appears to fit. (66)

The self-conscious awareness of oneself, observed by Taylor in the above passage, however, is not what constitutes the essential aspect of what makes shame the kind of emotion that it is since, within Taylor's cognitivist approach, the self-conscious structure is constitutive of the experience of shame as belief(s) of rational intelligibility rather than the identificatory belief of shame.[28] As Taylor also states:

> A person feeling shame judges herself adversely. This judgment is brought about by the realization of how her position is or may be seen from an observer's point of view. But there is no reference to such a point of view in her final self-directed judgment. (68)

And it is this final, self-directed judgment that constitutes shame's identificatory belief—the content of which defines shame's intentionality—that one is "defective and degraded" (66).

Given the particularities of Taylor's account of shame, one might argue that Taylor's standard account of shame admits ambiguity when it comes to the question of whether or not her account is more accurately characterized as a non-social account of shame (as Zahavi suggested) or a social account of shame (as suggested by Deonna, Rodogno, and Teroni), since for Taylor, both the beliefs of rational intelligibility and the identificatory belief of shame are "constitutive" of an experience of shame (Taylor 1985, 1–3). It is the identificatory belief, however, which defines experiences of shame as experiences of shame. It is also not ambiguous that Taylor's account of shame is a standard account of shame, which takes a global, negative self-assessment to be the differentia of shame—what identifies shame as an emotion of shame.

Also consider J. David Velleman's (2006) standard account of shame. Velleman characterizes shame as a kind of anxiety experienced by its subject in response to the subject's belief that one's capacity for self-presentation is threatened, a capacity that Velleman claims to be constitutive of one's will (52–53). What leads an agent to hold such a belief, according to Velleman, is the agent's belief that they had in some sense failed to "guard" their capacity for self-presentation by failing to act in accordance with their will, such as on occasions of what Velleman refers to as "failures of privacy" (60–61), or when one is made to feel as if one had failed to act in accordance with one's will by the behavioral responses of one's partners to social interaction, such as in cases that Velleman refers to as "failures of obscurity" and "inchoate shame" (61–64). In all such cases, the subject has an experience of having failed in some sense, that is, a global, negative self-assessment.

Furthermore, Velleman explains that the subject experiences the emotion of shame as an anxiety because the belief that one's capacity for self-presentation is threatened is associated with the belief that one may lose one's social standing as a qualified partner to social interaction (54–55). So, according to Velleman's account, the target or object of one's shame is the subject's failure or an attribute of the subject, and what identifies shame as an experience of shame—shame's intentionality or, in Taylor's terms, shame's identificatory belief—is a threat to one's self-presentation. What explains one's experience of a threat to one's self-presentation is that the subject believes or is made to believe that they had in some sense failed to guard their capacity for self-presentation.

Given this portrayal of Velleman's standard account of shame, one might argue that his account seems to inadequately explain why assessments of the subject made by particular others would affect the subject, as in cases of failures of obscurity and inchoate shame. Failures of obscurity, according to Velleman, are occasions of shame in which the subject's capacity for self-presentation is undermined because the particular target or object of the shame—which may be associated with the self through a synecdochic relation—obscures the subject's self-presentation (62). An example of such an occasion, according to Velleman, is a case in which a subject experiences shame in response to racist remarks. According to this example, the subject of racist remarks may experience shame because the target, the subject's race in this case, "eclipse[s] his efforts at self-presentation" (62). The subject of the racist remarks, as Velleman continues to explain, "is displayed, not just as 'the nigger' or 'the hymie,' but as one who has thus been captured in a socially defined image that leaves no room for self-presentation" (62).[29]

In considering such occasions of shame, and given that Velleman's account attempts to identify the intentionality of shame as a threat to one's capacity for self-presentation, it must be asked why subjects of failures of obscurity would come to ascribe such a property to the target—to some failure or attribute of the self—especially when one's capacity for self-presentation is inextricably tied to one's will and not to others' assessments. It leads one to question why one would believe that one's capacity for self-presentation is threatened, especially on occasions where the locus of the failure resides in one's partner to social interaction instead of the subject.

What I see occurring here is something analogous to the effect of fun house mirrors. When standing in front of a fun house mirror, one sees a distorted image of oneself reflected back unto oneself. The distortion is an attribute of the mirror rather than the person who is reflected in the mirror. So, any subject's belief regarding the distorted image, other than the belief that the image is an image of the subject, would be about the mirror and not the subject. Thus, if the subject comes to hold the belief that the distortion of the image implies something about the subject's self, it seems that some explanation as to why the subject would come to hold such a belief is needed. Similarly, one might argue that it remains to be explained, in Velleman's account, why the subject's assessment of their capacity for self-presentation, and thus their will, would be affected by the assessments of particular others, especially in cases in which the failure resides in the other rather than in the subject.[30]

Velleman's response would be that the subject comes to have the belief that their capacity for self-presentation, and thus their will, is threatened because they feel a "genuine vulnerability of being displayed as less than the master of [their] self-definition, and therefore, less than a socially qualified agent" (62–63).[31] I suggest that this feeling of vulnerability refers to the experience of the "significant and irreducible element of 'alterity'" that Zahavi concluded to be contained in shame ([2012] 2013, 321). This experience of alterity is also what underlies the experience of the dual perspective in guilt and shame that Lynd (1961) spoke of in regard to one's relations with others, wherein with guilt one "tends to regard both others and himself as instruments, remaining external to each other" and with shame "there is the ability to see the world through the eyes of another person, with another instead of myself as the center" (236–37). It also grounds what Calhoun referred to as the "practical weight" that the perspective of one's co-participant in a shared moral practice has on one's self-understanding (2004, 139–45); what Deigh referred to as the "concern for the opinion of others" (1983, 238); what Piper referred to as a "care about other's image of you" ([1992] 1996, 275); and what Tangney and Dearing (2002) referred to as "shame-proneness."

It can be understood in terms of having both a phylogenetic developmental history, and an ontogenetic developmental trajectory. Its evolutionary roots can be found not only in Deonna, Rodogno, and Teroni's postulation of a notion of "proto-shame" (2012, 169–70), but also in Nussbaum's postulation of "primitive shame" (2004, 84). What H. B. Lewis identifies as a "perceptual field" (1971, ch. 4) may be the more rudimentary structure that underlies a more robust sense of alterity, which Nussbaum spoke of as a "vicarious experience."[32] And, it might explain why individuals who have been clinically diagnosed with having a pervasive developmental disorder have not only been observed to be capable of experiencing shame (see Muris et al. 2016), but also to be shame prone (see Davidson, Vanegas, and Hilvert 2017),[33] and wherein an excessive sense of such alterity may be indicative of what Scheff referred to as "chronic shame" (2000, 86).

This "social" characterization of shame, which requires one to take an outside perspective on oneself, along with the opposing non-social characterization of shame, therefore, do not neatly map onto the respective categories of non-standard and standard accounts of shame, since Lynd (1961), H. B. Lewis (1971), Taylor (1985), Tangney and Dearing (2002), Nussbaum (2004), Velleman (2006), and Deonna, Rodogno, and Teroni (2012) are proponents of standard accounts and Deigh (1983), Piper ([1992] 1996), Scheff (2000; 2003), Calhoun (2004), and Zahavi ([2012] 2013) are proponents of non-standard accounts. Yet, each of these accounts can be understood as acknowledging the significance of alterity.

This sense of alterity, although being an essential feature of shame, also does not differentiate experiences of shame from any other kind of self-conscious emotion. Thus, this sense of alterity cannot be an articulation of the core of shame—the superordinate inference rule of shame, which constitutes the ontological rationality of shame. It alone cannot identify experiences of shame as experiences of shame, nor can it alone help us distinguish rational experiences of shame from irrational experiences of shame. This sense of alterity—which helps define the genus of shame as a self-conscious emotion, along with what has been observed about shame and other self-conscious emotions within the philosophical, psychological, and sociological literature on shame—can, however, help us identify the intentionality of shame, the superordinate inference rule of shame, and the ontological rationality of shame by allowing us to pull together various accounts of shame in order to isolate and precisify the normative standard that is entailed by the criterion for the ontological rationality of shame.

PRECISIFYING THE COR^{SHAME} AND IDENTIFYING SUR^{SHAME}

Based on what has been observed within the literature on shame from the disciplines of philosophy, psychology, and sociology, including the similarities and differences between shame and embarrassment, humiliation, humility, anger, guilt, and anxiety, we can conclude that the normative standard entailed by the criterion for the ontological rationality of shame, which defines experiences of shame as experiences of shame (shame's differentia), would have the following characteristics:

(1) An appropriate degree (in terms of fine-grainness) of alterity—in which too much can be understood in terms of something like chronic shame and too little can be understood in terms of having qualities that would place one on the positive side of the autism spectrum, and of which ontologically rational experiences of shame, embarrassment, humiliation, humility, some forms of anger, guilt, and anxiety can all be understood as types of modifications—that constitutes an essential aspect of the normative standard of the ontological rationality of shame (specifically, its genus as a self-conscious emotion);

(2) A sudden realization, perception, or belief about oneself—which heightens one's sense of alterity and affects a general but deep sense of oneself, or oneself within a given context—is the focus of the normative standard for the ontological rationality of shame;

(3) A general or contextual, global, negative self-assessment constitutes at least one of the conditions of the normative standard of the ontological rationality of shame, in which experiences of shame would be judged to be rational *qua* shame (i.e., ontologically rational, but not necessarily instrumentally, epistemically, or evaluatively rational);

(4) The thought, perception, or belief that a significant co-participant in a shared social or moral practice holds a negative assessment of oneself, or oneself within a given context—even when one does not agree with or accepts this negative assessment as being accurate—also constitutes at least one of the conditions of the normative standard of the ontological rationality of shame, in which experiences of shame would be judged to be rational *qua* shame (i.e., ontologically rational, but not necessarily instrumentally, epistemically, or evaluatively rational);

(5) The normative standard for the ontological rationality of shame functions so as to mediate negotiations between intrapersonal and interpersonal perspectives on oneself, including one's personal and interpersonal values, which serves the purpose of establishing, maintaining, or dismantling ranks among members of a epistemic community; and

(6) The normative standard in question may function in conjunction with other type-level superordinate inference rules, although its operation has been typically observed to be positively correlated with the superordinate inference rules of embarrassment, humiliation, anger, guilt, and anxiety, and negatively correlated with the superordinate inference rule of pride.

Given these precisifications, I propose that (at the least) the superordinate inference rule of shame (SUR^{SHAME}) is as follows:

SUR^{SHAME}: Shame begins with (a) the sudden realization (of which the subject may be unaware) that one is being seen (by the self or at least one other) as an aberrant member of one's epistemic community, and this experience may lead to at least one of the following epistemic conditions: (b) the recognition that one is taken to be an aberrant member of one's epistemic community, (c) the acceptance that one is an aberrant member of one's epistemic community, (d) the rejection that one is taken to be an aberrant member of one's epistemic community, or (e) the rejection of the (real or imagined) other as a legitimate authority on shared social or moral knowledge (such as knowledge pertaining to shared hermeneutic resources), i.e., ostracism, self-isolation, or revolution, all of which can include a breakdown in epistemic trust.

This proposal for the normative standard that constitutes the superordinate inference rule of shame, which fulfills the criterion for the ontological rationality of shame, captures (at the least) a significant aspect of the normative standard that constitutes the superordinate inference rule of shame. It may, however, not exhaust the intentionality of shame if we regard experiences of shame to be about more than the subjective, first-person experiences of shame. For example, one might also regard second-person and third-person experiences of shaming to also constitute or inform the intentionality of shame. It would, however, entail that what underlies the rational attribution of rational or irrational shame, as an experience of shame, and the meaning of the English word "shame," along with its cognates such as "ashamed" and its linguistic equivalents in other languages, is the proposed superordinate inference rule for shame.

It, along with Philip's belief of rational intelligibility, also helps explain why and how Philip's token experience of shame (the identificatory belief that [*he-has-a-club-foot*]) expresses the intentional content that *one-is-defective-and-degraded*: Philip's belief of rational intelligibility that [*he-is-unable-to-play-football*] is both what explains and caused Philip to hold his identificatory belief that [*he-has-a-club-foot*], and this identificatory belief that [*he-has-a-club-foot*] expresses the content that *he-is-defective-and-degraded* because the belief that [*he-has-a-club-foot*] led Philip to realize, again in this case,[34] that he is an aberrant member of his epistemic community, and that he is therefore defective and degraded. So, he experienced shame.

FULFILLING THE COR[SHAME]

My proposal for the normative standard that constitutes the superordinate inference rule of shame implies that when we consider the intentionality and ontological rationality of shame, we ought not regard experiences of shame in terms of a static state but rather in terms of a dynamic state that unfolds within a certain expanse of time, and in accordance with other aspects of the subject, perhaps also including their relationship with significant co-participants in a shared social or moral practice, which have not been further specified in this chapter (e.g., the subject's baseline level of self-confidence, attachment style, race, rank, status, and class). Furthermore, what I suggest as the superordinate inference rule of shame fulfills the precisified criterion for the ontological rationality of shame, in the following ways.

The superordinate inference rule of shame operates (regardless of its reliability) as a mode of alterity: it constitutes one kind of experience of our *sense of others*, which allows us to also experience ourselves not only as a member of a epistemic community, but also as one who is outside of an epistemic community; it allows us to experience ourselves as *the object* of others' assessments, as *others* for whom we are objects of assessment, and as *others who are the objects* of our assessment. The reliable operation of the superordinate inference rule of shame would allow us to have sudden realizations (in the form of a perception, belief, or imaginings) that one is taken (by oneself or another) to be an aberrant member of one's epistemic community, and such realizations would affect one's deep sense of self (either generally or contextually understood) because they necessarily call into question one's epistemic authority about the norms (statistical or axiological) one shares with co-participants in a shared social or moral practice, which the subject presupposed that they were in accord with prior to their sudden realization. This *calling into question* alone can incite shame without a corresponding global, negative self-assessment.

That calling our epistemic authority on these shared norms into question taps into a deep (general or contextual) sense of our self is not surprising. According to Strohminger and Nichols (2014), our "moral traits—more than any other mental faculty—are considered the most essential part of identity, the self, and the soul" (159), and these "moral traits" can be taken as the manifestations of our epistemic authority about shared norms (statistical or axiological) in a social or moral practice.[35]

That the reliable operation of the superordinate inference rule of shame includes various combinations of experiences from (a) to (e) (as noted in the previous section), and that the variety of these combinations of experiences—including those that are regarded by standard and non-standard accounts of shame to be irrational experiences of shame—instantiate the ontological rationality of shame should help make sense of the variety of shame experiences that are reflected not only in the ordinary language use of the English word "shame," and its linguistic equivalents in other languages, but also in theoretical languages of shame. For example, an experience of shame that ends simply with (a) or (b) may be what one might refer to as "the affect of shame,"[36] and it may be differentiated from an experience of shame that continues on and ends with (c), which may be referred to by employing the ordinary language English word "ashamed." Furthermore, an experience of shame that moves from (a) to (d), without also including (b) or (c), may have been referred to by H. B. Lewis (1971) as "by-passed shame" (197), whereas an experience of shame that moves from (a) to (e), without also going through (c)–(d), may have been referred to by H. B. Lewis as "shame-rage" (198).

That the reliable operation of the superordinate inference rule of shame involves the realization that one is taken as an aberrant member of one's epistemic community, which also calls into question the legitimacy of one's epistemic authority about shared social or moral norms, and therefore threatens what is most identified with one's personal identity, also explains why shame can function so as to mediate negotiations between one's intrapersonal and interpersonal perspectives on oneself and to establish, maintain, and dismantle ranks among members of an epistemic community. For the dynamics of shame experiences, which may include the experience of shaming, may be understood not only in terms of how members of an epistemic community negotiate shared social or moral norms, but also how one negotiates the internalization or rejection of these norms.

Finally, the superordinate inference rule of shame can also explain why shame may be experienced in conjunction with the emotions of embarrassment, humility, humiliation, anger, guilt, and anxiety, while also being negatively correlated with experiences of pride. The dynamics of the superordinate inference rule of shame may overlap with other type-level superordinate inference rules in that the various nodes from (a) to (e) may be shared by other type-level superordinate inference rules. For example, nodes (a)–(e) may be shared by experiences of "embarrassment," "humiliation," "anger," "guilt," and "anxiety." This, however, may not necessarily indicate a problem with the superordinate inference rule of shame since it would be consistent with ordinary language uses of these terms (see Scheff 2003), and the superordinate inference rule for shame may also be differentiated from the superordinate inference rules of embarrassment, humiliation, anger, guilt, and anxiety by the fact that these other type-level superordinate inference rules would have nodes that are not shared with the superordinate inference rule of shame.[37] For example, the superordinate inference rule of anger may include a node, the contents of which, represents an impediment to one's desired aims or goals, and the superordinate inference rule for guilt may include a node, the contents of which, represents the subject's accepted responsibility for an action. Furthermore, the superordinate inference rule of shame may be related, yet also differentiated, from the superordinate inference rule of humility in the sense that the two types of superordinate inference rules may have at least one common node (e.g., nodes (b) or (c)), and which may help describe how experiences of shame can lead to experiences of humility.[38]

A SIGNIFICANT BENEFIT OF THE SUR[SHAME]

One significant benefit of my proposal for the superordinate inference rule of shame is that it can shed more light on the rationality of our experiences of shame compared to alternative accounts of shame. Since the superordinate inference rule of shame grounds the intentionality of shame, and the intentionality of shame constitutes the ontological rationality of shame, any experience of shame that is in accordance with the superordinate inference rule of shame can be understood as being in some sense "rational," specifically, they can be understood as being "rational" in the ontological sense, regardless of their instrumental, epistemic, or evaluative rationality. This is because judgments regarding this kind of rationality—the ontological rationality of shame—would not take into consideration anything other than whether or not experiences of shame are consistent with the reliable operation of the normative standard that is expressed as the superordinate inference rule of shame.

From the perspective of empirical research, judgments regarding the ontological rationality of shame would only consider whether or not the intended use of the English word "shame," including its cognates such as "ashamed" and its linguistic equivalents in other languages, are consistent with the proposed superordinate inference rule of shame. The consistency between the intended uses of the English word "shame" and the proposed superordinate inference rule of shame may be determined by a conjunction of empirical methods—including ones that take at least some subject reports as accurately conveying their experience of shame—which aim to determine the veridicality or truth of a subject's intended use. Some subject reports, such as those given under artificial conditions,[39] may instead be regarded to be ontologically irrational experiences of shame. In other words, a conjunction of both qualitative and quantitative methods need to be used in order to triangulate a conclusion regarding whether or not a subject's experience of shame is an ontologically rational or an ontologically irrational experience of shame.

In differentiating the ontological rationality from the instrumental, epistemic, and evaluative rationality of shame, regardless of the empirical methods used to study the ontological rationality of shame, my proposed account of shame allows researchers to differentiate experiences of shame from emotional experiences that are not experiences of shame. It also allows researchers to speak of and study the rationality of experiences of shame that are independent from the rationality of how a subject uses their experience of shame to inform their rational decision-making (instrumental rationality), the rationality of a subject's justification or warrant for having an ontologically rational experience of shame (epistemic rationality), and the rationality of a subject's ontologically rational experience of shame with regard to the subject's personal history and values (evaluative rationality). Furthermore, this may then allow researchers to formulate more effective responses or therapies to help those who have uncontrollable, personally disruptive, or indefinitely reoccurring ontologically irrational experiences of shame.

ACKNOWLEDGMENTS

I would like to thank all of those who contributed to the development of this paper, which I began as a graduate student at Arizona State University: Cheshire C. Calhoun, Lani (Michelle) Shiota, Peter French, and Margaret U. Walker. Thank you for helping me think through the ideas that are now in this paper.

NOTES

1. In regard to standard accounts of shame in the psychological discourse, see H. B. Lewis 1971, and more recently Tangney and Dearing 2002. In regard to non-standard accounts of shame, see Gilbert 1998, 21–22, on "external shame."

2. See Tangney 1996, Gilbert 1998, Deonna, Rodogno, and Teroni 2012.

3. All my uses of "or" ought to be taken as mutually inclusive disjunctions. Every mutually exclusive disjunction is indicated by the use of "either, or."

4. Similar problems occur regarding what emotions are, which is at a more abstract level of inquiry in which the object of study is the genus Emotion (see Mun 2016b).

5. See Fricker 2007 and Dotson 2012.

6. Cf. this account with H. B. Lewis's (1971) account of shame, especially the fact that H. B. Lewis's account of shame exemplifies a standard account of shame whereas as the account proposed here is a non-standard account of shame.

7. Note that I use upper-case letters and superscripts in these cases in order to indicate that I am referring to whatever constitutes the base (e.g., a criterion for ontological rationality) within the given context, which is indicated by the use of a superscript. So, the term "COR^{SHAME}," refers to the criterion for ontological rationality within the context of shame, that is, the criterion for the ontological rationality of shame.

8. The notion of a superordinate inference rule was inspired by Cosmides and Tooby's (2000) notion of a "superordinate program" (92), although my notion of a superordinate inference rule refers more so to a connectionist system than a computational system.

9. *X is grounded in Y, or Y grounds X, if the existence of Y is a sufficient condition for inferring the existence of X*; that is, the existence of a particular thing X, or the existence of a particular set x (of particular things), is grounded in the existence of a particular thing Y, or the existence of a particular set y (of particular things), if the existence of a particular thing Y, or the existence of a particular set y (of particular things), is a sufficient condition for inferring the existence of the particular thing X, or the existence of the particular set x (of particular things).

10. My proposal does not imply that we can necessarily recover the fact that shame has evolutionary origins and developmental aspects from only the ordinary language use of the English word "shame" and its linguistic equivalences in other languages. I deny that we can necessarily do so because of the complexities of the meaning of such ordinary language words (see Mun 2016b). What I am suggesting, however, is that at least part of the meaning of these ordinary language words (such as the referent) may reflect the fact of shame's evolutionary and developmental aspects.

11. I am not speaking here of token experiences of shame, which may be differentiated from shame as a type of experience. Token experiences of shame also include a biographical history, which impart personal meanings to the shared meanings of our language.

12. For example, it does not presuppose what Barrett (2006) referred to as the "natural-kind view" and the "basic-emotion approaches" in psychology; what Deigh (1994) referred to as a "cognitivist theory," "thought-centered theory," and

"feeling-centered theory"; and what Charland (1995) referred to as a "computational theoretical framework" in philosophy. What I propose here, however, may be regarded as being fundamentally consistent with all of these views, approaches, theories, and framework.

13. The "aboutness" or intentionality of shame can also be understood in terms of Kenny's (1963) notion of an emotion's "formal object" (191), which is essential to what an emotion is.

14. Although I wouldn't discourage people from reading Maugham's novel, I would recommend that readers approach it with a critical perspective that uncovers the misogyny and privileged perspective that is implicit in this work of fiction.

15. Note that it is also possible to frame our discussion of the rationality of shame in accordance with other theories or approaches, and a cognitivist approach, such as Taylor's (1985), can be differentiated from what has been referred to in the philosophy of emotion as "cognitive theories" of emotion (see Mun forthcoming; also see Deigh 1983).

16. A unit of explanation can be generally understood as that through which an explanation is given and understood. For example, other than beliefs, which are regarded to be the primary unit of explanation in a cognitive approach to shame, one may also provide an explanation of what shame is, or various aspects of shame, in terms of feelings, physiological responses, or even what Kahnamen (2011) referred to as a "U-index." These could be alternative units of explanation.

17. See Mun 2019b for a more detailed discussion of the difference between proper targets and mere targets according to de Sousa's (1987) account.

18. See Mun, this edited collection, ch. 3, for a more detailed account of what I referred to as "beliefs of rational intelligibility."

19. Brackets, italics, and dashes are used throughout this chapter in order to indicate a belief with a specific type of content, whereas italics and dashes used without brackets indicate a particular content or type of content.

20. See Mun, this edited collection, ch. 3, for a schematic breakdown of all of Taylor's beliefs of rational intelligibility for shame.

21. In regard to the content of a belief there is no significant difference between the content that *Philip-is-unable-to-play-football* and the content that *he-is-unable-to-play-football*, since the context would dictate that the contents are equivalent.

22. One might conclude instead that Philip was ashamed of his inability to play football *because* of his club foot: his belief that [*he-has-a-club-foot*] would thus be given as the *reason* why he felt ashamed (his belief of rational intelligibility), and his belief that [*he-is-unable-to-play-football*] would be given as his identificatory belief, which would also be the belief that would be taken to indicate what it was that Philip found shameful (i.e., the target of his belief). Although this interpretation is not essentially problematic, the interpretation given above is a superior interpretation of Maugham's intentions, especially because Philip's club foot, and not his inability to play football, is a major feature of Maugham's story. For an additional discussion of Maugham's story, as it relates to Taylor's (1985) account, see Mun forthcoming.

23. For a discussion of the notion of "warrant," which is to be contrasted with the notion of "justification," within the philosophical area of epistemology, see Plantinga [1993] 2008; also see Prinz 2004 for a discussion of warrant with respect to emotions.

24. In practice we typically take one's rationality for granted and attend to questions regarding the irrationality of individuals when we are presented with a reason to do so, and the normative standard is typically put in positive terms as defining what is rational and what is irrational is typically evaluated in opposition to this normative standard.

25. It is important that readers do NOT equivocate "alterity" with "self-awareness" (see Zahavi 1999).

26. Although Zahavi ([2012] 2013) does speak of "non-social shame," he does not explicitly speak of "social shame," although he does speak of "shame."

27. I use all capitalizations in order to indicate reference to a concept.

28. See Mun, ch. 3, this edited collection, beliefs [T1]–[T3].

29. Also see Goffman 1963 for a more in-depth discussion on how people navigate through social norms and expectations as a way of managing their self-presentation.

30. Although Velleman might fall back on the response that these cases are cases of irrational shame, and as such his account need not provide such an explanation, the inadequacy of such a response becomes especially salient when we consider my argument regarding the dangers of falling back on the attribution of irrationality as a response to such requests (Mun, this edited collection, ch. 3; also see Mun 2019a). In short, such responses may be susceptible to charges of committing acts of epistemic injustice, especially against members of marginalized communities.

31. This response is consistent with what Velleman (2019) conveyed to me during a recent conversation, and although it suggests that his account may be more accurately characterized as a non-standard account of shame it would be problematic to regard it as such. Velleman's account differs from non-standard accounts like Calhoun's (2004) and Piper's ([1992] 1996) because it would regard some experiences of shame, such as Piper's groundless shame, to be "utterly inchoate shame" (64). As such, it is more accurately characterized as a standard account of shame since, like other standard accounts, it regards experiences of shame in which one does not hold a negative self-assessment to be irrational cases of shame.

32. Also see Harris-Perry's (2011) discussion of the perceptual field in relation to experiences of shame. Furthermore, according to Scheff (2000), H. B. Lewis also proposed that "shame arises when there is threat to the social bond" (95) or in response to "actions in the 'inner theatre'" (95). The "social bond" and "inner theatre" of which Scheff speaks may also be understood as implicating the sense of alterity of which I am speaking.

33. Readers should note the distinction between first-person experiences of shame—the indicators of which have been observed to be highly correlated with some of the experiences of individuals with pervasive developmental disorders (Muris et al. 2016, 385), which includes autistic disorder, Asperger disorder, and pervasive developmental disorder-not otherwise specified—and third/second-person recognitional capacities for shame experiences, a deficit of which has been observed with some individuals who have been clinically diagnosed with a pervasive developmental disorder (e.g., high-functioning autism and Asperger's syndrome); see Heerey, Keltner, and Capps 2003.

34. I say "again" here because although Philip would always know that he has a club foot, this need not entail that he is always aware of the fact that he is an aberrant member of his epistemic community.

35. For a more detailed discussion of how such moral traits can be related to one's epistemic authority about shared norms (statistical or axiological) in a social or moral practice, see Mun forthcoming.

36. Also see H. B. Lewis's discussion on the affect of shame (H. B. Lewis 1971, 233).

37. See Millikan's (2017) notion of "unitracker" for an idea similar to what I have in mind regarding the ontological structure of superordinate inference rules.

38. See Tanesini 2018 for an account of humility that could be consistent with the account of humility proposed here, although one ought to note the distinctions between the framework for humility employed by Tanesini and the framework for shame employed here.

39. For example, see the famous Schachter and Singer (1962) paper.

REFERENCES

Barrett, Lisa F. 2006. "Are Emotions Natural Kinds." *Perspectives on Psychological Science* 1, no. 1: 28–58.

Calhoun, Cheshire. 2004. "An Apology for Moral Shame." *Journal of Political Philosophy* 12, no. 2: 127–46.

Charland, Louis C. 1995. "Emotions as a Natural Kind: Toward a Computational Foundation for Emotion Theory." *Philosophical Psychology* 8, no. 1: 59–84.

Cosmides, L. and J. Tooby. 2000. "Chapter 7: Evolutionary Psychology and the Emotions." In *Handbook of Emotions*, 2nd ed., edited by Michael Lewis and Jeanette M. Haviland-Jones, 91–115. New York, NY: Guilford Press.

Davidson, Denise, Sandra B. Vanegas, and Elizabeth Hilvert. 2017. "Proneness to Self-Conscious Emotions in Adults With and Without Autism Traits." *Journal of Autism and Developmental Disorders* 47: 3392–404. DOI: 10.1007/s10803-017 -3260-8.

Deigh, John. 1983. "Shame and Self-Esteem: A Critique." *Ethics* 93, no. 2: 225–45.

———. 1994. "Cognitivism in the Theory of Emotion." *Ethics* 104, no. 4: 824–54.

Deonna, Julien A., Raffaele Rodogno, and Fabrice Teroni. 2012. *In Defense of Shame*. New York, NY: Oxford University Press.

de Sousa, Ronald. 1987. *The Rationality of Emotion.* Cambridge, MA: MIT Press.

Dotson, Kristie. 2012. "A Cautionary Tale: On Limiting Epistemic Oppression." *Frontiers: A Journal of Women's Studies* 33, no. 1: 24–47.

Fricker, Miranda. 2007. *Epistemic Injustice: Power and the Ethics of Knowing.* New York, NY: Oxford University Press.

Gilbert, Paul. 1998. "What Is Shame? Some Core Issues and Controversies." In *Shame: Interpersonal Behavior, Psychopathology, and Culture*, edited by Paul Gilbert and Bernice Andrews, 3–38. New York, NY: Oxford University Press.

Goffman, Erving. 1963. *Stigma: Notes on the Management of Spoiled Identity.* Englewood Cliffs, NJ: Prentice-Hall.

Harris-Perry, Melissa V. 2011. *Sister Citizen: Shame, Stereotypes, and Black Women in America.* New Haven, CT: Yale University Press.

Heerey, Erin A., Dacher Keltner, and Lisa M. Capps. 2003. "Making Sense of Self-Conscious Emotion: Linking Theory of Mind and Emotion in Children with Autism." *Emotion* 3, no. 4: 394–400.

Kahneman, Daniel. 2011. *Thinking, Fast and Slow*. New York, NY: Farrar, Straus, and Giroux.

Kenny, Anthony. 1963. *Action, Emotion and Will. Studies in Philosophical Psychology*. London, England: Routledge and K. Paul.

Lewis, Helen Block. 1971. *Shame and Guilt in Neurosis*. New York, NY: International Universities Press.

Lynd, Helen Merrell. 1961. *On Shame and the Search for Identity*. New York, NY: Science Editions, Inc.

Maugham, W. Somerset. 1915. *Of Human Bondage*. Garden City, NY: Doubleday, Doran, and Company, Inc. Accessed July 30, 2018. https://hdl.handle.net/2027/osu.32435001348671

Millikan, Ruth G. 2017. *Beyond Concepts: Unicepts, Language, and Natural Information*. New York, NY: Oxford University Press.

Mun, Cecilea. 2016a. "The Rationalities of Emotion." *Phenomenology and Mind* 11: 48–57. DOI: 10.13128/Phe_Mi-20105.

———. 2016b. "Natural Kinds, Social Constructions, and Ordinary Language." *Journal of Social Ontology* 2, no. 2: 247–69.

———. 2019a. "Rationalities through the Eyes of Shame: Oppression and Liberation via Emotion." *Hypatia*. DOI: 10.1111/hypa.12472.

———. 2019b. "How Emotions Know." *The Value of Emotions for Knowledge*, edited by Laura Candiotto, 27–50. London, England: Palgrave Macmillan.

———. Forthcoming. *Interdisciplinary Foundations for the Science of Emotion: Unification without Consilience*. Lanham, MD: Lexington Books.

Muris, Peter, Cor Meesters, Jolina Heimans, Sandra van Hulten, Linsy Kaanen, Brigit Oerlemans, Tessa Stikkelboeck, and Tim Tielmans. 2016. "Lack of Guilt, Guilt, and Shame: A Multi-Informant Study on the Relations Between Self-Conscious Emotions and Psychopathology in Clinically Referred Children and Adolescents." *European Child and Adolescent Psychiatry* 25, no. 4: 383–96.

Nussbaum, Martha C. 2004. *Hiding from Humanity: Disgust, Shame, and the Law*. Princeton, NJ: Princeton University Press.

Piper, Adrian. (1992) 1996. "Passing for White, Passing for Black." In *Out of Order, Out of Sight*, volume 1, Selected Writings in Meta-Art 1968–1992, 275–307. Cambridge, MA: MIT Press. Citations refer to the reprint edition.

Plantinga, Alvin. (2000) 2008. "Warrant: A First Approximation." In *Epistemology: An Anthology*, 2nd edition, edited by Ernest Sosa, Jaegwon Kim, Jeremy Fantl, and Matthew McGrath, 429–41. Malden, MA: Blackwell Publishing.

Prinz, Jesse. 2004. *Gut Reactions: A Perceptual Theory of Emotion*. New York, NY: Oxford University Press.

Schachter, Stanely and Jerome E. Singer. 1962. "Cognitive, Social, and Physiological Determinants of Emotional State." *Psychological Review* 69, no. 5: 379–99.

Scheff, Thomas J. 2003. "Shame in Self and Society." *Symbolic Interaction* 26, no. 2: 239–62. DOI: 10.1525/si.2003.26.2.23.

————. 2000. "Shame and the Social Bond: A Sociological Theory." *Sociological Theory* 18, no. 1: 84–99. https://search-proquest-com.sheffield.idm.oclc.org/docview/213331924?accountid=13828.

Strohminger, Nina and Shaun Nichols. 2014. "The Essential Moral Self." *Cognition* 131: 159–71.

Tangney, June Price. 1996. "Conceptual and Methodological Issues in the Assessment of Shame and Guilt." *Behavioral Research and Therapy* 34: 741–54.

Tangney, June Price and Ronald L. Dearing. 2002. *Shame and Guilt.* New York, NY: Guilford Press.

Tanesini, Alessandra. 2018. "Intellectual Humility as Attitude." *Philosophy and Phenomenological Research* 96, no. 2: 399–420. DOI: 10.1111/phpr.12326.

Taylor, Gabriele. 1985. *Pride, Shame, and Guilt: Emotions of Self-Assessment.* New York, NY: Oxford University Press.

Velleman, James David. 2006. *Self to Self: Selected Essays.* New York, NY: Cambridge University Press.

Zahavi, Dan. (2012) 2013. "Self, Consciousness, and Shame." In *The Oxford Handbook of Contemporary Phenomenology.* Oxford Handbook Online. Accessed July 13, 2018. DOI: 10.1093/oxfordhb/9780199594900.013.0016.

Chapter 3

Oppression and Liberation via the Rationalities of Shame

Cecilea Mun

Traditionally, shame has been characterized within the disciplines of philosophy and psychology as an emotion of global negative self-assessment, in which an individual necessarily accepts or assents to a global negative self-evaluation[1] (i.e., a negative evaluation of the whole self) (e.g., Lynd 1961; H. B. Lewis 1971; Taylor 1985; Williams 1993; M. Lewis 1995; Tangney and Dearing 2002; Nussbaum 2004; Velleman 2006; Deonna, Rodogno, and Teroni 2012; also see Gilbert 1998, 21–22, on "internal shame"). I refer to these accounts as *standard accounts of shame*. In *non-standard accounts of shame*, which are more commonly found within the philosophical discourse on shame, what defines shame is not the fact that one *holds* a global negative self-assessment, but the fact that one's assessment of one's identity is *susceptible to* the criticisms of others (e.g., Deigh 1983; Calhoun 2004; Zahavi [2012] 2013; also see Gilbert 1998, 21–22, on "external shame"). It is this *liability to* holding such negative self-assessments that gives experiences of shame their *intentional content*.[2] Gilbert characterized this disagreement as a disagreement over whether or not a global negative self-evaluation is necessary for an experience of shame (1998, 21).

I argue here in favor of non-standard accounts of shame over standard accounts by highlighting the problems with the closed conceptual structure of standard accounts of shame.[3] I begin with a detailed discussion of standard accounts of shame, focusing primarily on Gabriele Taylor's (1985) standard account. I then illustrate how Adrian Piper's ([1992] 1996) experience of groundless shame can be portrayed as (1) both a rational and an irrational experience of shame, in accordance with Taylor's account as a paradigm model of standard accounts of shame, and (2) as a rational experience of shame when taken in its own right as a legitimate, rational account of shame. Without denying that some experiences of shame are or can be irrational experiences of shame,[4] I move on to rely on Miranda Fricker's (2007), Christopher Hookway's (2010), and Kristie Dotson's (2011; 2012) accounts of different kinds of epistemic injustice in order to elucidate how standard accounts of shame can act as mechanisms of epistemic injustice, and in doing so can transmute the righteous indignation of the marginalized by recasting it as a shameful experience (i.e., by recasting it as an experience of the righteous shame of the marginalized).

TAYLOR'S STANDARD ACCOUNT OF SHAME

Gabriele Taylor's (1985) account of shame is a paradigmatic model of standard accounts of shame. According to Taylor's account, like pride, guilt, humiliation, and embarrassment, shame is constituted by at least two types of beliefs: *identificatory beliefs* and *explanatory beliefs*. An identificatory belief is not simply a belief that is associated with an emotional experience; it is a particular belief that is *constitutive of* a particular emotional experience in the sense that *it identifies that experience as a specific type of emotional experience* (e.g., shame, guilt, and embarrassment) (2).[5] An explanatory belief is *constitutive of* a particular emotional experience in the sense that it *causally explains why an individual would hold a particular identificatory belief without necessarily being a reason* for that individual's holding of that particular identificatory belief, and therefore *without necessarily being a reason for that individual's experience of a particular type of emotion* (36).[6] Taylor also spoke of explanatory beliefs that are *reasons for an individual's experience of a particular type of emotion* (i.e., that are reasons for the holding of a particular type of identificatory belief); these are explanatory beliefs (and so are causally constitutive in the same sense that all explanatory beliefs are), but they *also* make a particular emotional experience *rationally intelligible* (3).[7] For the purpose of clarity, I refer to explanatory beliefs that provide *only* causal explanations for an emotional experience—*without* also being a *reason for* an emotional experience, and thus *without* also being *a reason for* an identificatory belief—as *merely causal beliefs*. I will refer to explanatory beliefs that provide *both* causal explanations and are reasons for an emotional experience as *beliefs of rational intelligibility*.[8]

For Taylor, the identificatory belief of shame involves a global negative self-assessment in which an individual judges oneself to be defective and degraded (66, 68). What explains the rational intelligibility of an individual coming to hold such an identificatory belief—shame's beliefs of rational intelligibility—are the belief that there is a discrepancy between what one uncritically, unselfconsciously thought or assumed about oneself and a possible detached observer-description of oneself or one's action, and the belief that one ought not be seen under such a detached-observer description (66). Therefore, a sufficient condition for experiencing shame, according to Taylor's standard account, is the identificatory belief (T6), that one is defective and degraded (a global negative self-assessment). Furthermore, these three conditions for the rationality of shame, according to Taylor's standard account can be precisified through the following scheme of beliefs:

T1: *Belief*[I see myself under some benign, uncritical, unselfconscious description]

T2: *Belief*[I see myself under an alternative description; the detached-observer description]

T3: *Belief*[There is a discrepancy between belief (T1) and belief (T2)]

T4: *Belief*[There is a normative standard in accordance with which I find the alternative description in belief (T2) to be an undesirable description of myself]

T5: *Belief*[I ought not be seen under the alternative description of belief (T2)]

T6: ∴ *Belief*[I am defective and degraded]

In Taylor's account, beliefs (T1)–(T5) are the beliefs of rational intelligibility for any experience of shame, and therefore are independently necessary and jointly sufficient for rationally holding belief (T6), that one is defective and degraded. Thus, an experience of shame in which one did not also hold beliefs (T1)–(T5) would be regarded as an "irrational" experience of shame. Furthermore, because it would be unreasonable for one to have an experience of shame without also holding the identificatory belief that one is defective and degraded, an experience of shame that does not include this identificatory belief would also be regarded to be an "irrational" experience.[9] In the next section, I demonstrate how Adrian Piper's ([1992] 1996) experience of groundless shame can be characterized as being "irrational" in both these ways, but I begin by demonstrating how her experience of shame can be understood as a "rational" experience of shame, in accordance with Taylor's standard account.

THE "RATIONALITY" OF GROUNDLESS SHAME

In "Passing as Black, Passing as White," Piper ([1992] 1996) tells her readers about her experience during her first graduate student reception, in which she met for the first time a prominent, white, male professor whom she admired and whom, based on her admissions application, assumed that she would be dark skinned since Piper identified herself as black. Although Piper is in fact black, she in fact also has light skin. Piper recounts her experience of shame in response to the prominent, white, male professor's remark that Piper was just as black as he was in the following way:

> [T]here was the groundless shame of the inadvertent impostor, exposed to public ridicule or accusation. For this kind of shame, you don't actually need to have done anything wrong. All you need to do is care about others' image of you, and fail in your actions to reinforce their positive image of themselves. Their ridicule and accusations then function to both disown and degrade you from their status, to mark you not as having done wrong but as being wrong. This turns you into something bogus relative to their criterion of worth, and false relative to their criterion of authenticity. (275–76)

We can re-describe Piper's experience of shame in accordance with Taylor's standard account of shame by fitting Piper's experience into the scheme of necessary and jointly sufficient beliefs that were listed in the previous section:

TP1: *Belief*[I accurately identified myself as black on my admissions application]

TP2: *Belief*[A prominent, white, male professor believed that I fraudulently identified myself as being black]

TP3: *Belief*[There is a discrepancy between belief (TP1) and belief (TP2)]

TP4: *Belief*[There is a shared norm among members of the department, which includes me, as a graduate student, of maintaining one's worth and authenticity through one's accurate self-presentation]

TP5: *Belief*[I ought not be seen as being fraudulent by a prominent, white, male professor]

TP6: ∴ *Belief*[I am marked as being wrong in some way]

The intentional content of Piper's notion of groundless shame—what groundless shame represents—can be understood as *being-marked-as-being-wrong-in-some-way*.[10] The intentional content of groundless shame can also be understood, in terms of Taylor's account of shame, as the identificatory belief of being defective and degraded, which constitutes the experience of shame. The necessary and jointly sufficient beliefs of (TP1)–(TP5), as Piper's token beliefs of rational intelligibility, both logically and causally entail her experience of shame (i.e., the token, constitutive, identificatory belief that Piper is marked as being wrong in some way). Piper's experience of groundless shame, according to this interpretation, would therefore be characterized as a "rational" experience according to Taylor's standard account.

Lifting the Constraints on the Rationality of Shame

One ought to consider, however, whether Piper's experience of groundless shame ought to be understood in such a way so as to make it fit Taylor's standard account. Although Taylor's standard account of shame renders Piper's experience of groundless shame as a "rational" experience of shame, one ought to ask why one would regard Piper's shame as a "rational" experience of shame in accordance with Taylor's account. Why ought Piper be ashamed—have the experience of being *marked-as-being-wrong-in-some-way*—when it was *the professor who falsely believed* that Piper fraudulently identified herself as black, and then ridiculed her based on *his* false belief? One would think that the prominent, white, male professor is the one who should have been appropriately ashamed![11]

In response to the above question, I propose an alternative reading of Piper's experience, one that presumes a kind of *irony* in her description. The irony in Piper's description, I propose, lies in her *apparent* adoption of the prominent, white, male professor's perspective, which is evident not only in calling her experience an experience of "the groundless shame of the inadvertent imposter," but also in her response to being ridiculed by the prominent, white, male professor when he remarked that she was as black as he was. I propose that in Piper's experience of groundless shame, *she* in fact did *not* hold any global negative self-assessment. What brought about her experience of shame is, *as she said*, her concern for how the prominent, white, male professor identified her—a concern for his image of her ([1992] 1996, 2)—and the vulnerability of having her identity be susceptible to the interpretations of others.[12] As Calhoun suggests, insofar as we are co-participants of a shared moral practice "one's own self-conception does not decisively determine who one is" (2004, 145), although one ought to also note that the conceptions of others alone also fail to decisively determine who one is.[13] Thus, *as Piper stated*, the ridicule to which she was subjected (the remark that she was as black as the prominent, white, male professor), after she failed to reinforce his positive image of himself (I assume as an accurate assessor of race), *turned her* into something bogus relative to *his* criterion of worth and into something false relative to *his* criterion of authenticity (275–76).

Given this second reading of Piper's experience of groundless shame, we can reconstruct Piper's experience, in accordance with Taylor's standard account, in terms of the following scheme of beliefs:

TP1: *Belief*[I accurately identified myself as black on my admissions application]

TP2: *Belief*[A prominent, white, male professor believed that I fraudulently identified myself as being black]

TP3: *Belief*[There is a discrepancy between belief (TP1) and belief (TP2)]

TP4*: *Belief*[The prominent, white, male professor holds a normative standard about race such that in order for one to "accurately" identify oneself as black one ought to be dark skinned]

TP5: *Belief*[I ought not be seen as being fraudulent by this prominent, white, male professor]

TP6*: ∴ *Belief*[I believe that the prominent, white, male professor has marked me as being wrong in some way]

This second reading of Piper's experience, however, renders Piper's experience into an "irrational" experience of groundless shame, given Taylor's standard account of shame. It does so for two reasons: First, Taylor's account postulates that the operative normative standard in belief (T4) is the standard that the subject of shame would use in order to derive the imperative in belief (T5). And, according to the second reading of Piper's description of her experience, belief (TP4*) is not constituted by a normative standard from which belief (TP5) can be logically derived. It is instead constituted by a belief that a co-participant in a shared moral practice holds a normative standard to which the subject does not also subscribe.[14] Thus, what were identified as the beliefs of rational intelligibility for Piper's experience of shame, beliefs (TP1)–(TP3), (TP4*), and (TP5), would not reasonably justify her experience (i.e., her identificatory belief for shame, according to Taylor's standard account). These beliefs would therefore be merely causal beliefs for Piper's shame.

Second, belief (T6), in the scheme of beliefs for Taylor's account of rational shame, constitutes the identificatory belief that identifies the subject's experience as an experience of shame, and according to Taylor's account, this belief is necessarily a global negative self-assessment, specifically the belief that one is defective and degraded. Belief (TP6*), however, is not a negative self-assessment. It is instead a belief that *a co-participant in a shared moral practice perceived or judged one to be defective and degraded*. Thus, given my second reading, Piper's experience of groundless shame would be characterized by Taylor's standard account as an "irrational" experience of shame. It would be irrational because (1) the beliefs of rational intelligibility that Piper would have held would not have appropriately justified her experience of shame, and (2) *Piper* would not have held the identificatory belief that she was defective and degraded and yet, according to Piper's testimony, she would have had an experience of shame.

This characterization of Piper's experience of shame as being "irrational," in accordance with a standard account of shame, may seem to be a perfectly accurate or acceptable conclusion. One might argue that one ought not experience shame if one did not believe oneself to be defective and degraded, and that to experience shame when one did not hold such a belief is in fact irrational. One may also argue that my second reading of Piper's description of her experience is also inaccurate, especially given Piper's own words. For example, one might note that Piper calling her experience an experience of "groundless shame" betrays her belief that her experience was an irrational experience. Yet my second reading of Piper's description of her experience would suggest an alternative explanation of why Piper referred to her experience as "groundless;" it suggests that what Piper believed to be groundless in her experience of shame was *the prominent, white, male professor's belief* that Piper was marked as wrong in some way rather than Piper's belief that she was marked as wrong in some way.[15]

My second, alternative reading of Piper's description of her experience is also consistent with other readings of Piper's experience (see Calhoun 2004, 137), and it is more accurate to the extent that it gives significant weight to *all* of Piper's words and not just some. For example, the first reading of Piper's experience, presented in accordance with Taylor's standard account as beliefs (TP1)–(TP6), fails to acknowledge the significance of Piper's testimony that "*All you need to do* is care about others' image of you, and fail in your actions to reinforce their positive image of themselves" for an experience of groundless shame (275, italics added for emphasis); that these alone may be sufficient conditions for shame.

Some might also observe that the "problem" with my second reading of Piper's description of her experience of groundless shame is that when analyzed in accordance with Taylor's standard account of shame, Piper's experience is rendered into an "irrational" experience. I argue here that this problem lies not with Piper's experience of shame, her description of her experience, nor my second reading of Piper's description of her experience, but instead with standard accounts of shame, of which Taylor's account serves as a paradigm example, through which Piper's experience can be interpreted. When we remove the restrictions on rationality imposed by Taylor's standard account, take Piper's epistemic authority on her experience for granted, and accurately attend to her testimony, what is revealed is Piper's rational, non-standard account of shame.[16] And when we include the fact that Piper committed no wrong, we can understand her experience of shame as an experience of the *righteous shame of the marginalized*.[17]

I began the process of lifting the constraints on rationality imposed by standard accounts of shame at the beginning of this section by questioning the legitimacy of the interpretation of Piper's experience through the framework of Taylor's standard account of shame. We must now take Piper's epistemic authority for granted, which requires that we take Piper's experience to be a rational experience, especially given the fact that Piper's description of her experience actually depicts her as one who was both calm, levelheaded, and witty in response to the prominent, white, male professor's unjustified remarks, even if her response—that she hadn't known that he was as black as she was—was "automatic" (275). Doing so should motivate us to accurately attend to her testimony—her description of groundless shame—by giving each of her words a significant amount of epistemic weight,[18] which entails ensuring that each of her words play a significant role in an explanation of how Piper's experience is a rational experience of shame. Doing so reveals the following scheme of beliefs for Piper's experience of groundless shame (275–76):

P1: *Belief*[I had a concern for how the prominent, white, male professor identified me]

P2: *Belief*[I did not agree with the prominent, white, male professor's ridicule that I was as black as he was; I did not reinforce the prominent, white, male professor's positive image of himself as an accurate assessor of race, and was ridiculed for it]

P3: ∴ *Belief*[I was turned into something bogus relative to his criterion of worth, and false relative to his criterion of authenticity; I was marked by him as being wrong in some way]

The above depiction of Piper's experience of groundless shame, necessarily takes her experience to be a rational experience, since the presumption of acknowledging her epistemic authority would force us to acknowledge her experience as a rational experience. The above depiction of Piper's experience thus takes Piper's epistemic authority on her experience for granted—it does not commit any testimonial injustice. It therefore lifts the constraints on rationality that was previously placed on Piper's experience by the application of Taylor's standard account of shame—by the testimonial injustice enabled by standard accounts of shame. We can therefore derive the following general scheme of beliefs for Piper's notion of groundless shame—*covertly* named the "groundless shame of the inadvertent imposter" (275)—as a rational experience of shame:

GS1: *Belief*[I care about others' image of me][19]

GS2: *Belief*[I failed to reinforce others' positive image of themselves, and I am therefore ridiculed, disowned, and degraded (shamed) for this failure]

GS3: ∴ *Belief*[I am turned into something bogus relative to others' criterion of worth, and false relative to others' criterion of authenticity; I am marked as being wrong in some way]

Any experience of shame that fits the above scheme of beliefs for groundless shame would, according to standard accounts of shame (such as Taylor's), be regarded to be an "irrational" experience of shame. Yet when such experiences are taken in their own right, as legitimate, rational experiences of shame, they stand as rational accounts of shame that are consistent with other non-standard accounts of shame. Furthermore, upon closer examination, if we include the fact that Piper did nothing wrong, what Piper has given us is a depiction of a rational experience of shame that is *a rational response to an unjustified punitive action, committed by a co-participant of a higher status or rank, against one's status as an epistemic knower within a particular group.* As such, rational responses of this kind can also be understood as experiences of the *righteous indignation of the marginalized.*

In the following sections, I will further explain how such experiences can be transmuted into experiences of the *righteous shame of the marginalized* (e.g., the groundless shame of the inadvertent imposter) through the constraints on rationality that are placed upon one's experiences in virtue of standard accounts of shame (such as Taylor's standard account). I argue that, at the *social-practical-level* of analysis, some acts of shaming and being shamed (rather than being ashamed)[20] are acts of testimonial injustice, including acts of systematic testimonial injustice. And, these acts are enabled by standard accounts of shame. Furthermore, at the *social-conceptual-level* and the *practical-theoretical-level* of analyses, the transmutation of the righteous indignation of the marginalized into experiences of the righteous shame of the marginalized, in virtue of standard accounts of shame, are occasions of hermeneutic injustice, contributory injustice, or epistemic silencing (specifically, testimonial quieting and testimonial smothering). At the social-conceptual level, standard accounts of shame permit the transmutation of the righteous indignation of the marginalized into the righteous shame of the marginalized, and thereby socially authorize acts of hermeneutic or contributory injustice. At the practical-theoretical level, standard accounts of shame permit occasions of testimonial quieting, by prompting co-participants to reinterpret occasions of righteous indignation as occasions of the righteous shame of the marginalized, and they compel subjects to censor their testimony, thereby occasioning acts of testimonial smothering.

A TAXONOMY OF EPISTEMIC INJUSTICE

Epistemic injustice can be generally defined as an injustice that harms an agent as a knower. Applying Dotson's distinction between instances and practices (241) *mutatis mutandis* to the various kinds of epistemic injustice, such harms can be differentiated into at least four kinds of practices of epistemic injustice: testimonial injustice and hermeneutic injustice (see Fricker

2007; Hookway 2010; Dotson 2012); contributory injustice (Dotson 2012); and epistemic silencing (Hookway 2010 and Dotson 2011).

Testimonial injustice is a wrong committed by a hearer within the context of information-centered, communicative exchanges in which some prejudice leads the hearer to discount the epistemic credibility of the speaker (Fricker 2007, 1). This harms the speaker's capacity as a giver of knowledge by discounting the speaker's credibility as a reliable testifier. In short, the speaker suffers a "credibility deficit" (Fricker 2007, 61). Thus, their status as a legitimate member of an epistemic community is harmed. Fricker defines hermeneutic injustice as "the injustice of having some significant area of one's social experience obscured from collective understanding owing to a structural identity prejudice in the collective hermeneutical resource" (155). Such an injustice is regarded to be a structural injustice, according to Fricker, since it involves a deficiency in the shared hermeneutic resources that results in members of relevant social groups being unable to or denied the ability to make meaningful contributions to relevant hermeneutical resources due to their marginalized status (2007, 155).

Contributory injustice is comparable to Fricker's notion of hermeneutic injustice, since both involve the harm of "thwarting" an epistemic agent's ability to meaningfully contribute to shared hermeneutical resources due to "structurally prejudiced hermeneutic resources" (Dotson 2012, 32), although contributory injustice differs from hermeneutic injustice in that (1) it does not presuppose a closed conceptual structure (Dotson 2012, 37); (2) it does not ignore the availability of alternative hermeneutical resources, especially to members of marginalized communities, by acknowledging the fact that an epistemic agent can be denied the ability to meaningfully contribute to shared hermeneutic resources without also always being denied the ability to make sense of their own experiences as consequences of such harms (Dotson 31–32); and (3) contributory injustice is enacted by individuals rather than the relevant community in general.[21]

Epistemic silencing is an epistemic injustice committed by an epistemic agent due to a failure to recognize or admit the participatory value of an agent as a member of an epistemic community, which may engage in a variety of activities that include but are not limited to epistemic activities, due to the holding of some prejudice (see Hookway 2010, 154; Dotson 2011, 241).[22] Dotson (2011) also identifies two kinds of epistemic silencing: testimonial quieting and testimonial smothering (242).

Testimonial quieting, which is consistent with Hookway's (2010) notion of epistemic silencing, is observed by Dotson as occurring "when an audience fails to identify a speaker as a knower" (242). *Testimonial smothering* occurs when an epistemic agent "smothers" or "truncates" their own testimony "in order to ensure that the testimony contains only content for which one's audience demonstrates testimonial competence" (244). Dotson also notes three circumstances that are typical in cases of testimonial smothering, and all three circumstances together provide an explanation for why an epistemic agent would smother their own testimony:

(1) the content of the testimony must be unsafe and risky;
(2) the audience must demonstrate testimonial incompetence with respect to the content of the testimony to the speaker; and
(3) testimonial incompetence must follow from, or appear to follow from, pernicious ignorance. (Dotson 2011, 244)

Although there are various ways to distinguish differing kinds of epistemic injustices,[23] we can differentiate both testimonial injustice and hermeneutic injustice from both contributory injustice and epistemic silencing, including the two forms of testimonial quieting and testimonial smothering, by appealing to Hookway's (2010) notions of the information perspective and the participant perspective (157).[24] An informational perspective is one in which participants engage each other from the perspective of taking each other, and themselves, as reliable sources of knowledge, whereas a participant perspective is one in which participants engage each other from the perspective of judging whether or not other participants, and perhaps even themselves, are competent pursuers of some activity (and not just epistemic activities). Given this distinction, we can understand both contributory injustice and epistemic silencing as going beyond the boundaries of testimony—as going beyond the informational perspective espoused by both testimonial injustice and hermeneutic injustice—and instead espousing the participant perspective, which concerns more than the epistemic activities of giving and taking knowledge.

We can also differentiate testimonial injustice, contributory injustice, and testimonial quieting from both hermeneutic injustice and testimonial smothering by the fact that the first three are necessarily harms committed by a particular person against another particular person, and so can typically be characterized in terms of a dyadic relation, whereas hermeneutic injustice and practices of testimonial smothering are effects of a shared system of meanings or values on a particular person, within the context of a triadic relation between a person, their self, and members of their community, and are mediated by a system of meanings and values that are shared among relevant members of their community (i.e., hermeneutic resources). As such, it is the community in general that perpetrates practices of contributory injustice and testimonial smothering.

Despite these differences between testimonial injustice, hermeneutic injustice, contributory injustice, and epistemic silencing, all four kinds of epistemic injustice, which include the two categories of testimonial quieting and testimonial silencing, share the essential feature of being harms to an agent as a knower: testimonial injustice harms an epistemic agent as a knower by unduly subjecting the agent to an epistemic credibility deficit; both hermeneutic injustice and contributory injustice harm an epistemic agent in their ability to make epistemic contributions to shared hermeneutical resources or practices; testimonial quieting harms an epistemic agent as a knower through the failure to recognize an epistemic agent's status as a knower; and testimonial smothering harms an agent through coercive circumstances that compel an epistemic agent to censor their participation as an epistemic agent. All these harms can, therefore, be understood as harms to an agent as a knower since each type of harm implicates the agent's knowledge, ability to transmit knowledge, or ability to create knowledge within some shared practice. Yet, given the foregoing, all five harms can be understood as distinct kinds of epistemic injustices. In the following sections, I will illustrate how standard accounts of shame act as mechanisms of testimonial injustice, hermeneutic injustice, contributory injustice, testimonial quieting, and testimonial smothering, in that order.

SHAMING, BEING SHAMED, AND TESTIMONIAL INJUSTICE

Standard accounts of shame *enable* at least two kinds of experiences: shaming and being shamed. They, therefore, *enable* acts of epistemic injustice. In the context of both shaming and being shamed, standard accounts of shame can act *as mechanisms of epistemic injustice*. This can be illuminated by an analysis of how standard accounts operate in cases of groundless shame. At the *social-practical-level of analysis*—at the surface level on which the object of analysis is the communicative act between co-participants in a shared social practice—*acts of shaming* members of a marginalized community in the way that the prominent, white, male professor shamed Piper *are themselves acts of testimonial injustice*. In Piper's experience, the prominent, white, male professor sought to discredit Piper's epistemic authority through his shaming remark that Piper was as black as he was, which was not black at all. His remark sought to diminish Piper's general epistemic status by challenging her credibility as someone who knows the socially circumscribed differences between someone who is black and someone who is white, as well as Piper's credibility in her self-knowledge as someone who is black. Such challenges subject epistemic agents to credibility deficits and harm the agent's capacity as a giver of knowledge; they inhibit the target of shaming from conveying their knowledge to the shamer, and potentially or actually inhibit the target from conveying their knowledge to any other co-participant. As Piper attested:

> Their ridicule and accusations function to both disown and degrade you from their status, to mark you not as having *done* wrong but as *being wrong. This turns you into something bogus relative to their criterion of worth, and false relative to their criterion of authenticity. Once exposed as a fraud of this kind, you can never regain your legitimacy.* (275–76, italics added for emphasis)

Such acts of shaming can also be understood as constituting a practice of "systematic testimonial injustice," which are regarded as "systematic," because, according to Fricker (2007), they are injustices that track the subject of such injustices through a system of associated injustices that occur within the context of various types of activities (27). At the social-practical level of analysis, the testimonial injustice experienced by Piper in her experience of groundless shame was a consequence of what Fricker referred to as a "negative identity-prejudicial stereotype" (2007, 35), which *prompted* the prominent, white, male professor to shame Piper. The prominent, white, male professor would not have thought it appropriate to shame Piper in such a way if not for the fact that he regarded her as being subordinate in some way: by being black, a woman, or a graduate student. Such dispositions were made possible not only by the problematic negative identity-prejudicial stereotypes held by the professor, but also by an understanding of shame that reflects a standard account.

These negative identity-prejudicial stereotypes (that graduate students, women, and black people are necessarily subordinate to prominent professors, males, and white people) are aspects of the emotion feeling rules that confer a sense of appropriateness to the shaming practices that are motivated by, and therefore reinforced by, the conditions that sustain such negative identity-prejudicial stereotypes.[25] Standard accounts of shame also encourage co-participants, especially those who may be regarded as having a higher status, rank, or place of privilege, to resort to shaming to not only mark the other as being defective and degraded, but to also attempt to cause the other to believe that they are defective and degraded. They provide the conceptual resources (i.e., hermeneutic resources) that, when understood as feeling rules (Hochschild 2012), *enable* such acts. As such, standard accounts of shame, understood as espousing feeling rules for shame (including shaming, being shamed, and experiences of shame), are mechanisms for the practice of systemic testimonial injustices at the social-practical level of analysis.

Such systematic testimonial injustices are prevalent in many societies, especially those that rely on a hierarchy of status or class. For example, in the United States and the United Kingdom, such systematic testimonial injustices can also be understood in terms of what Rachel McKinnon (2017) refers to as "gas lighting," as well as what are often referred to as "micro-aggressions." One might also argue that the lack of diversity within academic disciplines, such as philosophy, is partly a result of such deliberate or inadvertent attempts of testimonial injustice. The prevalence of using shame as a mechanism of epistemic injustice is also an extension of its effectiveness as a general mechanism for establishing a ranking order among members of a hierarchical community (Cohen, Vandello, and Rantilla 1998, 274; also see Deonna, Rodogno, and Teroni 2012). Yet, although such shaming is often successful in oppressing those of a lower rank, it does not necessarily do so. As evidenced by Piper's experience of groundless shame, such acts of shaming can also backfire, and instead embolden the marginalized subject to challenge, and at times illegitimatize, the authority of the higher-ranking co-participant—a lesson to be kept in mind by those who hold positions of authority.

SHAME, RATIONALITY, HERMENEUTIC INJUSTICE, AND CONTRIBUTORY INJUSTICE

By permitting Piper's experience of groundless shame to be rendered an "irrational" experience, standard accounts of shame (such as Taylor's) also act as mechanisms of practices of hermeneutic or contributory injustice at the *social-conceptual level of analysis,* on which the object of analysis is a concept, including the analysis of its application by members of a hermeneutic community, outside of communicative acts. Recall that Piper experienced shame without also holding the global negative self-assessment that was *required* by Taylor's standard account in order for Piper's experience to be regarded a *rational* experience of shame. Thus, Taylor's account marks Piper's experience as being "irrational." In doing so, standard accounts of shame can deny subjects of such experiences of groundless shame, or members of their community, the ability to make sense of these experiences. Understanding standard accounts of shame in this way is to understand them as mechanisms of hermeneutic or contributory injustice at the social-conceptual level of analysis.

At the social-conceptual level of analysis, standard accounts of shame—as illustrated in the first three sections, by the example of Taylor's standard account—encourage agents to locate the "irrational" *inconsistency* between *the criteria for shame* established by standard accounts of shame and *experiences of shame* (such as Piper's) to some aspect of the target of shaming/the subject of shame (e.g., the target or subject's cognitive or emotional system) rather than something "external" to the target/subject (e.g., standard accounts of shame or a deficit in a shared system of meanings or values/hermeneutic resources).[26] As such, when standard accounts successfully permit the attribution of irrationality—when the criticism sticks—they act as mechanisms of hermeneutic or contributory injustice by *practically* diminishing one's *capacity to convey* one's emotional intelligence or knowledge, or by *practically* diminishing the *reliability* of one's general cognitive capacity to process emotional, social, or other relevant information (e.g., in terms of a loss of one's trust in one's cognitive or emotional system, or a loss of trust by others in one's cognitive or emotional system).[27] Thus, the attribution of irrationality, made possible by standard accounts of shame, can also subject epistemic agents to credibility deficits, which work to incapacitate or debilitate an individual as a knower within their epistemic community.

In cases in which one has no access to alternative hermeneutic resources to turn to, such as non-standard accounts of shame or the alternative epistemologies, countermythologies, and hidden transcripts noted by Dotson (2012, 31), we can understand such harms that are made possible by standard accounts of shame as occasions of hermeneutic injustice. Yet, as I have argued, rather than interpreting Piper's experience as an "irrational" experience, and thereby converting it into an irrational experience, in accordance with standard accounts, we can instead interpret Piper's experience as a rational experience in accordance with what I derived as Piper's account of groundless shame. Doing so provides us with a way of understanding how standard accounts of shame can be mechanisms of contributory injustice rather than hermeneutic injustice: what I derived as Piper's criteria for a rational experience of groundless shame can act as an alternative hermeneutic resource which epistemic agents can use in order to make sense of their experience of groundless shame, while standard accounts like Taylor's can continue to act as mechanisms that keep, at the least, some co-participants in a shared social or moral practice from accessing the rationality of the experiences of some epistemic agents due to these co-participant's "willful hermeneutical ignorance in maintaining and utilizing structurally prejudiced hermeneutical resources" (e.g., standard accounts of shame). Thus, standard accounts of shame can help "thwart" the ability of a subject of groundless shame (such as Piper's) "to contribute to shared epistemic resources" (Dotson 2012, 32), especially within a community in which some of its members advocate standard accounts of shame over non-standard accounts of shame.

Besides illustrating how Piper's experience of groundless shame can be understood as an occasion of hermeneutic or contributory injustice, my foregoing explanation also suggests that experiences of hermeneutic injustice may in fact be at least equally, and perhaps more, detrimental to *non-marginalized non-minorities* or *marginalized non-minorities* who do not have access to alternative hermeneutic resources, compared to marginalized minorities who do have access to such hermeneutic resources, since non-marginalized non-minorities or marginalized non-minorities may not have any recourse to any alternative hermeneutic resources to help them make appropriate, and perhaps liberatory, sense of their experiences of shame. Furthermore, this point might be further extended in order to encourage non-marginalized non-minorities and marginalized non-minorities to form alliances with marginalized minorities in order for all to gain access to resources that may allow them to overcome such incapacitating or debilitating injustices.

SHAME AND EPISTEMIC SILENCING

Whereas testimonial injustice and hermeneutic injustice are restricted to the domain of testimonial exchanges, and contributory injustice, which is perpetrated by the willful hermeneutical ignorance of a co-participant in a shared social practice, is enacted by an individual person, epistemic silencing (such as testimonial quieting and testimonial smothering) can occur outside strictly testimonial exchanges, within practices in which epistemic agents take a participant perspective (Hookway 2010). Furthermore, although practices of testimonial quieting are similar to practices of testimonial injustice, in that both are acts that produce a credibility deficit in a speaker, practices of testimonial quieting are especially perpetrated by an individual co-participant's failure, due to their willful ignorance of alternative hermeneutical resources. In contrast, testimonial smothering is a response to the forces of shared, prejudicial, hermeneutic resources, which coerce epistemic agents to censor their testimony, in content or style of presentation, in order to make their testimony more palatable to their audience, primarily out of both fear and being overburdened by their co-participant's willful hermeneutical ignorance.

Given these categories of epistemic injustice, we can understand how proponents of standard accounts of shame, either intentionally or unintentionally, contribute to occurrences of testimonial quieting and testimonial smothering. Such understandings are achieved at the *practical-theoretical-level of analysis*, in which one of the aims of the analysis is to understand the consequences of theoretical practices.[28] In regard to occurrences of testimonial quieting, proponents of standard accounts of shame—in reinforcing standard accounts of shame as adequate accounts of shame—fail to acknowledge the legitimacy of non-standard accounts, and as such contribute to the failure of recognizing testifiers of non-standard accounts as knowers. In the first three sections, I illustrated how proponents of standard accounts of shame do so.

Also, at the practical-theoretical level of analysis, we can understand Piper's testimony, including the naming of her account as an account of "groundless shame of the inadvertent imposter,"[29] as her response to the coercive forces of the prejudicial, hermeneutic resources (such as standard accounts of shame) that she shared with her co-participants (such as the prominent, white, male professor). As a black, female, graduate student, and perhaps even later as a prominent black, female, philosopher and artist (at the time of her testimony's first publication), one might suggest that there were good reasons for Piper to regard (1) the content of her testimony as being unsafe or risky, (2) her co-participants (such as the prominent, white, male professors) to be incompetent in being able to sufficiently accept Piper's testimony if given straightforwardly, without irony, and (3) the incompetence of her co-participants (such as the prominent, white, male professor) as following from their "pernicious ignorance," which is defined by Dotson as a "reliable ignorance or a counterfactual incompetence that, in the given context, is harmful" (2011, 242).[30] As such, Piper's testimony can be understood as an occasion of the practice of testimonial smothering. Piper "censored" her testimony through an ironic, covert presentation of her experience, in which she seemed to have taken the perspective of her shamer (the prominent, white, male professor, and the white, educated, upper-class society of which he and she were both members in virtue of being members of an elite educational institution). Yet it is clear that her testimony was an ironic presentation since she did not whole-heartedly agree with such an interpretation of herself or her actions. As she continued in her testimony about African-American experiences:

> The oppressive treatment of African-Americans facilitates this distancing response, by requiring every African-American to draw a sharp distinction between the person he is and the person society perceives him to be; that is, between who he is as an individual and the way he is designated and treated by others. (285)

THE RIGHTEOUS INDIGNATION AND
SHAME OF THE MARGINALIZED

In conclusion, given all of the foregoing, one can understand how Piper's experience of groundless shame can be an experience of *the righteous indignation of the marginalized* that has been transmuted into an experience of *the righteous shame of the marginalized* in virtue of standard accounts of shame: Piper's experience can be understood so as to include the fact that she did nothing wrong, her experiences of the "wrenching grief and anger" that one of her "intellectual heroes" had "sullied himself" in her presence, as well as her ensuing experience of guilt and remorse. When we do so, we can understand her experience as *a rational response to an unjustified punitive action, committed by a co-participant of a higher status or rank, against one's status as an epistemic knower within a particular group*—an experience of the righteous indignation of the marginalized.[31] A standard account of shame, however, may regard such an experience as something like "shame-rage" (see H. B. Lewis 1971, 41, 198). This turning of such an experience of righteous indignation into an experience of irrational shame ("shame-rage"), also illustrates how standard accounts of shame, as mechanisms of epistemic injustice, can transmute such experiences when these experiences are considered from the social-practical, social-conceptual, and the practical-theoretical levels of analyses. Furthermore, at all three levels of analyses, standard accounts of shame work as mechanisms through which such experiences can be understood as instantiating *inauthentic rational experiences of shame (as with my first reading of Piper's account) or authentic irrational experiences (as with my second reading of Piper's account) that can instead be understood as rational experiences of shame (as with the final reading of Piper's account) if not for the relevant epistemic injustice perpetuated by standard accounts of shame*—they can be understood as occasions of the *righteous shame of the marginalized* (in short, *righteous shame*).[32]

ACKNOWLEDGEMENT

This chapter was previously published in *Hypatia* in a slightly different form under the title "Rationality through the Eyes of Shame: Oppression and Liberation via Emotion," © 2019, Hypatia, Inc. All rights reserved.

NOTES

1. All uses of "or" ought to be taken as mutually inclusive disjunctions, and every mutually exclusive disjunction is indicated by the use of "either, or."

2. An "intentional content" is a broader notion compared to Taylor's (1985) "identificatory belief" (2). They are, however, similar in that they both identify a certain type of experience as an experience of that type.

3. For a discussion of closed conceptual structures in regard to the concept of epistemic injustice, see Dotson 2012, 41–42. My use of the term here is mostly consistent with Dotson's use, except that it is applied to the concept of shame. As my arguments in this chapter will suggest, standard accounts of shame constitute closed conceptual structures by circumscribing a very limited set of experiences as rational experiences of shame and characterizing all other experiences of shame as irrational. I am, however, hesitant here to apply Dotson's notion of open conceptual structures to analyses of the discourse on shame because doing so would go beyond the considerations offered in this paper.

4. For example, at least some cases of "inchoate shame," see Velleman 2006, 64; at least some cases of "bypass shame" and "shame-rage," see H. B. Lewis 1971, 196, 198, and at least some cases that are appropriately characterized by standard accounts of shame.

5. Note that on Taylor's account, emotions may be constituted by a set of identificatory beliefs rather than a single identificatory belief, see Taylor 1985, 2.

6. Note that I am speaking here of a reason *for having* an emotional experience rather than a reason *for* an emotional experience. The difference between these two kinds of reasons can be understood in terms of the difference between what Taylor referred to as an explanatory belief that provides a merely causal explanation ("for having") and an explanatory belief that also provides a rational explanation ("for") (what I subsequently refer to in this passage as "beliefs of rational intelligibility").

7. One may regard the "rational intelligibility" of an emotion to be synonymous with the rationality of emotion. The notion of rational intelligibility that I am using here, however, is a notion that belongs to Taylor's particular view, which presupposes a cognitive approach to the rationality of emotions, and whether or not the rationality of emotions presupposes the kind of robust cognitive elements, such as a propositional attitude, on which Taylor's cognitive approach relies, is currently being debated in the discourse on emotion.

8. Taylor does not provide any word other than "explanatory belief" to refer to these two distinct types of explanatory beliefs. Furthermore, on Taylor's account, what I refer to as "beliefs of rational intelligibility," would not be reasons *for having* an emotion, but would instead be reasons *for* an emotion. This is because, for Taylor, the relation between beliefs of rational intelligibility and identificatory beliefs are logical relations, in which particular beliefs of rational intelligibility are the premises that rationally support a particular identificatory belief as a conclusion. Textual support for this interpretation of Taylor's view can be found in her criticism of Donald Davidson's view, see Taylor (1985, 6–14). Beliefs of rational intelligibility can, however, be reasons *for having a rational experience* of an emotion in that such beliefs are both *rationally and causally explanatory*. The significant point here is that talk of "having" an experience indicates a causal relation.

9. Note that although these conditions are each necessary and jointly sufficient for a *rational* experience of shame, Taylor's *cognitive approach* (in contrast with a "cognitive theory," see Deigh 1994), does not suggest that cognitive approaches provide a *complete* analysis of any emotion (1–2). Furthermore, I do not currently know enough about Taylor's standard, cognitive account of shame to say whether or not Taylor would regard such irrational experiences to be irrational for similar reasons as experiences of shame in which one does not hold beliefs (T1)–(T5) and yet is merely caused to believe that one is defective and degraded. Since identificatory beliefs are not reasons for an emotional experience of a certain type, but instead are constitutive of those experiences, Taylor might not think that such irrational experiences of shame were irrational in the sense that they were unjustified experiences (i.e., have beliefs with cognitive content that aim yet fail to justify the identificatory belief). They may instead be regarded as irrational in the sense that the mere causes of the identificatory belief lack any cognitive content that aims to justify the identificatory belief (i.e., they are non-justified). For a more detailed discussion regarding the rationality of emotions, including the rationality of emotions that lack cognitive content according to a cognitive theory of emotion, see Calhoun 1984 and Deigh 1994. I, however, argue here that such experiences can be epistemically rational experiences in at least two ways: (1) by being *justified* by reasons or (2) by being *warranted* by explanations that may act as something like reasons (for

the emotional experience) in a rational explanation of a person's emotional response. Also see Mun 2016, for a more thorough discussion on the instrumental rationality, epistemic rationality, evaluative rationality, and ontological rationality of emotions.

10. Following a fairly common convention in the area of philosophy of mind, I use hyphenated terms in this way in order to indicate reference to an *intentional content*.

11. One may also wonder whether or not the prominent, white, male professor, in this case, was insulated from embodying shame or, at the least, shameful qualities, because of his position of power. I would say that he was not, regardless of his shamelessness. For example, from Piper's perspective, as well as mine, the prominent, white, male professor did in fact embody such properties, especially given Piper's comment about how he "sullied himself" in her presence. Thus, one can embody shameful properties in their shamelessness. Donald Trump may serve as a more public, contemporary example. Cf. this brief note about shamelessness with the discussions on shamelessness by Mason (2010) and Baron (2018), and the related discussion of shamelessness and "second hand shame" by Weiss (2018).

12. Cf. the vulnerability in Velleman's account of shame, see Velleman 2006, 63.

13. Regarding Piper's agreement with this claim, see Piper (1992) 1996, 285; also see Goffman's (1963) depiction of "normals" and "the stigmatized" in regard to their responsibilities toward each other. From my understanding of Goffman's perspective, normals and the stigmatized have the same sorts of responsibilities toward the other, and the only difference between the stigmatized and normals is an ontological difference of having a stigmatizing property or not, although this difference significantly affects the lives of each in terms of the way various social strategies are employed. For example, see the passage starting at the end of the first paragraph, with "It should be restated here that this kind of joking by the stigmatized . . . " (134). I interpret Goffman in this passage as suggesting that the social experiences of a stigmatized person include a relation to normals that puts the stigmatized person in a position to be benevolent, which might sound surprising (at least to some), but true. I also find it liberating since it acknowledges the fact that sometimes it's the normals that need to be shown patience, especially by the stigmatized. Such alternative understandings of ourselves can also be understood as being made possible by what Dotson referred to as "alternative epistemologies, countermythologies, and hidden transcripts that exist in hermeneutically marginalized communities *among themselves*" (Dotson 2012, 31).

14. Regarding co-participants in a shared moral practice, see Calhoun 2004, 129.

15. One interesting thing to note is that given the ambiguity in Piper's presentation of her experience of groundless shame, primarily due to the irony she employs, the description of her experience might be used as a way to test a reader for implicit biases. For example, as a preliminary hypothesis, one might predict that readers with a significant degree of implicit racial bias against African Americans would read Piper's testimony as conveying that her experience was groundless because she believed that *her* experience was unjustified (therefore interpreting her testimony in a way that is similar to the first two interpretations I provided), whereas those without a significant degree of implicit racial bias against African Americans might read Piper's testimony as conveying that her experience was an experience of groundless shame because *the prominent, white, male professor* who shamed her was unjustified in shaming her.

16. In *non-standard accounts of shame*, which are more commonly found within the philosophical discourse on shame, what defines shame is not the fact that one *holds* a global negative self-assessment, but the fact that one's assessment of one's identity is *susceptible to* the criticisms of others (e.g., Deigh 1983; Calhoun 2004; Zahavi [2012] 2013; also see Gilbert 1998, 21–22, on "external shame"). It is this *liability to* holding such negative self-assessments that gives experiences of shame their *intentional content*.

17. One might judge the term "the righteous shame of the marginalized" to be a misnomer. If so, I suggest that the reader check the perspective from which they are understanding this emotion. From the perspective of the marginalized, such experiences are experiences of the righteous shame of the marginalized.

18. I refer here to a very general notion of epistemic weight—the amount of credence, legitimacy, or authority that we often give to claims, beliefs, assertions, etc.—which is also consistent with Calhoun's use of the term, see Calhoun 2004, 142.

19. Although some might believe that such a concern for others is typically qualified, I cannot say if this is the case for Piper's account of shame. But there are good reasons to think that the type of concern for others involved here is the type of unqualified, basic, or fundamental concern about others that people typically have as a statistically normal aspect of human psychology. For example, it may be the kind of concern that is involved in what Zahavi ([2012] 2013) referred to as our sense of "alterity," as well as the feeling of vulnerability toward a threat to one's self-presentation in Velleman's (2019) account of shame (cf. Velleman 2006). Also see Mun 2019.

20. By distinguishing the notions of "acts of shaming" from "being shamed," I am differentiating acts of shaming (which may also be referred to as occasions of "being shamed") from experiences of being shamed that also emotionally affect the subject. Given my distinction, acts of shaming and being shamed can come apart. Acts of shaming may misfire, and so may not successfully lead to experiences of being shamed. Acts of shaming and being shamed are also both distinct from experiences of "being ashamed." Neither acts of shaming nor experiences of being shamed need be experiences of being ashamed, especially given non-standard accounts of shame. The experience of being shamed is one in which the subject of the experience experiences shame without necessarily accepting a global, negative self-assessment. An experience of being ashamed is one in which the subject of the experience necessarily accepts a global, negative self-assessment. Thus, all standard accounts of shame necessarily entail that subjects of shame are subjects of being ashamed, whereas non-standard accounts allow for the possibility that subjects of shame are either subjects of being shamed without being ashamed or subjects of being ashamed.

21. One might also consider the difference between the notions of hermeneutic injustice and contributory injustice as products of the different perspectives held by Fricker (as a prominent white professor) and Dotson (as a prominent black professor), which provides further evidence for the benefits of promoting diversity and inclusiveness in academia.

22. Such prejudice can be understood in terms of Fricker's notion of prejudice, defined as "judgments which may have a positive or negative valence, and which display some (typically, epistemically culpable) resistance to counter-evidence owing

to some affective investment on the part of the subject," (Fricker 2007, 35). Prejudices can be differentiated from stereotypes in that stereotypes are simply defined
by Fricker as "widely held associations between a given social group and one or
more attributes," (Fricker 2007, 31). Furthermore, prejudices can be differentiated
into negative identity prejudices, which are "prejudices with a negative valence held
against people *qua* social type," and when such negative identity prejudices become
stereotypes, the result is a negative identity-prejudicial stereotype, which Fricker
defines as a "widely held disparaging association between a social group and one or
more attributes, where this association embodies a generalization that displays some
(typically, epistemically culpable) resistance to counter-evidence owing to an ethically bad affective investment" (Fricker 2007, 35).

23. For example, Dotson (2012) differentiates testimonial injustice, hermeneutic
injustice, and contributory injustice from each other in terms of an "order-of-change"
heuristic (26), which identifies testimonial injustice with first-order changes in that they
require interventions in the practice of established patterns or schemes (28), hermeneutic injustice with second-order changes in that they require changes in established patterns or schemes (30), and contributory injustice with third-order changes that require
one to go beyond established patterns and schemes, into alternative sources of meaning,
such as those alternative hermeneutic resources noted by Dotson (2012).

24. I am inferring that Dotson's two categories of epistemic silencing—testimonial
quieting and testimonial smothering—take the participant perspective, in order to
establish the need to ensure that these notions of epistemic injustice are not inscribed
as closed conceptual structures (see Dotson 2012, 37).

25. These negative identity-prejudicial stereotypes may have independent exis-
tences apart from the feeling rules that are employed by members of a social group,
but this does not negate the fact that they are also aspects of emotion feeling rules.

26. See Mun 2019, for a similar point regarding Velleman's (2006) standard
account of shame.

27. For a discussion of how the loss of trust—in oneself or in the world—is related
to the experience of shame, see Lynd 1961, 43–49.

28. Note that the three levels of analysis that I have introduced in this paper—the
social-practical, the social-conceptual, and the practical-theoretical—are levels of
analysis that may be applied to an analysis of a variety of phenomena, and an analysis at one level does not necessarily exclude the possibility of providing an analysis
of the same phenomenon from another level. For example, one might also provide
an analysis of standard accounts of shame as mechanisms of testimonial quieting
and testimonial silencing at the social-conceptual level of analysis rather than at the
practical-theoretical level of analysis, as I do here.

29. One covert aspect in her account's name, the "groundless shame of the inadvertent imposter," is in the fact that the words "inadvertent imposter" reflect the perspective
of her co-participants and not Piper's perspective of herself, yet in naming her account
the "groundless shame of the inadvertent imposter," Piper leaves the reader to possibly,
perhaps under the influence of their willful ignorance, interpret her account as indicating that she believes herself to be an inadvertent imposter. Another covert aspect, as I
discussed earlier, is the use of the word "groundless" in the naming of her account of
shame. Although one might take "groundless" as characterizing Piper's experience of

shame, I suggested earlier that the word "groundless" ought to be taken as character-izing the prominent, white, male professor's belief that Piper is wrong in some way, which is what Piper's experience of shame can be said to be about (see TP6* and P3).

30. In Piper's case, the reliable ignorance or the counterfactual incompetence can be understood as the prominent, white, male professor's ignorance of what counts as being "black," which if he had known, he would not have found it appropriate to shame Piper.

31. Such an experience is righteous to the extent that it is a rational response to an unjustified punitive action; it is righteous as a reasonable response to injustice.

32. In regard to authentic and inauthentic emotional experiences, see Taylor's (1985) chapter on integrity.

REFERENCES

Baron, Marcia. 2018. "Shame and Shamelessness." *Philosophia* 46, no. 3: 721–31. DOI: 10.1007/s11406-017-9933-x.

Calhoun, Cheshire. 1984. "Cognitive Emotions?" In *What is an Emotion? Classic Readings in Philosophical Psychology*, edited by Cheshire Calhoun and Robert C. Solomon, 236–47. New York, NY: Oxford University Press.

———. 2004. "An Apology for Moral Shame." *Journal of Political Philosophy* 12, no. 2: 127–46.

Cohen, Dov, Joseph Vandello, and Adrian K. Rantilla. 1998. "The Sacred and the Social: Cultures of Honor and Violence." In *Shame: Interpersonal Behavior, Psychopathology, and Culture*, edited by Paul Gilbert and Bernice Andrews, 262–82. New York, NY: Oxford University Press.

Deigh, John. 1983. "Shame and Self-Esteem: A Critique." *Ethics* 93, no. 2: 225–45.

———. 1994. "Cognitivism in the Theory of Emotions." *Ethics* 104: 824–54.

Deonna, Julien A., Raffaele Rodogno, and Fabrice Teroni. 2012. *In Defense of Shame: The Faces of an Emotion.* New York, NY: Oxford University Press.

Dotson, Kristie. 2011. "Tracking Epistemic Violence, Tracking Practices of Silencing." *Hypatia* 26, no. 2: 236–57.

———. 2012. "A Cautionary Tale: On Limiting Epistemic Oppression." *Frontiers: A Journal of Women's Studies* 33, no. 1: 24–47.

Fricker, Miranda. 2007. *Epistemic Injustice: Power and the Ethics of Knowing.* New York, NY: Oxford University Press.

Gilbert, Paul. 1998. "What is Shame? Some Core Issues and Controversies." In *Shame: Interpersonal Behavior, Psychopathology, and Culture*, edited by Paul Gilbert and Bernice Andrews, 3–38. New York, NY: Oxford University Press.

Goffman, Erving. 1963. *Stigma: Notes on the Management of Spoiled Identity.* New York, NY: Simon and Schuster, Inc.

Hochschild, Arlie Russell. 2012. *The Managed Heart: Commercialization of Human Feelings.* 3rd edition. Berkeley, CA: University of California Press.

Hookway, Christopher. 2010. "Some Varieties of Epistemic Injustice: Reflections on Fricker." *Episteme*: 151–63. DOI: 10.3366./E1742360010000882.

Kenny, Anthony. 1963. *Action, Emotion, and Will.* London: Routledge and K. Paul.

Kidd, Ian James, José Medina, and Gaile Pohlhaus, Jr., eds. 2017. *Routledge Handbook to Epistemic Injustice*. New York, NY: Routledge. ProQuest Ebook Central. https://ebookcentral.proquest.com/lib/sheffield/detail.action?docID=4834237.

Lewis, Helen Block. 1971. *Shame and Guilt in Neurosis*. New York, NY: International Universities Press.

Lewis, Michael. 1995. *Shame: The Exposed Self*. New York, NY: Free Press.

Lynd, Helen Merrell. 1961. *On Shame and the Search for Identity*. New York, NY: Science Editions, Inc.

Mason, Michelle. 2010. "On Shamelessness." *Philosophical Papers* 39, no. 3: 401–25. DOI: 10.1080/05568641.2010.538916.

McKinnon, Rachel. 2017. "Allies Behaving Badly: Gaslighting as Epistemic Injustice." In *Routledge Handbook to Epistemic Injustice*, edited by Ian James Kidd, José Medina, and Gaile Pohlhaus, Jr., 167–274. New York, NY: Routledge. ProQuest Ebook Central. https://ebookcentral.proquest.com/lib/sheffield/detail.action?docID=4834237.

Mun, Cecilea. 2016. "The Rationalities of Emotion." *Phenomenology and Mind* 11: 48–57. DOI: 10.13128/Phe_Mi-20105.

———. 2019. "Unification through the Rationalities and Intentionalities of Shame." In *Interdisciplinary Perspectives of Shame: Methods, Theories, Norms, Cultures, and Politics*, edited by Cecilea Mun. Lanham, MD: Lexington Books.

Nussbaum, Martha C. 2001. *Upheavals of Thought: The Intelligence of Emotions*. New York, NY: Cambridge University Press.

———. 2004. *Hiding from Humanity: Disgust, Shame, and the Law*. Princeton, NJ: Princeton University Press.

Piper, Adrian. (1992) 1996. "Passing for White, Passing for Black." In *Out of Order, Out of Sight*, volume 1, Selected Writings in Meta-Art 1968–1992, 275–307. Cambridge, MA: MIT Press. Citations refer to the reprint edition.

Tangney, June Price, and Ronda L. Dearing. 2002. *Shame and Guilt. Emotions and Social Behavior*. New York, NY: Guilford Press.

Taylor, Gabriele. 1985. *Pride, Shame, and Guilt: Emotions of Self-Assessment*. New York, NY: Oxford University Press.

Velleman, J. David. 2006. The Genesis of Shame." In *Self to Self: Selected Essays*, 45–69. New York, NY: Cambridge University Press.

———. *Personal Conversation, Eastern American Philosophical Association Conference*, January 10, 2019.

Weiss, Gail. 2018. The Shame of Shamelessness. *Hypatia* 33, no. 3: 537–52. DOI: 10.1111/hypa.12414.

Williams, Bernard. 1993. *Shame and Necessity*. Berkeley, CA: University of California Press.

Zahavi, Dan. (2012) 2013. Self, Consciousness, and Shame. In *The Oxford Handbook of Contemporary Phenomenology*, edited by Dan Zahavi. Oxford Handbooks Online. DOI: 10.1093/oxfordhb/9780199594900.013.0016. Accessed July 13, 2018.

Chapter 4

The Virtues of Epistemic Shame in Critical Dialogue

Laura Candiotto

Plato, in the famous sixth definition of sophistry in the *Sophist* (230b4–230e5), depicted *katharsis* as the function played by shame in those aporetic states triggered by Socrates via the *elenchus* (cross-examination or refutation) of an interlocutor's opinions (Candiotto 2015; 2018; 2019). This kind of epistemic purification made the epistemic agent aware of their faults, nurtured their desire to overcome this unpleasant situation, and thus, pushed them to struggle for knowledge within a process of collective inquiry. Bringing this conceptualization of shame to bear on the contemporary discourse on epistemic emotions entails that shame, in getting rid of false beliefs, is an affective tool for the epistemic enhancement of cognitive agents. Following the aporetic tradition, I maintain that the epistemic function of an aporetic state—specifically, the function of motivating one to face contradictions—is to purify the soul of its illness, which is understood here as the holding of a false belief. Moreover, this kind of purification is a crucial phase in the struggle for truth since it permits one to free their soul from the pernicious ignorance of having an unmotivated presumption of knowledge.

I first examine the function of aporetic states in the Socratic method and then in cooperative group learning, depicting their epistemic valence as purification from false beliefs.[1] *Aporetic* states are disruptive mental states wherein one faces some contradiction that one does not know how to resolve, which then leads to an epistemic doubt that breaks one's process of inquiry—as when one does not know how to solve a moral dilemma or when one finds some paradoxical conclusion in their argument. These states are endowed with a complex phenomenology, from bodily feelings to different kinds of emotional responses. My aim is to analyze the role played by one of these emotional responses—shame—by recognizing its epistemic primacy in the process of cognitive transformation. Second, I discuss the notion of cognitive

75

transformation as the outcome of the beneficial cathartic function played by shame in epistemic purification. Third, I extend this analysis to the conditions that are required to avoid shame's well-known shortcomings, thereby introducing *lovely shame* as a novel hermeneutical tool for detecting the virtuous side of epistemic shame. I finally conclude by framing the virtues of *lovely shame* within the context of Socratic skepticism.

THE FUNCTION OF APORETIC STATES IN THE SOCRATIC METHOD

For a prominent tradition in philosophy that comes from Socrates' critical thinking and Descartes' foundationalism, radical doubt is taken as a necessary preliminary step for the establishment of a well-grounded theory. For Descartes ([1641] 1996), through radical doubt we test if our beliefs are justified, and thus whether they can serve as the foundation of scientific knowledge. Before him, both Plato and Aristotle studied the crucial interweaving of doubt and knowledge, depicting *aporein* as its extreme consequence.[2] *Aporein* is the procedure that asks us to doubt those beliefs that we hold in order to test their consistency. The *aporein* leads to the *aporia*, or aporetic state, which is the negative state of no longer believing what one thought one knew. The *aporia* forces one to face contradictions, making the epistemic agent feel as if they do not have any means to escape.[3]

According to Plato's depiction of Socrates in Plato's first dialogues,[4] Socrates was a master of achieving this breakdown of reasoning: Socrates adopted *elenchus* as the best method for bringing the interlocutor to face their ignorance as unquestioned and unjustified knowledge. The dialogues between Socrates and his interlocutors display a strenuous struggle for truth in which Socrates obliges his interlocutors to face their errors in order to pass through the dark spaces of aporetic states.[5] In fact, the aporetic outcome of the Socratic method can be understood as a place in which rationality comes to a standstill, and where a paradox or contradiction serves as the best medication against the presumption of knowledge.[6] But this is not the final destination. In the Socratic method, as interpreted by Plato, aporetic states are crucial for the process of knowledge-building, not only by testing out an interlocutor's beliefs, but also for reaching the subsequent step, which is the one that displays the locus of a true beliefs' generation as *maieutic*.[7]

The powerful impact of aporetic states on the epistemic agent is primarily produced by their emotional component. Aporetic states are, in fact, both cognitive and affective; the recognition of errors is colored by certain negative feelings and dispositions (such as impotency, inadequacy, and helplessness) that are related to the experience of failure and the loss of security in one's belief system.[8] One's reasoning becomes blind and cannot find any solution, as it has fallen into the black hole of contradictions. In some of Plato's dialogues (for examples, see the *Charmides* and the *Theaetetus*), going beyond this state requires one to bravely continue the inquiry by trusting Socrates to bring them into the subsequent phase in which knowledge is generated.[9] The risk of prematurely stopping the inquiry is very high—and many of Plato's Socratic dialogues end exactly at this point (for examples, see the *Euthyphro* and the *Gorgias*); but Plato (*Soph.* 230b4-e5, *Theaet.* 149a-151d), and then Aristotle (*Met.* B, 995a24–34), showed how important it was to use aporetic states in order to go beyond them.[10]

If the *aporia* is taken as the motivation for searching for a better answer, it will not end the inquiry but, on the contrary, it will reinvigorate it. Aporetic states are thus understood by Plato as cognitively motivational states within the process of a dialogical inquiry that is functional for the achievement of truth (Candiotto 2015). The aporetic tradition brings to us an important insight: we should question our assumptions in order to detect errors and develop arguments that would falsify our unquestioned opinions, thus enhancing our understanding of a topic. And every philosopher knows how vital the doubts and the difficulties that one faces in the process of inquiry are for achieving a better understanding of the topic inquired about.[11] Aporetic states are like roadblocks that oblige us to stop and reconsider the knowledge one thought one possessed; but, by doing so, they may also lead to breakthroughs in the process of reasoning, opening new paths to better grounded answers, and developing a deeper understanding of things. Thus, the disruptive and negative aspect of aporetic states is combined with a more positive one, though still very painful.

THE FUNCTION OF EPISTEMIC SHAME IN COOPERATIVE GROUP LEARNING

In the Socratic method, the turning point between the refutation of false beliefs and the production of new and better-grounded beliefs consists in the acknowledgment of one's own inadequacy, which leads to a sense of inferiority—this situation is captured by the Greek terms *aidôs* and *aischynê*, both meaning "shame."[12] The behavioral characterization of shame—hiding the face or slumping the body—communicated deference to the Gods, and then to the group, in ancient times. This feeling of inferiority is a prerequisite for purification. Shame was a virtue, the one that allows an agent to recognize their inadequacy, and through it to purify them from wrong behaviors—from those wrong behaviors that are false beliefs according to the Socratic tradition—and, thus, to activate a process of purification.

This cleansing is the emotional acknowledgment of error, which enjoins cognitive transformation.[13] But this acknowledgment involves an active and dynamic subject who engages the process of transformation in full (Maiese 2017), as something that is also felt—in our case, by experiencing shame. Only in this case, I argue, can the "disorienting dilemma" (Merizow 2000; but on the epistemic value of disorientation see also Earnshaw forthcoming 2019), which is another way of denoting an aporetic state, lead to this shift in perspective, which is one of the most important outcomes of a learning process. Within critical dialogues, as processes of collective inquiry through philosophical conversations, aporetic states arise during the strenuous interweaving of questions and answers among the members of the group. Although there are some important differences between the Socratic method, which aims to trigger an aporetic state in the mind of interlocutors in order to purify them from false beliefs, and the cooperative process of collective inquiry, for which an eventual aporetic state would be a shared group state, the intersubjective dimension of inquiry is still at the ground of the generation of aporetic states. As in the Socratic method, the function of aporetic states in cooperative group learning is to purify group knowledge from the errors of reasoning.[14] One characteristic of such states that is very important within the process of group learning is that they arise because of a shared responsibility towards a common epistemic goal. Cooperation among interlocutors is crucial for making the recognition of errors beneficial for group inquiry.

Critical dialogue is one of the methods used in cooperative group learning, and it is relevant here because it confers to shared aporetic states a crucial role in the development of group knowledge. Within cooperative groups, perplexity is introduced into the group with the aim of enhancing each other's intellectual capacities for the benefit of group knowledge. According to Johnson and Johnson (1999), each member of a cooperative learning group is responsible for the others' epistemic progress; each member is accountable for striving to learn and for providing others with support. Thus, cooperation among interlocutors is crucial for making the recognition of errors beneficial for group inquiry since interlocutors help each other with recognizing the errors that impact the common inquiry.

Through the challenges of others, an epistemic agent may feel ashamed for their epistemic errors and, thus, have the desire to overcome this unpleasant situation through epistemic purification. Think about the thoughts that accompany your experience of shame. Some of them are related to the impact of others' judgments of you (such as "You know that I am wrong, and you blame me") or to the fear of exclusion (such as "I will be set apart because I am wrong"). Experiencing aporetic states may also trigger some thoughts related to impotency, as when you say, "I do not know any more what to believe."

As suggested earlier and will further discuss in the next section, the phenomenology of aporetic states is quite complex, and it is composed of different feelings, emotions, and thoughts. But what is important to highlight here is that epistemic shame entails a readiness to adjust the agent's relationship to epistemic contents with respect to something that is of paramount importance to the person, which is established by the achievement of knowledge through their membership in an epistemic group. The adjustment purifies the agent's beliefs, and this purification is a beneficial change within a process of transformative learning. Hence, epistemic shame functions to focus action toward the achievement of knowledge, especially the acknowledgment of false beliefs.

THE CONTEXT-DEPENDENT VALENCE
OF EPISTEMIC SHAME

Research on the so-called epistemic emotions are relatively new, and they are usually devoted to those positive emotions that are motives for inquiry (e.g., curiosity) (Stoker 2004; Brady 2009; Morton 2010; Candiotto 2017b). Yet the distinction between positive and negative emotions, as in the case of aporetic states, seem to be less discrete, and the distinction between moral and epistemic emotions doesn't seem to be very useful, especially for understanding the specific kind of action involved in epistemic agency. This means that a moral emotion (such as shame) can perform an epistemic function if inscribed within the epistemic context of inquiry. Therefore, shame can perform an epistemic function in the process of inquiry, especially within critical dialogues of group learning.

The epistemic purification triggered by aporetic states is endowed by a rich phenomenology where shame seems to play an important role. Shame, as with all affective framings, operates prior to conceptual processing and allows the agent to focus their cognitive attention on what matters to them, disclosed through bodily feelings (Slaby 2008, 447). Furthermore, as it has been underlined by Lansky (2005, 865), "shame emphasizes weakness, vulnerability, and the likelihood of rejection—so much so that its acknowledgement often generates more shame." For our topic, this implies that group aporetic states, described as the social procedure of belief-purification, may be more painful than the recognition of our faults while ruminating alone. People may prefer to avoid them, and thus they may also avoid the risky environment of cooperative group learning. But, though aporetic states are more difficult to accept in a social context—they unmask the agent's inadequacy to the other members of the group that are evaluating the agent's beliefs— they are more effective, since the social pressure encourages an agent who is feeling ashamed for their faults to change their mind and to overcome their shortcomings through collective inquiry. Therefore, this negative phase, which is characterized as being "negative" in accordance with its associated unpleasant feelings, is also very beneficial for the process of group learning since aporetic states, when shared among members of a group, set the right epistemic context for the development of a deeper understanding—the context of a cooperative effort free from the presumption of knowledge. And, arguably, a well-trained epistemic agent can appreciate its positive valence.

The common identification of emotional valence with hedonicity,[15] for which positive emotions are pleasant and thus good and negative emotions are unpleasant and thus bad,[16] finds here an interesting counter-example. In fact, aporetic states are painful, but they are judged as positive. If an epistemic agent will genuinely pursue truth, they will find that aporetic states have the power to purify their reasoning from false beliefs, since it is their unpleasantness that nurtures the desire to go beyond them and to strive for better grounded beliefs. I thus claim that aporetic states display a specific epistemic feature within the collective dimension of inquiry—the one that ascribes to shame the positive and active function of bringing the agent to enact belief-purification. Shame is therefore neither good nor bad intrinsically, but its valence depends on the function performed within a specific context: it is the context—the one of cooperative group learning and critical dialogues in our case—that confers its beneficial valence. A functionalist approach to epistemic shame is thus intrinsically relational, and it focuses on what an epistemic agent is trying to do when being moved by their desired end in a specific environment. For the functionalist approach, in fact, the function of an emotion as goal directed is to activate a certain kind of action within a specific context (Campos et al. 1994; Price 2015). In our case, the function of shame in critical dialogue is the one of purifying beliefs.

EPISTEMIC SHAME, EPISTEMIC PURIFICATION, AND COGNITIVE TRANSFORMATION

For Erickson's psychosocial, developmental stages (see in Scheck 2005), shame is a developmental precursor of guilt. This view has been also corroborated by many anthropological studies about shame cultures and guilt cultures (Gilbert and Andrews 1998). Shame is in fact a more basic emotional experience than guilt and it plays a key role in the recognition of faults urged by aporetic states. As it is well known, shame is a social emotion (Giner-Sorolla 2012, 103–30), and Barrett (1995) has clearly underlined its crucial function for the development of a moral character. Through others' challenges, an epistemic agent may feel ashamed for their epistemic errors and may thus desire to overcome this unpleasant situation through an epistemic purification that will bring about a cognitive transformation. By "cognitive transformation," I mean the act of ridding oneself of false beliefs and rebuilding a new cognitive environment filled by new and well-grounded beliefs.[17] But why does shame produce purification? How does it do so? And why does epistemic purification bring on a cognitive transformation?

Let's come back to Plato. Plato was the first who thought about the epistemic function of shame in the history of philosophy (Candiotto 2015). Moreover, as I have already noted, he settled its function exactly within aporetic states of critical dialogues. For Plato, if the agent accepts the purification activated by shame, they will recognize their faults and will be able to continue the inquiry. Therefore, for Plato, shame is a therapeutic tool that produces a *katharsis*, which means, in the etymological sense, to make the soul limpid and pure (*katharos*), free from the mistakes that did not allow one to have a correct vision/knowledge. The procedure has a medical characterization: it is a purge that allows one to get rid of the impurities in order to restore the health of the body. In the same way, by expelling false beliefs, the soul will be healthier and free to achieve new knowledge.

But what does it mean to "expel false beliefs" in contemporary terms? Psychoanalytic theory provides some salient suggestions for answering this question. Freud introduced the idea that shame is a method of defense (Lansky 1995, 1077) that deals with the feeling of inferiority (Adler 1916). Shame is thus experienced in the intersubjective dimension of life, and it makes the agent feel that something about them is wrong in comparison to the others. Then, after decades in which shame was almost neglected as a topic of study, the conceptualization of shame's relational dimension was further developed in the 1970s, thanks to the work of H. B. Lewis (1971), and in the 1980s, as a narcissistic phenomenon, by Morrison (1989).[18] What is meaningful here is that if therapy may be conceived as a kind of purification, in its Freudian-Breuerian sense (Freud and Breuer 2004), or as the identification and change of a thinking disorder by cognitive theories (Beck 1995), then the experience or re-experience of shame in treatment sessions (Lansky 1995, 1080) may be used by an analyst as a transference tool that allows them to activate the healing process. As Freud and Breuer suggested, in reference to the Aristotelian theory of *katharsis* in drama, their method is like a chimney sweep, who cleans and frees the soul from the dirt that blocked it. The core idea embedded in this method is the same one I described regarding purification through aporetic states, within an epistemic context.[19]

But why does epistemic purification bring about cognitive transformation? For the standard theory within the psychoanalytic tradition, shame and guilt are different because only guilt involves an active engagement of the agent whereas shame involves a more passive stance (H. B. Lewis 1971).[20] However, the analysis I provided about aporetic states shows us that it is the recognition of mistakes, expressed by shame, that brings one to revise one's knowledge. Although we could not be responsible for all our beliefs, since many of them are culturally acquired, or be aware in full of their wrongness, we nevertheless feel ashamed of them if they are rightly criticized by our partners during critical dialogues, and this motivates us to repair our relationship with both the members of the group and the truth by helping us get rid of errors. This belief-purification that is motivated by shame also makes space for such cognitive transformations.

Thus, differently from Barrett's functionalist account of shame and guilt (1995, 25–26, 41–43), I do not claim that only guilt functions to motivate reparative actions, since feeling ashamed of a false belief leads to purification as a reparative action. What is significant here, however, is the power performed by the social context in triggering the process of transformation through the experience of shame. Thus, we need to give due consideration to the intersubjective dimension embedded in epistemic shame in order to grasp the dynamics of the cognitive transformation. Being that shame is context-dependent, the importance of the group in giving value to the knowledge achieved, and thus motivating agents to be averse to making mistakes, is clear.

Agents also need not privately undertake a strong commitment to truth since epistemic purification is automatically activated. One should only acknowledge these states that highlight the deficiencies detected by other members of the group.[21] But the main characteristic of shame, which is a developmental precursor of guilt and activated by a social context, is that it can lead to belief-purification in a simpler and less sophisticated way, without the internalization of moral rules as required by guilt. Without the social context that points to the fallacy of one of the member's reasoning, making them feel ashamed of it, it is not assured that the agent will recognize the errors and feel guilty for them. Of course, an agent with a well-developed character—one who has internalized the rules of good and bad reasoning, testing beliefs before undertaking them—is able to feel guilty of false beliefs on their own. I can therefore reply to the questions that ask for the *how* and *why* of shame's epistemic function saying that shame is a social emotion and that its valence depends on the context. The function performed by the social context is thus the answer to the question of how and why epistemic purification brings about a cognitive transformation.

In the context of aporetic states, shame, as a moral emotion, performs an epistemic function, the one of purifying one of false beliefs. This function is triggered by the social dimensions of inquiry and, although very painful, its function is quite effective as it leads to cognitive transformation through epistemic purification. Shame does not require complex cognitive functions to be activated, but it is triggered by the social context. That's why it is very useful in group aporetic states. It activates the process of transformation, even without a clear awareness of the reason of the faults, and without envisaging solutions. The epistemic agent is susceptible to the judgment of the others, to the one the agent that has been shamed gives credit, and to the group that recognizes that the beliefs of one of its members are false.

THE EPISTEMIC VIRTUES OF LOVELY SHAME

In-group judgments that highlight cognitive mistakes and bring one to aporetic states may be very dangerous. In this regard, Nussbaum (2004) has clearly depicted the destructiveness of shame not only for the subject experiencing it, but also for a society in general. Shame, in fact, may activate processes of social exclusion, targeting, and humiliation. I don't take this important point as an objection to my thesis, since in cooperative group learning certain conditions should be assured in order to confer to shame its beneficial epistemic function. As I have already argued, shame is neither good nor bad intrinsically, but its valence depends on the function performed in a specific context: it is the context—in our case the one of cooperative group learning—that confers to it a beneficial function. I have also already established that a cooperative learning setting, which is regulated by the aim of helping each other, allows aporetic states and their emotional components to benefit from disruption. I now introduce a novel hermeneutical tool, the one of *lovely shame*, to clarify that some specific conditions are required to make shame beneficial for group learning. I bring it in theoretical terms, but I hope that the implications for educational theory and practice may be clear to the readers.

Lovely shame may be defined as "lovely" because its conditions are (1) to be experienced within a friendly environment, where the cognitive agents care for one another's cognitive achievements as individuals and as a group; (2) to be oriented by the love for wisdom; and (3) to be desired as a tool for purification. Condition (1) refers to the context: as I have already explained, in the functionalist approach that I undertake, shame is neither good nor bad intrinsically, but it acquires its valence by the action it performs in a specific context. Thus, shame may be lovely if it is performed within a friendly environment and with the aim to benefit group learning.[22] Condition (2) highlights the goal toward which the action of lovely shame should be directed: group learning and, in its first-person significance, the acquisition of wisdom.[23] Condition (3) helps to reinforce the motivation to accept aporetic states as disruptive states, and thus a desire for the purification triggered by shame, although it is very painful. Using a utilitarian calculus, the epistemic agent should assess these pains as being less than the benefits acquired by purification, and thus desire to face them for reaching the aspired epistemic goods.

However, the right environment does not do everything, and if and how shame can be beneficial also depend on individual personal beliefs and past personal histories. We thus need to ensure the development of some intellectual virtues in regulating shame, such as intellectual humility.[24] If well trained, lovely shame points to the acknowledgment of limits and, at the same time, supports the process of perfectibility. Moreover, in its zetetic stance, lovely shame is related to intellectual courage, which permits one to overcome the difficulties that can affect collective research, and allows the ashamed to be receptive to new ideas. Baehr (2011) has highlighted the relationship between intellectual courage and the willingness to be open that at first glance may seem to be an antithetical disposition to shameful behaviors, at least in their most common characterizations. But, if the ashamed is able to courageously desire to revisit their beliefs, shame will open one to epistemic purification within a safe place of cooperative group learning rather than be just a painful feeling of closure and separation.

The benefit that intellectual courage may bring to shame is the recognition of the value of cognitive transformation, which is required for transformative learning and epistemic success. But the love inherent to the lovely shame is its primary force. In this case, love is like the honey in the medication that makes the cathartic purge more tolerable, or like the antidote that neutralizes the side effects of a harmful drug. Shame is often related to the feeling of being unlovable, because of our deficiency, and thus it is joined to the fear of social exclusion. However, if this purge is administered by friends, and if the epistemic group aims to achieve knowledge, considering it the most valuable goal, then the ashamed may be prone to accept the purification operated by shame, being aware of its force of getting rid of false beliefs.

Nussbaum (2013) has depicted love as one of the fundamental emotions that we need to nurture in order to construct our humanity. From the perspective of critical dialogues, this might be intended as the necessity of converting the disruptive outcome of shame in a form of loving others which, through a process of belief-purification, could achieve cognitive transformation and self-love from self-transformation. Loving others and self-love also entail that one acknowledges errors and continuously challenges one's assumptions because, at the core of critical dialogue there is the idea that the worst form of life is the one that is far from the truth.

Socrates' philosophy, as interpreted by Plato, is one of the best examples of the feasibility of this approach. Recognizing the value of knowledge, it interweaves the motivation for inquiry with the purifying action of aporetic states. But a specific context—a loving and caring cooperative context—is essential to this method. Therefore, the virtue of lovely shame can emerge only within a context that allows the recognition of limits as a resource and not as a vice to be hidden. For this reason, shame must be combined with love. This does not mean that dialectical exchanges should be dismissed. In fact, aporetic states may also be understood as battles against errors. But they will be beneficial only if the interlocutors will work together as friends against the fallacies of reasoning. Thus, within critical dialogues, the dialectical exchange is grounded in a friendly environment that permits the use of shame to be beneficial for their members and group inquiry.

SOCRATIC SKEPTICISM AS VIRTUE
IN LOVELY SHAME

Calhoun (2004) has claimed, for moral shame, that the vulnerability of being ashamed before those with whom one is involved is a mark of moral maturity, which includes a sense of intellectual maturity. In our case, to be intellectually mature, in respect to lovely shame, may mean that the ashamed recognizes the value of knowledge, and will be happy to be purified of their false beliefs. Thus, they will permit shame to play its epistemic function. Epistemic maturity, in fact, does not mean the possession of knowledge, but as Roberts and Woods (2007) claimed about intellectual firmness,[25] it is our concern for the epistemic goods that makes us flexible to revise our assumptions and to challenge them accordingly to the circumstances. What one should be able to let go in experiencing lovely shame is thus the presumption to be always in the "right." In fact, if the agents are able to do so, they will free themselves from false belief thanks to the help of others. But, in order to do so, they will need to be firm in their motivation, and thus be able to access the available knowledge through challenging their own beliefs.[26]

This means that another condition is required in order for one to be able to beneficially accept the vulnerability provoked by lovely shame: the one that asks the agent to be "mature." Being mature in this context means that firmness in one's integrity does not amount to dogmatically defending one's perspective, even if it appears to be false, but instead the capacity to not lose one's balance during the painful experience of one's and others' questioning. This form of epistemic maturity is therefore associated with the flexibility of being open to change.

Flexibility can be effectively understood as one of the virtues required by critical thinking.[27] Miranda Fricker (2003, 154–57) has identified flexibility as the virtue that should be cultivated appropriately for those contexts in which we depend on others' testimony, such as in collective epistemic contexts of critical dialogues. The flexibility to accept refutation and to challenge beliefs is exactly the critical attitude embedded within the Socratic mottos, "I know that I know nothing" and "Know thyself." Therefore, lovely shame is a depiction of Socratic skepticism as a virtue. Nevertheless, these critical attitudes that fight against dogmatism do not necessarily lead to the impossibility of knowledge.[28]

In fact, if critical thinking is inscribed within the epistemic horizon, which evaluates knowledge as the best good, lovely shame will be understood as one of the best cleansing tools for the continuous improvement of inquiry. "Know thyself" primarily means to be aware of one's own ignorance, and it thus leads to the recognition of the falsity of unjustified beliefs. Knowing of one's not knowing is a metacognitive state, as the recognition of one's ignorance, and thus Socratic skepticism is a specific kind of wisdom, the one that recognizes the falsity of one's beliefs and is aware of one's need for purification. It is the acknowledgment of ignorance that leads to a curious commitment to new discoveries.

At the core of wisdom, which is the main purpose of the Socratic practice, there is epistemic purification, seen as the getting rid of false beliefs. Then there is cognitive transformation, as the reshaping of our beliefs. Arguably, wisdom is more than cognitive,[29] and it is not reducible to knowledge, but it is certain that knowledge plays an essential role in it—at least for the Socratic tradition. Finally, the negativity and discontinuity brought about by lovely shame reveals the trust in the improvement of knowledge through self-transformation,[30] since it discloses our openness to the possibility of better-grounded understandings and ridding ourselves of cognitive mistakes.

In this chapter, I defended the view on which not only "positive" emotions, but also "negative emotions," can be a source of improvement in personal and collective life, demonstrating the beneficial function performed by shame in aporetic states. Generally, shame arises from a judgmental environment, but I highlighted, on the contrary, how it can also arise in environments of cooperative learning, within the tradition of critical dialogue. Certain conditions, however, should be assured. I therefore introduced the novel hermeneutical tool of "lovely shame" for detecting love as the common denominator of these conditions. Therefore, friendly environments, a love for wisdom, and a desire for improvement appear to be some of the characteristics that an agent should be assured in their learning environment for the purpose of cognitive achievement. Obviously, the epistemic emotion of lovely shame does not do all the work—other conditions, especially some intellectual virtues, should also be nurtured for enhancing the quality of inquiry and our disposition to pursue wisdom. But I hope to have argued enough for acknowledging that it does quite a lot.

ACKNOWLEDGMENTS

This work was supported by the European Union under the Marie Skłodowska-Curie Individual Fellowship for the project EMOTIONS FIRST [655143]. I discussed some of the ideas that then have been developed in this chapter at the Edinburgh Epistemology Research Group and at the Eidyn Workshop "The Epistemic Aims of Education" (University of Edinburgh, October 2016). I would like to thank Duncan Pritchard and Adam Carter for the kind invitation, and their colleagues and the public for the rich discussion.

NOTES

1. This means that an affective state such as shame plays an epistemic function that is to contribute to the process of knowledge-building through the purification of false beliefs. Disclosing an epistemic valence, shame could rightly be defined, in the context of aporetic states, as an epistemic emotion. On the notion of "epistemic emotion," see Morton 2010 and Candiotto 2017b.

2. There is an important aporetic tradition in Classical Antiquity, from the early philosophers to Plotinus and Damascius. It is important to frame the Socratic method within this wider cultural context, while also recognising its innovative aspects and prominence throughout the history of Western Philosophy. See Karamanolis and Politis 2017.

3. The word *aporia* has a rich etymological background: it derives from the verb *aporein* and it is composed by the alpha privative (*a-*) and *poros* (meaning means or passage). Therefore, the literal meaning of *aporia* is being without any means or without any "passage" to escape. Rescher (2009) has defined the *aporia* as any cognitive situation in which the threat of inconsistency confronts us.

4. It is commonly assumed that the first dialogues provide evidence of the historical Socrates' thoughts and method, and Plato started to develop his own philosophy from the *Phaedo* and the *Symposium*. However, this standard interpretation is problematic not only because we do not have a final agreement about the chronology of Plato's dialogues, but also because the very same Socrates depicted in the dialogues is a character created by Plato for his own aims, from the apologetic to the philosophical ones. I thus depict Plato's characterization of Socrates, and the Socratic Method, with an awareness of this so-called Socratic problem. For an orientation in this issue, see Blondell 2002 and Rowe 2007. Several images are used by Plato for depicting Socrates' aporetic method, from the torpedo-fish analogy of the *Meno* (79e–80b) to the gadfly analogy of the *Apology* (23a). But apart from these significant images, the aporetic method is embedded in the very same development of the dialogues, in the interweaving of questions and answers among the interlocutors. For an analysis of the aporetic method in Plato's Socratic dialogues, see Erler 1987 and Politis 2015.

5. For an analysis of the structure of inquiry in Plato's aporetic dialogues, see Politis 2015.

6. Quite often, Socrates' interlocutors did not want to be refuted, being a very unpleasant situation indeed, but Socrates prescribed it as the best medicine for those who thought they possessed knowledge (Plato, *Soph.* 230b4–e5).

7. For Plato, the interlocutor is free to generate knowledge by themselves after being purified by the refutation (*elenchus*). This process is called *maieutic*. See Plato's *Theaetetus* (149a–151d) in Plato 1997.

8. See English 2013 for a detailed analysis of learning processes as negative and discontinuous from an experiential, theoretical, and moral point of view.

9. Discussing the epistemic valence of the "labour pains" in the *Theaetetus*, Brown (2017) has clarified the relationship between "labour pains" and the maieutic generation of knowledge. Significantly, the "labour pains" express a phenomenological metaphor for *aporetic* states. On the *pathein* experienced within the processes of inquiry, especially in the aporetic states as their beginning, see Candiotto and Politis (forthcoming).

10. Politis (2006) thus depicted the cathartic and the zetetic functions of the aporetic states: the first is the one that purifies one of false beliefs, and the second is the one that finds a means to going beyond the perplexities and to continue the inquiry. *Zetetic* is the adjectival form of *zetesis* which means inquiry, and thus the *zetetic* function is the one that contributes to the development of inquiry. But it is important to maintain that these two functions are integrated in a single procedure, that of the aporetic method, in order to recognize that the cathartic function is also *zetetic*, since the awareness of mistakes is the first step of a well-founded inquiry. See Candiotto 2015; 2017b.

11. There is a trend in epistemology that takes *understanding* to be something more valuable than mere knowledge (Grimm 2006; Pritchard 2016), and research in educational practices seem to reinforce this idea, since getting at the meaning of what is known and interpreting the information, for example, is more valuable than the sole possession of the information. And this more valuable outcome is the main goal of learning practices.

12. There are some semantic differences between the two. For example, *aischynê* is more related to the context of the individual moral virtues, in which case it may be translated as "modesty."

13. Feeling ashamed of something has a strong impact on the self as a whole ("I feel that my entire self is bad"). This allows purification to have an impact on the whole epistemic agent, and not only on their false beliefs. For the central role played by shame on self-knowledge, see Rochat 2009, 105–17. For a holistic notion of transformation, both affective and cognitive, see Maiese 2017.

14. The debate about the nature of group mental states in social epistemology—for example, whether they are the sum of individual mental states (in which the group can be described as sharing a single, emergent mental state that cannot be reduced to the individually held states of each group member) or a set of individual mental states that are independently held by each group member is still ongoing (see Tollefsen 2015). I do not take a position in this debate here because my aim is to explain how and why aporetic states purify group knowledge from false beliefs in order to depict the epistemic function of shame within the process of collective inquiry, although it is a very fascinating question, with important implications for my research.

15. The approach to emotional valence as hedonicity comes from cognitive psychology, especially in the studies dedicated to current affect. See Barrett 1998; Barrett 2006; Barrett and Russell 1999. Other theoretical frameworks are also available. For example, Lambie and Marcel (2002) have distinguished between valence and hedonicity. Hedonic value derives from the calculus of pleasures and pains, whereas valence derives from positive and negative evaluations. Nevertheless, they maintain that the affective dimension is mostly measured by the hedonic tone. Another option

is to distinguish between affective valence and emotional valence, the former related to bodily feelings and the latter to judgments.

16. This identification is mirrored in the links between positive emotions and cognitive ease, and negative emotions and cognitive effort.

17. Cognitive sciences have described the phenomenon of cognitive transformation as the process of reframing of the cognitive environments, thanks to the emergence of new and different cognitive functions. See Klein and Baxter 2006.

18. It is significant that for Morrison shame plays a central role in therapy. The therapeutic failure, or premature termination of the therapeutic relationship, is often the result of a failure in processing feelings of shame during treatment.

19. For Lacan (1991) and then for Roustang (2009), Socrates in fact is not only the first philosopher, but also the first therapist. Regarding my topic, Lear (2013; 2014) has argued for a creative and life-changing use of Socratic irony, depicting the related positive outcomes of shame. Please see Candiotto 2019 for a detailed analysis of the dialogical dynamics in play within the Socratic cognitive theory. For a critical analysis of the modern psychotherapy triggered by a comparison with the Socratic method, see Maranhao 1986.

20. For a review of the many attempts to differentiate shame and guilt, see Tangney and Dearing 2002, 10–23.

21. But this does not imply that it is an easy thing to accept or to fully acknowledge. In fact, very often the ashamed try to hide these states—as it is made clear by the bodily expressions related to these phenomena (such as blushing or hiding the face).

22. In this regard, the distinction between reparative shame and disintegrative shame brought by Braithwaite (1989) is significant. In his analysis, not only can shame perform reparative actions, as I claim, but it also identifies the conditions for getting to this positive function in the cultural context of respect for the offender. Braithwaite's context of analysis is different from mine—criminology is his field of enquiry—but nevertheless I found that his work in general, and the emphasis on respect as a condition for the positive outcome of shame, supports the view I am defending here about the positive role of shame in critical dialogue, and especially about the friendly environmental condition for lovely shame.

23. An important monograph on the virtues of negative emotions and suffering has been published by Michael Brady after I wrote the final version of this chapter, and I cannot include a detailed discussion of it at this stage. But let me just mention that the view for which suffering is necessary for wisdom seems to be in line with what I am arguing here about the epistemic value of the painful experience triggered by shame and implied by aporetic states. Please see Brady 2018, but also Brady 2019, forthcoming.

24. Virtue epistemology, for which the fundamental epistemic concepts are analyzed in terms of abilities and character traits of the epistemic agent (Zagzebski 1996), has carefully depicted those virtues of the mind that are required for epistemic success. The character-based account understands intellectual virtues as excellences of intellectual character. On the link between epistemic emotions and intellectual virtues, see Candiotto 2017b. On the epistemic valence of doubt as intellectual virtue, see Hookway 2000.

25. On the deep consonances between epistemic maturity and intellectual firmness, please see Candiotto 2017c.

26. They must therefore have a good degree of self-esteem to not only withstand criticism but use it as a tool for self-enhancement. Arguing this, I do not want to deny the fact that shame is often related to low self-esteem (see Deigh 1983). On the contrary, the aim of this section is to state the conditions that may assure the avoidance of the shortcomings that are related to shame, in order to allow one to profit for its purifying function.

27. See Mezirow 1990, for the function of critical reflection at the roots of transformative learning. See Siegel 2016, about the intellectually virtuous critical spirit.

28. For a quick summary of the meaning assumed by skepticism throughout history and for a defense of its civic value, see Hazlett 2016.

29. Wisdom, in fact, aims to transform one's entire life, and this is achieved through a holistic engagement of the agent's self. Plato, again, is the reference for the conceptualization of wisdom as the main aim of a philosophical life, but here the boundaries among the disciplines become less strict, and thus what appears to be true for epistemology should also be investigated from an ethical, political, and spiritual point of view. See Plato's *Republic*, especially books 7–10. For the contemporary philosophical debate on wisdom, see Grimm 2015.

30. For Socrates, cognitive transformations are always transformations of ways of living, and thus they also acquire moral valence. I cannot develop this line of reasoning here, but I trust that it could be assumed as the background that highlights the existential valence of aporetic states. See O'Sullivan et al. 2002, for addressing this point regarding transformative learning.

REFERENCES

Adler, A. 1916. *The Neurotic Constitution*. New York, NY: Yard and Company.

Aristotle. 1984. *The Complete Works of Aristotle*, edited by J. Barnes. Princeton, NJ: Princeton University Press.

Baehr, J. 2011. *The Inquiring Mind: On Intellectual Virtues and Virtue Epistemology*. New York, NY: Oxford University Press.

Barrett, K. 1995. "A Functionalist Approach to Shame and Guilt." In *Self-Conscious Emotions: The Psychology of Shame, Guilt, Embarrassment, and Pride*, edited by J. Price Tangney and K. Von Fischer, 25–63. New York, NY: Guilford Press.

Barrett, L. F. 1998. "Discrete Emotions or Dimensions? The Role of Valence Focus and Arousal Focus." *Cognition and Emotion* 12, no. 4: 579–99.

———. 2006. "Valence is a Basic Building Block of Emotional Life." *Journal of Research in Personality* 40: 35–55.

Barrett, L. F. and J. A. Russell. 1999. "The Structure of Current Affect: Controversies and Emerging Consensus." *Current Directions in Psychological Science* 8, no. 1: 10–14.

Beck, J. S. 1995. *Cognitive Therapy: Basics and Beyond*. New York, NY: Guilford Press.

Blondell, R. 2002. *The Play of Character in Plato's Dialogues.* Cambridge, England: Cambridge University Press.

Brady, M. 2019, forthcoming. "Learning from Adversity: Suffering and Wisdom." In *The Value of Emotions for Knowledge*, edited by L. Candiotto. Basingstoke: Palgrave Macmillan.

———. 2018. *Suffering and Virtue.* Oxford, England: Oxford University Press.

———. 2009. "Curiosity and the Value of Truth." In *Epistemic Value*, edited by A. Haddock, A. Millar, and D. Pritchard, 265–83. Oxford, England: Oxford University Press.

Braithwaite, J. 1989. *Crime, Shame and Reintegration.* Cambridge, England: Cambridge University Press.

Brown, L. 2017. "Aporia in Plato's *Theaetetus* and *Sophist.*" In *The Aporetic Tradition in Ancient Philosophy*, edited by G. Karamanolis and V. Politis, 91–111. Cambridge, England: Cambridge University Press.

Calhoun, C. 2004. "An Apology for Moral Shame." *Journal of Political Philosophy* 12, no. 2: 127–46.

Campos, J. J., D. L. Mumme, R. Kermoian, and R. G. Campos. 1994. "A Functionalist Perspective on the Nature of Emotion." *Monographs of the Society for Research in Child Development* 59, no. 2–3: 284–303.

Candiotto, L. 2015. "Aporetic State and Extended Emotions. The Shameful Recognition of Contradictions in the Socratic Elenchus." *Ethics and Politics* XVII: 233–48.

———. 2017a. "Boosting Cooperation. The Beneficial Function of Positive Emotions in Dialogical Inquiry." In "The Learning Brain and the Classroom," eds. A. Tillas, B. Kaldis, special issue, Humana.Mente, *Journal of Philosophical Studies* 33, no. III–V: 59–82.

———. 2017b. "Epistemic Emotions: The Building Blocks of Intellectual Virtues." *Studi di Estetica* XLV, IV, no. 7: 7–25.

———. 2017c. "La Maturità Intellettuale come *Akmé.*" *Giornale Critico di Storia delle Idee/Critical Journal of History of Ideas* 1: 47–58.

———. 2018. "Purification Through Emotions: The Role of Shame in Plato's *Sophist* 230b4-e5." In "Bildung and Paideia. Philosophical Models of Education," eds. J. Dillon, M. L. Zovko, special issue, *Educational Philosophy and Theory* 50, no. 6–7: 576–85.

———. 2019. "Plato's Dialogically Extended Cognition: Cognitive Transformation as Elenctic Catharsis." In *The Routledge Companion to Classics and Cognitive Theory*, edited by P. Meineck, W. M. Short, and J. Devereux, 202–15. London, England and New York, NY: Routledge.

Candiotto, L. and V. Politis. Forthcoming. "Epistemic Wonder and the Beginning of the Enquiry: Plato's *Theaetetus* 155d2–4 and Its wider significance." In *Emotions in Plato*, edited by L. Candiotto and O. Renaut. Leiden, Netherlands: Brill.

Deigh, J. 1983. "Shame and Self-Esteem: A Critique." *Ethics* 93, no. 2: 225–45.

Descartes, R. (1641) 1996. *Meditations on First Philosophy: With Selections from the Objections and Replies*, revised edition, translated by J. Cottingham. Cambridge, England: Cambridge University Press.

Earnshaw, O. 2019 forthcoming. "Disorientation and Cognitive Enquiry." In *The Value of Emotions for Knowledge*, edited by L. Candiotto. Basingstoke: Palgrave Macmillan.

English, A. 2013. *Discontinuity in Learning*. Cambridge, England: Cambridge University Press.

Erler, M. 1987. *Der Sinn der Aporien in den Dialogen Platons. Übungsstü cke zur Anleitung im Philosophischen Denken*. Berlin, Germany: W. de Gruyter.

Freud, S. and J. Breuer. (1895) 2004. *Studies in Hysteria*. Translated by Nicola Luckhurst. London, England: Penguin Books. Citations refer to the reprint edition.

Fricker, Miranda. 2003. "Epistemic Injustice and a Role for Virtue in the Politics of Knowing." In *Moral and Epistemic Virtues*, edited by M. Brady and D. Pritchard, 139–58. Malden, MA: Blackwell Publishing.

Gilbert, P. and B. Andrews, eds. 1998. *Series in Affective Science. Shame: Interpersonal Behavior, Psychopathology, and Culture*. New York, NY: Oxford University Press.

Giner-Sorolla, R. 2012. *Judging Passions: Moral Emotions in Persons and Groups*. London, England: Psychology Press.

Grimm, S. 2015. "Wisdom." *Australasian Journal of Philosophy* 93, no. 1: 139–54.

———. 2006. "Is Understanding a Species of Knowledge?" *British Journal for the Philosophy of Science* 57: 515–35.

———. 2015. "Wisdom." *Australasian Journal of Philosophy* 93, no. 1: 139–54.

Hazlett, A. 2016. "The Civic Virtues of Skepticism, Intellectual Humility, and Intellectual Criticism." In *Intellectual Virtues and Education. Essays in Applied Virtue Epistemology*, edited by J. Baehr, 71–92. York, England/Abingdon, England: Routledge.

Hookway, C. 2000. "Regulating Inquiry: Virtue, Doubt, and Sentiment." In *Knowledge, Belief, and Character: Readings in Virtue Epistemology*, edited by G. Axtell, 149–60. Lanham, MD: Rowman and Littlefield.

Johnson, D. W. and R. Johnson. 1999. *Learning Together and Alone: Cooperative, Competitive, and Individualistic Learning*, 5th edition. Boston, MA: Allyn and Bacon.

Karamanolis, G. and V. Politis, eds. 2017. *The Aporetic Tradition in Ancient Philosophy*. Cambridge, England: Cambridge University Press.

Klein, G. and H. C. Baxter. 2006. "Cognitive Transformation Theory: Contrasting Cognitive and Behavioral Learning." *Interservice/Industry Training, Simulation, and Education Conference (I/ITSEC)*, paper n. 2500.

Lacan, J. 1991. *Le Séminaire. Livre VIII. Le Transfert, 1960–1961*, Texte Établi par Jacques-Alain Miller. Paris, France: Seuil.

Lambie, J. A. and A. J. Marcel. 2002. "Consciousness and the Varieties of Emotion Experience: A Theoretical Framework." *Psychological Review* 109, no. 2: 219–59.

Lansky, M. R. 2005. "Hidden Shame." *Journal of the American Psychoanalytic Association* 53, no. 3: 865–90.

———. 1995. "Shame and the Scope of Psychoanalytic Understanding." *The American Behavioral Scientist* 38, no. 8: 1076–90.

———. 2005. "Hidden Shame." *Journal of the American Psychoanalytic Association* 53, no. 3: 865–90.

Lear, J. 2014. *A Case for Irony*. Cambridge, MA: Harvard University Press.

———. 2013. "The Ironic Creativity of Socratic Doubt." *MLN* 128: 1001–18.

———. 2014. *A Case for Irony*. Cambridge, MA: Harvard University Press.

Lewis, H. B. 1971. *Shame and Guilt in Neurosis*. New York, NY: International University Press.

Maiese, M. 2017. "Transformative Learning, Enactivism, and Affectivity." *Studies in Philosophy and Education* 36: 197–216.

Maramhao, T. 1986. *Therapeutic Discourse and Socratic Dialogue. A Cultural Critique*. Madison, WI: University of Wisconsin Press.

Mezirow, J. 2000. *Learning as Transformation. Critical Perspectives on a Theory in Progress*. San Francisco, CA: Jossey Bass.

———. 1990. "How Critical Reflection Triggers Transformative Learning." In *Fostering Critical Reflection in Adulthood: A Guide to Transformative and Emancipator Learning*, edited by J. Mezirow and Associates, 1–20. San Francisco, CA: Jossey-Bass.

———. 2000. *Learning as Transformation. Critical Perspectives on a Theory in Progress*. San Francisco, CA: Jossey Bass.

Morrison, A. P. 1989. *Shame: The Underside of Narcissism*. Hillsdale, MI: Analytic Press.

Morton, A. 2010. "Epistemic Emotions." In *The Oxford Handbook of Philosophy of Emotion*, edited by P. Goldie, 385–99. Oxford, England: Oxford University Press.

Nussbaum, M. 2013. *Political Emotions: Why Love Matters for Justice*. Cambridge-London, England: The Belknap Press of Harvard University Press.

———. 2004. *Hiding from Humanity: Disgust, Shame and the Law*. Princeton, NJ: Princeton University Press.

———. 2013. *Political Emotions: Why Love Matters for Justice*. Cambridge/London, England: The Belknap Press of Harvard University Press.

O'Sullivan, E., A. Morrell, and M. O'Connor, eds. 2002. *Expanding the Boundaries of Transformative Learning: Essays on Theory and Praxis*. New York, NY: Palgrave Press.

Plato. 1997. *Complete Works*, edited by J. M. Cooper. Indianapolis, IN/Cambridge, England: Hackett Publishing Company.

Politis, V. 2015. *The Structure of Enquiry in Plato's Early Dialogues*. Cambridge, England: Cambridge University Press.

———. 2006. "Aporia and Searching in Early Plato." In *Remembering Socrates: Philosophical Essays*, edited by J. Lindsay and V. Karsmanis, 88–109. Oxford, England/New York, NY: Clarendon Press.

———. 2015. *The Structure of Enquiry in Plato's Early Dialogues*. Cambridge, England: Cambridge University Press.

Price, C. 2015. *Emotions*. Cambridge, England: Polity.

Pritchard, D. 2016. "Seeing It for Oneself. Perceptual Knowledge, Understanding, and Intellectual Autonomy." *Episteme* 13: 29–42.

Rescher, N. 2009. *Ignorance: On the Wider Implications of Deficient Knowledge*. Pittsburgh, PA: University of Pittsburgh Press.

Roberts, R. C. and J. Wood. 2007. *Intellectual Virtues: An Essay in Regulative Epistemology*. Oxford, England: Oxford University Press.

Rochat, P. 2009. *Others in Mind: Social Origins of Self-Consciousness*. Oxford, England: Oxford University Press.

Roustang, F. 2009. *Le Secret du Socrate pour Changer la Vie*. Paris, France: Odile Jacob.

Rowe, C. 2007. *Plato and the Art of Philosophical Writing*. Cambridge, England: Cambridge University Press.

Scheck, S. 2005. *The Stages of Psychosocial Development According to Erik H. Erikson*. Norderstedt, Germany: Grin Verlag.

Siegel, H. 2016. "Critical Thinking and the Intellectual Virtues." In *Intellectual Virtues and Education: Essays in Applied Virtue Epistemology*, edited by J. Baehr, 95–112. New York, NY/Abingdon, England: Routledge.

Slaby, J. 2008. "Affective Intentionality and the Feeling Body." *Phenomenology and the Cognitive Sciences* 7: 429–44.

Stocker, M. 2004. "Some Considerations about Intellectual Desire and Emotions." In *Thinking about Feeling*, edited by R. C. Solomon, 135–48. New York, NY: Oxford University Press.

Tangney, J. P. and R. L. Dearing. 2002. *Shame and Guilt*. New York, NY and London, England: The Guilford Press.

Tollefsen, D. 2015. *Groups as Agents*. Cambridge, England: Polity.

Zagzebski, L. 1996. *Virtues of the Mind: An Inquiry into the Nature of Virtue and the Ethical Foundations of Knowledge*. Cambridge, England: Cambridge University Press.

Chapter 5

Being In and Excluded from the Sociotechnical World

Matthew Rukgaber

Being ashamed before a flight of stairs that one cannot ascend can be teased out phenomenologically in order to show the way in which shame and the self are bound by *sociotechnical systems*. These systems will be shown to embody intersubjective relations that are vital to the sense of oneself in prereflective, embodied situations. In this chapter, I illustrate how a type of shame is connected to the *existential feeling* of "belonging to the world," and how this helps us to understand that shame and negative self-judgment can be separated from one another in situations like the one just described (Ratcliffe 2008, 107). I hold that this type of shame is common for persons who are not afforded the spaces to merely exist as a *lived body* among others, such as those labeled as disabled by society.

The phenomenological perspective utilized in this chapter is intended to compliment social constructivist accounts of disability. By using a phenomenological method, I will be looking at this situation in a way as described by David Morris, in which he claims phenomenology is a "transcendental philosophy," but unlike Kant, he focuses not on conceptual conditions of experience but on *appearing itself*: "Phenomenology instead proceeds by description, by elucidating empirically given phenomenon so as to glean transcendental insight through them" (Morris 2018, 131). Feelings and social institutions are part of the empirically given, but phenomenology describes the pre-reflective sense within appearing in the initial encounter with the situation. In what follows, the experience of shame and the pre-reflective awareness of other persons and social institutions will be explored in order to show how a type of shame is separable from negative self-judgment and results from an existential feeling of exclusion from the sociotechnical systems. This type of shame is often overlooked but is evident in the experiences of those labeled as "disabled" by society.

Why think of shame as becoming manifest at the level of our basic *affective attunement* to the sociotechnical systems that make up the human world?[1] Human beings are so thoroughly enmeshed in webs of relations with other humans, artifacts, and institutions that there is no experience, emotional or otherwise, of self, other, or world that is not entirely penetrated by these systems of human meaning and activity that we can call sociotechnical.[2] Further, existential feelings are our "prepersonal" and "anonymous" way of inhabiting, being attuned to, and responding to sociotechnical systems as the home of human behavior (Merleau-Ponty 1962, 347). They take place at the level of what phenomenologists have called the lived body and are, therefore, capable of existing independently of our personal consciousness and from the conscious relations of recognition and self-assessment.

I believe that such an account, which can be derived from the work of Merleau-Ponty and Heidegger, is better able to account for the nature of a type of shame that arises when persons labeled as disabled confront a discriminatory artifactual system that they reject.[3] This notion of shame as a generalized affective attunement does not require one to engage in any specific negative self-judgment or to see oneself as failing to live up to some standard. Operating independently of one's own explicit cognitions of self-value and the recognition of others, this prepersonal, bodily shame fills one with a sense of loss, of being not-at-home due to barriers within the sociotechnical systems that hinder inconspicuous coexistence.

The first section of this chapter will show certain limitations of conceptions of shame focused on "self-devaluation" due to certain "values against which the subject judges himself or herself" (Dolezal 2015, 4). It will also look to phenomenological sources for an alternative account. The second section will further elaborate how persons labeled as disabled can still feel shame when confronted with an ableist world with which they disagree and which does not lower their self-esteem.

THE PHENOMENOLOGY OF EMOTION AND A
SOCIOTECHNICAL SYSTEMS APPROACH TO SHAME

The need to turn to the theory of affect in Merleau-Ponty and mood in Heidegger is a result of the fact that the phenomenological accounts of emotion found in the philosophies of Husserl, Scheler, and Sartre are unable to account for a type of shame in which there is no negative self-judgment.[4] For Husserl, "affect-consciousness" builds upon *"objectivating consciousness"* and is a new layer of significance in which objects appear to me as "pleasurable or unpleasurable, as agreeable or disagreeable" through feeling-states (Husserl 2001, 277–78). Through the "intentionality of feeling," objects are "laden with objective value predicates," and therefore exercise an "allure of gradually varying intensity on the ego as the ego of possible knowledge" (280). Feeling in itself unfolds according to its own intentionality (e.g., fulfillment of desire, relaxation, shunning the unpleasant), which is not the same as objective attentiveness and value cognition, but runs parallel to each. Nevertheless, the content of affect is manifest because there is an objectivating consciousness that constitutes the object and, so also, an "*objectivating affection*" (281). Thus, the elaboration of a Husserlian notion of shame would hold that there is "underlying cognitive sense as grasped by a subject," which is an assessment of the shameful "value-qualities" of an object, such as my body, my person or character, or some event or action performed (Drummond 2018, 15).

The Husserlian model takes the act of feeling to have an active, volitional, and cognitive aspect in addition to its passive aspect (Husserl 2001, 282), which has the implication that the shamed person, in feeling shame, recognizes some attribute of themselves as shameful. Such a view would "encourage us to find fault with ashamed people" and the shamed person to find fault with herself (Calhoun 2004, 137). This is precisely what happens when Scheler develops the theory of affect as the intentional grasping of objective values. He contends that spiritual shame emerges because of our failure to exist at or be taken by others to exist at the level of unique, moral, personal, and fully human existence (Scheler 1987, 83). Whether stemming from self-judgment or the judgment of others, we feel the intrinsic shamefulness of our vital, animal selves when compared to our humanity. Similarly, a bodily shame also exists which emerges when our vital selves, which strive for certain natural virtues, are undermined by the mere pursuit of sensuousness. If this view of shame is correct, then presumably, when a person feels shame about not being able to climb a flight of stairs, she is affectively grasping her vital nature as shameful, as something dragging her down to a less than human way of being.

But it is clear that shame can exist alongside "a denial that there is anything to be ashamed of" by "a mature, well-formed ethical agent" who can "sustain their own positive views of themselves" (Calhoun 2004, 136–38). One may feel shame before a flight of stairs that one cannot ascend even if one does not believe this to be shameful. Perhaps the Sartrean view of shame can explain this through the power of "the Other" (or the generalized Other who is "extended across the whole world") who brings us to shame and does not recognize us as a subject (Sartre 1956, 389). Perhaps, it is not that I am shameful but that I am being shamed by others who have a sort of power over me. But if one attempts to relocate all shame in the ontological facts of our dependency, our animality, our loss of possibilities to others, our embodiment, or our failure to live up to our values and ideals, then any minimally self-aware human would live in a state of constant shame. Sartre's analysis leaves the subject as always in an insecure state about his or her being-for-others. Given that intersubjectivity is the human condition, the state of being free from shame would then be self-deception.

Also, the previous description of a shame from without and without judgment is not compatible with Sartre's view, which still requires that "I am ashamed of what I *am*" and that I pass "judgment on myself as on an object" (301–302). Sartrean (pure) shame is my recognition of "myself in this degraded, fixed, and dependent being which I am for the Other" (384). Shame remains for Sartre an autonomous act: It is I who have "stripped myself of transcendence," and made myself into an inherently shameful object when I am faced with the Other (352).[5] There is no way for a Sartrean view to recognize a shame that persists at the embodied level of the affects that are distinct from consciousness. Shame remains "a global decrease of self-esteem" because of "an acceptance of the other's evaluation," or a shame "of oneself before the other" because of one's "flawed self" (Zahavi 2014, 223, 226).

Although the views already mentioned certainly recognize the felt aspects of shame, they nevertheless continue to think of the feeling of shame as secondary to "cognitive situational feelings" that are acts of an intentional consciousness responding to value-qualities of specific objects, states of affairs, or acts (Heller 1979, 64). However, Agnes Heller has argued that the affects are quite different from this: they are natural, expressive, bodily reactions to external stimuli and include things like shame, curiosity, joy, disgust, sexuality, rage, and fear (71–73). In their pure state, the affects are heteronomous, bodily reactions. While the affects can be generated by the sorts of personal, volitional acts of evaluation previously mentioned, it is also the case that shame can come upon me without my having any intentional relation toward any particular shameful feature of myself. It can emerge in conflict with all my intentional acts of self-evaluation and value judgment. It can even emerge as others support and affirm my personhood, rather than lessening the esteem I have in their mind and my own.[6] From a phenomenological point of view, this would be expressed as a spontaneous upsurge of sense in the prereflective, embodied encounter with the situation.

If it is denied that shame can emerge in a situation in which I reject that my body or actions are actually shameful, then it must be denied that I am in fact truly committed to the positive evaluation of my body, identity, or actions. On the Husserlian, Schelerian, and Sartrean views of shame, it remains a puzzle how it is possible that one can feel shame, as Calhoun notes, "in the face of sexist, racist, homophobic, or classist expressions" (Calhoun 2004, 136), or ableist ones with which one disagrees and that one knows to be wrong and of no value. Perhaps others might not recognize me as a full subject, but it is not clear that my self-esteem relies on this or that their recognition need motivate any self-judgment. After all, I may feel shame as a result of the abelist actions and assumptions of others who are less powerful and secure in their social status and identity and who have no bearing on my sense of myself, such as children. I may even feel existential shame before inanimate objects such as stairs.

This is possible because shame as an existential feeling can emerge when one experiences a loss of anonymous and disattentive social existence at the level of the lived body, even while conscious, explicit, interpersonal life posits my ethical and social equality.[7] Living a human life requires more than recognition. It also requires the space where culturally informed structures of behavior and human meaning are incorporated, anonymously and unconsciously, into the structure of our lived body.

While that reveals our dependency, it is not shameful: it is the very foundation upon which subjectivity and personal modification of those structures into identity takes place. Indeed, an integral part of human freedom is the way in which we inhabit shared, creative practices of self- and other-objectification. Objectification only produces shame when it signifies a breakdown of the pathways toward effortless coexistence with others, a loss of the space where one can simply be a body anonymously. Such a loss means that the very ground of the dialectical relations in which we are both subject and object alongside others is disrupted. Thus, prepersonal shame emerges when there is an impassable barrier to the secure acceptance within the impersonal norms, practices, and objects that support and reinforce both personal and impersonal lives.

Merleau-Ponty's criticism of the Sartrean division between the *For-Itself* (consciousness) and the *In-Itself* (material nature), his denial that we are either entirely one or the other, and his rejection that one aspect of our being is especially shameful are also found in the thought of Helmuth Plessner (1970). Plessner calls our fundamental state of being *ex-centric positionality*, which is the idea that we exist in "two orders" simultaneously and are constantly reconciling both "being" as a subjective process and "having" ourselves as an object (1970, 37). Obviously, the reason why being objectified and exposed before others is often taken to be central to shame is because it is assumed that human beings are fundamentally subjects and not objects. But the core phenomenological insight underlying the approach to shame that I advocate is that human beings have an "ambiguous" existence as both embodied subject (*Lieb*) and body-object (*Körper*), never being entirely one or the other (36).[8] We negotiate this liminal space and learn how to be both subjects and objects through our sociotechnical existence. If we find ourselves excluded from this space, we may not judge ourselves to be shameful, but we may well feel shame as feeling literally prereflectively being "squeezed out" from our necessarily lived and shared space with others.

Ordinarily we fluidly navigate a set of explicit and implicit co-inhabited norms that enable us to be both subjects and objects to ourselves and with others. The breakdown of this ambiguous form of life is what Plessner calls a "boundary reaction," in which one finds oneself in an "unanswerable" situation "in which no expression is any longer suitable" (111). The specific feature of the "boundary reaction" of shame, that which is "unanswerable," is that one finds oneself without any pathway back to the anonymous and effortless way that we typically inhabit the world. We may still have our self-esteem and recognize our loss as saying less about us and more about the sociotechnical systems we inhabit.

This account reflects recent insights into the phenomenology of illness as a sort of loss in which our bodily way of inhabiting sociotechnical systems is undermined: "[W]hat could once be done unthinkingly, with no planning and marginal effort, is now an explicit task, requiring thought, attention, and a pronounced effort" (Carel 2016, 68). But when caught in shame, one cannot simply carry on but with effort. There is no suitable expression or social behavior that one can perform to resume one's ordinary, effortless coexistence.

Boundary situations create a sort of "vertigo" and "disorganization" in relationship to the social world that reaches down to our relation to our body (Plessner 1970, 110). A boundary situation is a disorganization in the environment that is translated to the body and, thus, "prevents an organized relation of the person to his [or her] body" (111). In that disorganized space, the prereflective, felt space dominates as overwhelming us momentarily. From a phenomenological perspective, shame is heteronomous only in the sense of not being an extension of our volitional self, but it is not some sort of return to instinctive, mechanical behavior. While shame pushes us toward disappearance and flight from the sociotechnical system, we remain human beings striving to communicate with a world that is refusing to communicate back, and our embodied being seeks to mesh with a world at its disposal that has been alternatively laid out to foreclose that possibility.

The phenomenology of inclusion within the sociotechnical world is the experience of living alongside other persons engaged in disattentive practical behavior.[9] We also occupy situations of explicit concern where attentive behavior is integrated into a set of norms that contribute to the smooth functioning of the system rather than being a disruption of it. We can describe the affect of such inclusion as an existential feeling, mood, or "Being-attuned," that is not an intentional act of a personal consciousness or the cognition of the value-quality of things (Heidegger 1962, 134/172). Examples of such existential feelings are feeling "not at home in one's surrounding" and feeling "vulnerable, lost, like a stranger" (Slaby and Stephen 2008, 510).

This notion of mood derives from Heidegger, who is focused on the mood of anxiety, as an "indefinite" affect that responds to *the world as such* and leads to entities within the world being taken as insignificant (1962, 187/231).

This brings about the feeling of uncanniness or "not-being-at-home," which is contrasted to "being-at-home" in "everyday familiarity" with the world (188/233). Heideggerian anxiety is a mood where we experience "the receding of beings as a whole," and this "makes manifest the nothing" or the abyss of Being (Heidegger 1998, 88). The pervasiveness of these existential attunements and the "essential impossibility" of determining them tells us that they are not to be understood as a cognition about some specific object or any particular property (88).

While I do not have any interest in the specifics of Heidegger's notion of anxiety, I contend that we do have such a fundamental, affective relationship to the sociotechnical world—to the complex set of personal and impersonal relations to humans, norms, and artifacts that form who we are as individuals and as a group. While Heidegger believes that anxiety is something like the feeling of the loss of our grasp on all entities in the world and their significance, I maintain that prepersonal shame is the feeling of the loss of the significant yet impersonal relations and things that constitute the sociotechnical world, and that form the shared foundation of existence with others. Like grief, which is a sense of profound loss due to the tragedy of the nonexistence of relations that make up part of the self, prepersonal shame is a sense of loss of the communicative space that allows us to enter into the lived body relations that make up the shared anonymous world.[10]

While Merleau-Ponty only offers an account of the positive affect of sexuality, which he believes to be the root of all affective investment in the world, he does offer a criticism of and a counterproposal to the dialectic of self and Other that constitutes the Sartrean view of shame.[11] In discussing the attempt to render sexuality into the dialectic of personal "shame and shamelessness," and Hegel's master-slave dialectic, Merleau-Ponty argues that this is not representative of our fundamental affective way of existing (1962, 167). He argues that the sexual affect is not merely my shameless way of striving to master the other, to look at them without being looked at, or to fascinate them and ensnare them. It actually is our most basic "tending of an existence towards another existence" and our fundamental "opening out upon 'another'" through which one body is affectively expressive for another (168). In other words, Merleau-Ponty turns sexual affect into an existential intersubjective feeling, rather than merely a way of constituting and cognizing the sexual value of the Other, or of looking at, desiring, and mastering the Other.

This generalization of sexuality transforms it into the means by which we are expressive, meaningful bodies for one another. It is the means by which intentional behavior and the norms governing it can be immediately expressive for our bodies and can become the habituated second nature on which we rely. Because both the perceptual world and the world of objects are interwoven with human behavior and significance, our affects are neither isolated in the mind or in the body as object: they permeate the world.[12] But just as the sexual affect in its immodest form gets shifted to a generalized, existential attunement to others, so also does shame undergo a shift. To find oneself unable to anonymously co-inhabit the expressive, human, sociotechnical world is a displacement accompanied by a profound feeling of displeasure for which there is no adequate response. Although the shamed person may judge themselves negatively because of this exclusion and the Other may be the source of shame, these do not seem to necessarily be so. Both I and others may be profoundly committed to my freedom, equality, and selfhood, but it may be that the norms and material structures of the world do not allow me to anonymously and effortlessly live as an expressive body with others.

For Merleau-Ponty, these fundamental affects operate at a level that is "below" what we call "objective or positing consciousness" and are, therefore, not "voluntary" (1962, 163; also see Oksala 2006, 214). While something like grief may break "the circuit of all actions relating" to a deceased person, there can also be a complete severing of "coexistence" that nullifies "the movement of existence" (Merleau-Ponty 1962, 160, 162). The experience of shame is often said to be that of an escape, a sinking into the earth. That existential flight from "past and future," and "self and others," is mirrored in the feeling of shame, which expresses the lived body's expulsion from simply inhabiting these "fundamental dimensions of existence" (161). While our personal life is an extension of our impersonal life, it can nevertheless be posited and sustained by objective, evaluative consciousness, at least temporarily.

Eventually, loss of the possibility of anonymous social life in which we live absorbed with others would corrupt our personal selves. Freedom and willed authenticity critically depend on the inauthentic state of heteronomous coexistence: it provides the space of communicative engagement with others that we modify in order to become individuals. Merleau-Ponty illustrates these relations with the case of a girl whose personal expression of love is thwarted by her family resulting in a non-voluntary "refusal of co-existence" (160). We are not told what her feelings are, but the primitive affect of fear created a similar response in her once. I suspect this to be a case of profound grief, because it results from the sudden nonexistence of a specific possibility, although it has far-reaching implications for her. Shame differs because it results from non-admittance to the space of anonymous, communicative, embodied coexistence, where we reckon with the possibilities that the expressive behavior of others afford us. While we might be tempted to call this becoming an object, it can also be the case that, in the breakdown of anonymity, everyone involved consciously affirms that one is a subject and interpersonal recognition is sustained, but the world on a prereflective level is nevertheless foreclosed.

Merleau-Ponty's account of the affects means not only that they take place within the field of social existence, but that they are existential feelings that express our most basic sense of our place in the human world.[13] Our affective opening out onto the shared world (*adduction*) through sexuality and through affect can be thought of, in general, as a sort of trust in the world and a lack of modesty. We are naturally exposed to and intertwined with others. If we experience the embodied affective sense of shame, then we experience an exclusion from the possibility of such trust in the world, which results in a counter-movement and withdrawal from the world (*abduction*). Shame's submissive, reconciliatory posture shows a desperate attempt to reenter the community where no techniques for doing so remain. Thus, even at the heart of shame, there is adductive motion towards the world of others.

Shame contains the ambiguity of existence. It is both a mirroring of our outcast flight from the present human world, and a countenance that attempts to embed us within the world. This shows what Merleau-Ponty means when he says that our actions essentially have several meanings: we are always both a passive being reacting to the sociotechnical world and an expressive subject striving to achieve personal existence. While we may see shame as protecting the individual in such behaviors, we should not conclude that shame essentially has an ethical function. After all, it has been noted that shame seems to make "extinction of the self . . . more, rather than less, likely to happen" (Kekes 1988, 292). Such an account fits, I believe, with the evolutionary origins of shame.[14]

DISABILITY AND SHAME WITHIN SOCIOTECHNICAL SYSTEMS

I have offered an account of how it is possible to feel prepersonal shame before sexist, racist, homophobic, or ableist expressions that one's personal self entirely rejects. Someone who strongly repudiates all ableist norms and values, and strongly embraces, as part of her core identity, her body and the nature of its motility may still feel the affect of shame when confronted with a world that does not enable effortless, anonymous coexistence. To deny that there can be such shame is to imply that, for example, a person who adopts what society calls "a disability" as part of her identity must be also adopting ableist standards if she feels any shame related to this so-called disability. If we do not allow this prepersonal shame, we must say that she actually values and judges according to the explicitly rejected norms when experiencing such shame. This is to say that this person's identity and values are a lie. But this is unpalatable.

On many views of shame, it would seem that the "mature, well-formed ethical agent" should not feel shame in the face of expressions that do not reflect one's own values (Calhoun 2004, 135). Obviously, the problem is most acute for cognitive views of shame in the analytic tradition.[15] For Kekes, "the cognitive aspect of shame involves a self-conscious detached comparison between the deficiency responsible for our failure and the standard of which we have fallen short" (1988, 294), so if one feels shame before ableist norms, one must actually hold oneself to have fallen short of a norm that is consciously rejected. While that is possible, it is surely not universally the case. Similarly, if Deonna and Teroni are correct that "shame is the subject's awareness that the way he is or acts is so much at odds with the values he cares to exemplify that it appears to disqualify him from his very commitment to the value," then the person who feels shame before a flight of stairs must conclude that his explicit positive evaluation of his motility is not actually a value to which he is committed (2009, 46), and even is at odds with his value commitments.

Even Taylor's view, one of the more influential in the field of philosophy, holds that shame is a "sophisticated type of self-consciousness" in which the "person feeling shame judges herself adversely" (1985, 67–68). Yet I can feel prepersonal shame in the face of expressions of value that do not cause such an adverse self-judgment. I do not feel shame because I secretly endorse those values but because their expression cuts me off from a shared anonymous world with others. On a reflective level of judgment, the person who felt this wave of shame may be justified that her own sense of self-esteem has not been damaged and may have less esteem for the society that failed in its construction of sociotechnical systems to be inclusive of all its members.

Persons who expressly value those attributes that society labels as "disability" and who may be surrounded by others devoted to affirming and supporting an inclusive sociotechnical world may still feel shame when confronted with ableist norms.[16] It seems forced to say that one is turned into an object, treated as less than human, or judging oneself and being judged by others according to some feature of one's identity that does not conform to one's "self-conception" (Thomason 2015, 13). The staircase before one surely does not do this, and neither do I. If the ableist sociotechnical world is thought of as treating one in a certain way, then it seems to offer mere indifference (Stiker 1999, 183). The sociotechnical world need not explicitly reduce one to an object; rather, it is simply unaccommodating to some and, therefore, discriminatory, making it difficult to live effortlessly as other privileged groups do. Therefore, while the self of one's self-conception, and the basis for one's self-esteem, may be affirmed by others and by one's own consciousness, one may still lose the possibility to live anonymously as a lived body, thus disrupting the ambiguous setting by which we are both subject and object with others. This is the source of a shame in which one feels expelled from the material and normative basis of social life.

Ceryle Marie Wade's account of a "great shame" that comes about for people who "need attendants" in daily life illustrates my point (1994, 92–93).

> And because this shame is so deep, and because it is perpetuated even by our movement when we emphasized only the able-ness of our beings, we buy into that language that lies about us and becomes part of our movement, and our movement dances over the surface of our real lives by spending all its precious energy on bus access while millions of us don't get out of bed or get by with inadequate personal care. Because we don't want to say this need that shames us out loud in front of people who have no understanding of the unprivate universe we live in, even if that person is a disabled sister or brother. (Wade 1994, 93)

It may seem that the shame stated here surrounds the making public that which ought to be private. Such a view is not uncommon (Schneider 1992, 43), but I think that Wade's point is rather different. The private-public distinction is heavily dependent on the norms of our society. The problem here is not that there is something inherently shameful or undignified about having other people clean one after defecating, for we can imagine a society in which royalty had attendants to do this without there being any shame. As Velleman states, "what naturally caused shame in Eden may not have caused shame at all in Sodom and Gomorrah" (2001, 44).

Furthermore, shame obviously can be brought about by things that are essentially public, like one's motility, but which reside as part of the anonymous background conditions of life. In other words, it is not the making public or objective per se that brings about a sense of shame. The problem is an inescapable publicity, which means one is cut off from ever being at home among the objects and norms of society as it is currently constituted. Wade is describing an exclusion from the ability to disattend all such concerns and place them at the level of anonymous existence, habit, and ingrained social norms.

We can use Heidegger's famous terminology and take Wade to be describing a sociotechnical world where one's embodied existence is not allowed to be taken for granted as what is *ready-at-hand*. Life is no longer inconspicuous and unobtrusive: one's very existence is turned into something conspicuous and obtrusive (Heidegger 1962, 73–74/102–103). One exists primarily in states of explicit, technical concern, where both self and world are *present-at-hand*.[17] The former way of living is one of familiarity, in which one can act effortlessly and spontaneously. The latter is to live like a foreigner in a land in which the customs are alien and all action must be made explicit. But objectification or being made present-at-hand is only a problem when it indicates being cut off from the anonymous and the familiar. Socially inscribed moments of explicit concern about oneself and one's situation are an essential part of life. They are only problematic if they dominate one's social life, and the possibility to be inconspicuous alongside others is denied.

Groups who are excluded from that social and material system, or who only tenuously inhabit it, are more subject to the sort of shame that I have described than those who occupy a privileged place in the system.[18] In particular, so-called able-bodied persons occupy a place of privilege in which they can focus on their willed, personal acts, their conscious adherence to the norms of social life, and their relations of explicit recognition.

Shame can operate for such individuals primarily as a cognitive-situational emotion that oversees behavior relative to personal, social-ethical norms. Such cognitive-situational shame is often praised for its significance for ethical life and in the formation of the self (Sedgwick 2003, 36–37).[19] But to extend such praise to shame in general is to ignore the shame of people who are not afforded such "ontological security" (Giddens 1991, 44). Although no one is impervious to the existential feeling of shame, those who society calls "able-bodied" and who are accommodated by the normative and material world are fairly well insulated from ever confronting the existential feeling of shame that comes from being profoundly prohibited from harmonious and effortless coexistence with others. So, while there certainly are different types of shame, if we overlook this deeper, affective form of shame that can manifest as a pervasive sense of one's exclusion from the shared sociotechnical world, then we are likely to overestimate its ethical significance.

Existential feelings are elusive in part because when we theorize about them or experience them, our mind looks for a specific, object, event, or quality that is the reason for the feeling. The mind and its cognitions are object-directed and are inevitably "of something." So, within the feeling of shame before a flight of stairs, one is likely to think that it is the property of being unable to ascend them that causes shame and, therefore, one's inadequacy in this area is shameful. However, on the view that I have proposed, shame need not be directed to any specific object or quality. While it is a response to a social state of affairs, I do not mean to say that we cognitively assess it as such and judge, for example, that the world itself is shameful. In the heteronomous, affective moment, one simply has a feeling, whether it is sadness, grief, fear, or shame, which alters one's way of being in the world.

In Heidegger's terms, having a mood alters our basic attunement to the world as such: it is indefinite and not "of" anything in particular. Therefore, I think it is a mistake to hold that the feeling of shame must be shame *of myself*, as Sartre claimed. Instead, a perceptual account of emotion rather than an attitudinal one can simply say that shame before the stairs, or as a feature of the "unprivate universe" that Wade describes, is a result of the fact that one perceives and feels the loss of the possibility of anonymous, effortless inhabitation of the sociotechnical world.[20] Shame does not say that this state of affairs is shameful. It is an embodied prereflective response to being cut off from the anonymous ground of coexistence. We may give ourselves an interpretation of that feeling as a particular value-assessment of the self, but this affect only points to the exclusion from anonymous being. It does not make any claim or judgment about why this exclusion has occurred. Although, this shame might well be intermixed with a prereflective feeling of frustration that is an implicit reference to the fact that the ableist society has not been more inclusive in its sociotechnical systems.

Importantly, Wade presents us with a statement of chronic shame. Given the connection between the affective attunement of shame and the sociotechnical systems of the lifeworld, we can easily see how systematic and persistent exclusion correlates to chronic shame. Instead of seeing chronic shame as persistent, low self-esteem, or negative self-judgment, coming "repetitively into one's awareness" (Dolezal 2015, 10), we can now see it as our embodied way of inhabiting a sociotechnical system, which may offer interpersonal recognition but does not offer us a way to be a lived body anonymously alongside others and objects. The dominant affect is no longer one of impersonal acceptance. It is feeling not-at-home in the world in the sense that one has not been afforded an unproblematic place among the objects of the world, even if others recognize one as having value, being a subject, and deserving such a place.

Such a life is unbearable, and so one naturally carves out a set of associations, motions, perceptions, practices, and the like that allow one to live effortlessly with others. Nevertheless, the subject of chronic shame tends to avoid entire areas of social life and geographical space, because they cannot be entered into without provoking the boundary situation in which shame floods our world. Persons who are labeled as disabled by society are more susceptible to this sort of chronic shame, due to the fact that language, objects, social practices, and space itself fail to offer the ontological security of anonymity. The so-called able-bodied have the privilege of a sociotechnical system that is constructed in such a way that the task of shame-avoidance is shouldered by the dominant norms, practices, and artifacts of the world. Of course, if those privileged others bring one to shame as a way of enforcing or exposing one's "social, political, and moral inferiority," then one may be tempted to see shame as exhausted by explicit rejection of the personal self (Weiss 2018, 544). But to be shut out from the affective and communicative space in which the lived body can anonymously co-inhabit the normative, artifactual world causes an affective reverberation that we can easily see as shame due to its connections with classic features of shame, such as exposure.

Phenomenology and Merleau-Ponty in particular have been accused of assuming a universal conception of the body that cannot recognize gender, race, or disability (Stawarska 2006, 92). It seems legitimate to worry that such a picture is likely to leave out persons who are labeled as disabled. It has also been argued that phenomenology provides a normative and discriminatory picture of what it is to be a body, to be mobile, to perceive, and to be sexual, for example, assuming a conception of the lived body that is not only ableist but also male and heterosexual.[21] But others have found possibilities for recognizing difference within what Merleau-Ponty calls our anonymous being, our prepersonal dwelling in a shared, expressive world (Kruks 2006). After all, there is no single structure that prescribes how to inhabit our basic modes of having a shared world. We only have the structures that our social history creates.[22] So, while the view of shame and of the affects that I have advanced in this chapter holds that the embodied prereflective phenomenon of shame, and its operation, are natural features of human beings, I nevertheless contend that there are no particular qualities of a person or of a body that are shameful.

The state of being-at-home in the sociotechnical world is simply inconspicuous incorporation into the norms and practices that surround one. What defines the boundary situation of shame depends on whether the specific state of conspicuousness is or is not a part of a set of shared practices that lead back into and support reintegration into inconspicuousness. If not, and the sociotechnical world makes inconspicuousness into an inescapable feature of being for which there is neither an adequate personal and conscious, or impersonal and bodily, response, then we have the conditions for prepersonal shame. I believe that such a phenomenology of a socially constructed notion of shame aligns with social constructivist notions of "disability" that have seemed to some to be at odds with phenomenology.[23]

From the perspective that I have been arguing, a significant feature of "disability," likely shared with other social minorities, is the fact that one's disattentive occupation of the norms and practices of society is imperiled by the discriminatory nature of social reality. One must attend and make conspicuous behavior that would be anonymous in a non-discriminatory system. For those labeled as disabled, being made into an object of explicit concern, by both supporters of one's personal expression of self and those who wish to deny that, can be the primary social reality. Although it would take much more argument to show this, I find an affinity with the idea that "disability" is a notion constructed by the systematic forms of exclusion found within the general sociotechnical system and its various subsystems.

While I am sympathetic to Elizabeth Barnes's account of "disability" as a social construction, it seems to me that the relevant social fact that explains what "disability" amounts to, as a part of social metaphysics, is not, as she claims, simply that this is a group that has solidarity in a struggle for justice around the notion of "disability rights" (Barnes 2018). Instead, one should stress that "disability" is a notion constructed first by systematic forms of exclusion. One aspect of that exclusion is to be profoundly subject to shame, and to other boundary situations, due to social barriers that do not allow one to as easily integrate into everyday, impersonal, and unthematized existence.

One reason that "disability" seems to be a social construct is that we can imagine this social category being emptied by modification of the material world, transformation of interpersonal rules of behavior, and the creation of social practices that can recognize and guide the navigation of different forms of dependence.[24] Similarly, given that our social reality inevitably consists of numerous smaller communities and a plurality of sociotechnical systems, we can combat the hegemonic aspects of the dominant sociotechnical system by providing the space and resources that enable more independence to subsystems that can create communities that afford disattentive coexistence to the variety of forms that bodies and minds can take. So, while Barnes is right to say that the solidarity of the group labeled as "disabled" by society is what gives a sort of *internal* cohesion, we should not ignore that the pressures of an exclusionary sociotechnical world are the *external* causes of the need for such solidarity in the first place.

ACKNOWLEDGMENTS

Many thanks to Glen Mazis for this and several other helpful additions to this text. His phenomenological challenges to my occasional use of Kantian language have added much clarity. Thanks also to Talia Welsh and participants of the 43rd Annual Meeting of the International Merleau-Ponty Circle for their comments.

NOTES

1. The concept of affective attunement is a translation of Heidegger's word "*Stimmung*," which is sometimes translated as "mood" (Heidegger 1962, 134/173, German pagination/English pagination). This concept is found, for example, in Bartky's feminist phenomenology of the body and shame (1990, 85).

2. On the notion of sociotechnical systems, see Dijkema, Lukszo, and Weiknen 2013.

3. I do not use the language of "people *with* disability," as if this were a quality of a person rather than the (oppressive) social situation and, instead, use the description of people *who are labeled* as disabled. See Tremain 2017, 10–11.

4. Other source for a view such as this within the phenomenological and philosophical-anthropological traditions can be found in Rukgaber 2018.

5. On the equivocal nature of shame on Sartre's view, see Weiss 2018, 541.

6. I understand self-esteem as Taylor describes it: thinking of oneself favorably and, thereby, having a "sense of one's own value" (Taylor 1985, 78). The idea that

shame involves a loss of self-esteem has been rightly and extensively criticized by Deigh (1983) on the basis that it does not recognize a diverse enough, social sense of self, although Deigh's notion of the social self is, I believe, not radical enough and remains centered on the intentional actions of the willful agent.

7. For more details on the phenomenology of disability and its social aspects, see Toombs 1995.

8. On this distinction, see Krüger 2010.

9. The term "disattention" is borrowed from Erving Goffman who uses it to indicate how we adhere to a set of social norms or rules and tune out everything that is obtrusive or disruptive. He describes this as a "civil inattention" that we give to the behavior of others (1963, 84).

10. The connection between shame and grief is rarely discussed, an exception being Schermer (2011). On the notion of grief as related to disability, see Roos 2011.

11. Ratcliffe (2008, 112–14), Dolezal (2015), and Fuchs (2003) do not recognize that Merleau-Ponty's view is quite different from Sartre's. A Merleau-Pontian conception of shame as exclusion from institutions also naturally emerges from his discussion of love and emotions as institutions, in lectures from the mid-1950s. See Maclaren 2017.

12. A significant Merleau-Pontian account of the intertwining of emotion and world is found in Mazis 1993, chs. 2–3.

13. For a dialectical conception of shame as a modification of one's situation in the world, see Vallelonga 1998, 134, 140.

14. On the evolutionary "descent" of shame, see Maibom 2010.

15. Binding the notion of shame to negative self-judgment about myself, my failure relative to an ideal, and a recognition that "I have done something that I feel is bad" is just as common in works from other traditions (e.g., Ahmed 2014, 103–106).

16. Elaboration of examples such as this and their implications can be found in Rukgaber 2016.

17. This terminology of the *present-at-hand* or *ready-at-hand* is explained by Heidegger, respectively, in terms of either grasping an object or property "thematically" or not (1962, 69/98).

18. For more information on the connection between anonymous social life and privilege, see Weiss 2017.

19. There are many other defenses of the moral significance of shame because of this regulative function that it plays. See Rotenstreich 1965, 66–68; Scheler 1987, 27; Calhoun 2004; Deonna, Rodogno, and Teroni 2012; and Manion 2002.

20. On the attitudinal versus perceptual theory distinction, see Rossi and Tappolet 2018.

21. See Butler 2006, for example.

22. For an excellent Merleau-Pontian account of the historical and interpersonal nature of the emotions as it relates to the medicalization of the body, see Mazis 2001.

23. Dolezal aligns phenomenology and constructivism, but also argues that phenomenologists fail to "spend much time considering" how "social structures such as institutions" figure into the body (2015, xiii, xix).

24. See Wendell 1996, ch. 2.

REFERENCES

Ahmed, Sara. 2014. *The Cultural Politics of Emotion.* Edinburgh, Scotland: Edinburgh University Press.

Barnes, Elizabeth. 2018. "Against Impairment: Replies to Aas, Howard, and Francis." *Philosophical Studies* 175, no. 5: 1151–62.

Bartky, Sandra Lee. 1990. *Femininity and Domination.* New York, NY and London, England: Routledge.

Butler, Judith. 2006. "Sexual Difference as a Question of Ethics: Alterities of the Flesh in Irigaray and Merleau-Ponty." In *Feminist Interpretations of Maurice Merleau-Ponty*, edited by Dorothea Olkowski and Gail Weiss, 107–25. College Station, PA: Penn State University Press.

Calhoun, Cheshire. 2004. "An Apology for Moral Shame." *The Journal of Political Philosophy* 12, no. 2: 127–46.

Carel, Havi. 2016. *Phenomenology of Illness.* Oxford, England: Oxford University Press.

Deigh, John. 1983. "Shame and Self-Esteem: A Critique." *Ethics* 93, no. 2: 383–418.

Deonna, Julien and Fabrice Teroni. 2009. "The Self of Shame." In *Emotions, Ethics, and Authenticity*, edited by Mikko Salmela and Verena Mayer, 33–50. Amsterdam, Netherlands/Philadelphia, PA: John Benjamins Publishing.

Deonna, Julien, Raffaele Rodogno, and Fabrice Teroni. 2012. *In Defense of Shame.* Oxford, England: Oxford University Press.

Dolezal, Luna. 2015. *The Body and Shame: Phenomenology, Feminism, and the Socially Shaped Body.* Lanham: MD: Lexington Books.

Drummond, John. 2018. "Anger and Indignation." In *Emotional Experiences: Ethical and Social Significance*, edited by John J. Drummond and Sonja Rinofner-Kreidl, 15–30. Lanham, MA: Rowan and Littlefield.

Fuchs, Thomas. 2003. "The Phenomenology of Shame, Guilt and the Body in Body Dysmorphic Disorder and Depression." *Journal of Phenomenological Psychology* 33, no. 2: 223–43.

Giddens, Anthony. 1991. *Modernity and Self-Identity.* Stanford, CA: Stanford University Press.

Goffman, Erving. 1963. *Behavior in Public Places.* New York, NY: Free Press.

Heidegger, Martin. 1962. *Being and Time.* New York, NY: HarperCollins Publishers.

———. 1998. *Pathmarks.* Cambridge, England: Cambridge University Press.

Heller, Agnes. 1979. *A Theory of Feelings.* Assen, ML: Van Gorcum.

Husserl, Edmund. 2001. *Analyses Concerning Passive and Active Synthesis: Lectures on Transcendental Logic*. Dordrecht, Netherlands: Kluwer.

Kekes, John. 1988. "Shame and Moral Progress." *Midwest Studies in Philosophy* 13, no. 1: 282–96.

Kruks, Sonia. 2006. "Merleau-Ponty and the Problem of Difference in Feminism." In *Feminist Interpretations of Merleau-Ponty*, edited by Dorothea Olkowski and Gail Weiss, 25–47. University Park, PA: Penn State University Press.

Krüger, Hans-Peter. 2010. "Persons and Their Bodies: The *Körper/Leib* Distinction and Helmuth Plessner's Theories of Ex-centric Positionality and *Homo Absconditus*." *Journal of Speculative Philosophy* 24, no. 3: 256–74.

Maclaren, Kym. 2017. "The 'Entre-Deux' of Emotions: Emotions as Institutions." In *Perception and Its Development n Merleau-Ponty's Phenomenology*, edited by Kirsten Jacobson and John Russon, 51–80. Toronto, CA: University of Toronto Press.

Maibom, Heidi. 2010. "The Descent of Shame." *Philosophy and Phenomenological Research* 80, no. 3: 566–94.

Manion, Jennifer. 2002. "The Moral Relevance of Shame." *American Philosophical Quarterly* 39, no. 1: 73–90.

Mazis, Glen. 1993. *Emotion and Embodiment*. New York, NY: Peter Lang.

———. 2001. "Emotion and Embodiment within the Medical World." In *Handbook of Phenomenology and Medicine*, edited by S. Toombs, 197–214. Dordrecht, Netherlands: Kluwer.

Merleau-Ponty, Maurice. 1962. *The Phenomenology of Perception*. London, England: Routledge.

Morris, David. 2018. *Merleau-Ponty's Developmental Phenomenology*. Evanston, IL: Northwestern University Press.

Oksala, Johana. 2006. "Female Freedom: Can the Lived Body Be Emancipated?" In *Feminist Interpretations of Merleau-Ponty*, edited by Dorothea Olkowski and Gail Weiss, 209–28. University Park, PA: Penn State University Press.

Plessner, Helmuth. 1970. *Laughing and Crying*. Evanston, IL: Northwestern University Press.

Ratcliffe, Matthew. 2008. *The Feelings of Being: Phenomenology, Psychiatry and the Sense of Reality*. Oxford, England: Oxford University Press.

Roos, Susan. 2011. "The Long Road to Relevance: Disability, Chronic Sorrow, and Shame." In *The Shame of Death, Grief, and Trauma*, edited by Jeffery Kauffman, 171–97. New York, NY: Routledge.

Rossi, Mauro and Christine Tappolet. 2018. "What Kind of Evaluative States are Emotions? The Attitudinal Theory vs. the Perceptual Theory of Emotions." *Canadian Journal of Philosophy* 49, no. 4: 544–63. https://doi.org/10.1080/00455091.2018.1472516.

Rotenstreich, Nathan. 1965. "On Shame." *The Review of Metaphysics* 93, no. 4: 743–65.

Rukgaber, Matthew. 2016. "Philosophical Anthropology, Shame, and Disability: In Favor of an Interpersonal Theory of Shame." *Res Philosophica* 93, no. 4: 743–65.

————. 2018. "Philosophical Anthropology and the Interpersonal Theory of the Affect of Shame." *Journal of Phenomenological Psychology* 49, no. 1: 83–112.

Sartre, Jean-Paul. 1956. *Being and Nothingness*. New York, NY: Washington Square Books.

Scheler, Max. 1987. *Person and Self-Value*. Dordrecht, Netherlands/Boston, MA: Martinus Nijhoff.

Schermer, Victor. 2011. "Between Shame, Death, and Mourning." In *The Shame of Death, Grief, and Trauma*, edited by Jeffery Kauffman, 33–57. New York, NY: Routledge.

Schneider, Carl. 1992. *Shame, Exposure and Privacy*. New York, NY: Norton.

Sedgwick, Eve Kosofsky. 2003. *Touching Feeling: Affect, Pedagogy, Performativity*. Durham, NC: Duke University Press.

Slaby, Jan and Achim Stephan. 2008. "Affective Intentionality and Self Consciousness." *Consciousness and Cognition* 17, no. 2: 506–13.

Stawarska, Beata. 2006. "From the Body Proper to Flesh: Merleau-Ponty on Intersubjectivity." In *Feminist Interpretations of Maurice Merleau-Ponty*, edited by Dorothea Olkowski and Gail Weiss, 91–106. College Station, PA: Penn State University Press.

Stiker, Henri-Jacques. 1999. *A History of Disability*. Ann Arbor, MI: University of Michigan Press.

Taylor, Gabriele. 1985. *Pride, Same, and Guilt*. Oxford, England: Clarendon Press.

Thomason, Krista. 2015. "Shame, Violence, and Morality." *Philosophy and Phenomenological Research* 91, no. 1: 1–24.

Toombs, S. Kay. 1995. "The Lived Experience of Disability." *Human Studies* 18, no.1: 9–23.

Tremain, Shelley Lynn. 2017. *Foucault and Feminist Philosophy of Disability*. Ann Arbor, MI: University of Michigan Press.

Vallelonga, Damian. 1998. "An Empirical Phenomenological Investigation of Being-Ashamed." In *Phenomenological Inquiry in Psychology*, edited by R. Valle, 123–55. New York, NY: Plenum Press.

Velleman, J. David. 2001. "The Genesis of Shame." *Philosophy and Public Affairs* 30, no. 1: 27–52.

Wade, Gayle. 2002. "It Ain't Exactly Sexy." In *The Ragged Edge*, edited by Barrett Shaw, 92–94. Louisville, KY: Avocado Press.

Weiss, Gail. 2017. "Sedimented Attitudes and Existential Responsibilities." In *Body/Self/Other: The Phenomenology of Social Encounters*, edited by Luna Dolezal and Danielle Petherbridge, 75–102. Albany, NY: SUNY Press.

————. 2018. "The Shame of Shamelessness." *Hypatia* 33, no. 3: 537–52.

Wendell, Susan. 1996. *The Rejected Body*. New York, NY/London, England: Routledge.

Zahavi, Dan. 2014. *Self and Other*. Oxford, England: Oxford University Press.

Part II

NORMS, CULTURES, AND POLITICS

Chapter 6

Nietzsche, Shame, and the
Seal of Liberation

Daniel R. Herbert

In part 2 of *Thus Spoke Zarathustra*, the eponymous protagonist of that work, and Nietzsche's spokesman, tells his disciples:

> The enlightened man calls man himself: the animal with red cheeks.
>
> How did this happen to man? Is it not because he has had to be ashamed too often?
>
> Oh my friends! Thus speaks the enlightened man: "Shame, shame, shame— that is the history of man!" (Z II, 25, "Of the Compassionate")

Elsewhere throughout Nietzsche's writings one encounters on a number of occasions the same thought which Zarathustra here expresses to his followers: man is alone amongst the animals in blushing, and it is man's history which has conferred this dubious distinction upon him, by rearing him to be ashamed. Nietzsche very often presents shame as an affliction originating in the attempt by humankind to renounce its instinctive and animal being. Typical, for instance, of Nietzsche's remarks concerning this peculiarly human phenomenon, is his description of shame as "the monster that attached itself to men when they aspired beyond the animals" (KGW 10, 199). Shame, according to Nietzsche, is both the instrument and the result of a historical process of self-domestication which has left humankind lamentably alienated from its natural instincts.

A similarly negative evaluation of shame is to be found in the well-known concluding remarks to book three of *The Gay Science*, where Nietzsche writes:

> *Whom do you call bad?*—He who always wants to put people to shame.
> *What is most human to you?*—To spare someone shame.

> *What is the seal of liberation?*—No longer to be ashamed before oneself. (GS
> III, 273–75)

This passage seems clearly to present shame as something to be overcome.
The oppressive shaming of others is unambiguously denounced and shame
itself is condemned as an encumbrance of which one must disburden oneself
in order to achieve liberation.

Such a straightforwardly negative assessment of shame is not without
exception, however, in Nietzsche's writings. Zarathustra, for instance, is
notoriously critical of an alleged lack of shame amongst the compassionate
which sets them apart from those who are noble of spirit (Z II, 25, "Of the
Compassionate"). Moreover, Nietzsche frequently complains against the
shamelessness of "the vulgar," who are without a certain sense of reverence
and humility in the presence of that which is truly great and awe-inspiring.
For Nietzsche then, the absence of shame can be indicative of an ignoble
character.

What might initially appear to be incompatible tendencies within
Nietzsche's thinking with respect to shame reveal themselves under closer
scrutiny as consistent features of an anti-nihilist campaign against allegedly
devitalizing cultural trends. According to Nietzsche, Christianity has had an
extremely unhealthy influence upon human affairs, leading to the development of a culture in which there is both too much and too little shame. Christian culture suffers from an excess of shame, in Nietzsche's view, because it
encourages one to be ashamed of one's natural instincts. At the same time,
Nietzsche claims that Christianity has contributed to the production of a
culture which is shameless in its self-satisfied contentment with uninspiring
mediocrity. As such, for Nietzsche, shame and shamelessness are, in the case
of societies heavily influenced by Christianity, expressions of the same rejection of powerful life-affirming instincts.[1]

Nietzsche's treatment of shame is explored over the remaining seven sections of the following chapter, the first of which introduces his challenge to be
unashamed before oneself. Section 3 presents Schopenhauer's philosophy as
the kind of life-denying attitude which Nietzsche challenges his audience to
overcome by living unashamedly. In section 4, Nietzsche's position is shown
to be complicated by a hostility to shamelessness as well as to life-inhibiting
forms of shame. The fifth section examines Nietzsche's criticisms of a certain
species of shamelessness—that of shameless pity—with particular focus on
his account in "The Ugliest Man" from *Thus Spoke Zarathustra*. Section 6
introduces Nietzsche's case for a certain kind of shame by exploring his distinction between the differing roles performed by that phenomenon in classical Hellenic and Christian cultures. In section 7, Nietzsche is seen to celebrate
ancient Greece for its life-affirming use of "Apollonian" shame as a means

for approaching but not succumbing to, raw instinctive energies which he calls "Dionysian." The final section summarizes the conclusions of the present chapter, showing Nietzsche to be critical of shame and of shamelessness alike when either threatens to undermine a life-affirming attitude of the kind which he claims is to be found in ancient Hellenic culture.

NIETZSCHE'S CHALLENGE TO BE WITHOUT SHAME BEFORE ONESELF

Among Nietzsche's most well-known comments regarding shame is the statement with which he concludes book two of *The Gay Science*—"And as long as you are in any way ashamed before yourselves, you do not yet belong among us" (GS II, 107). With this remark, Nietzsche may be understood to issue a challenge to his readers, to behold themselves completely exposed to the most probing self-examination and to remain entirely unashamed by the spectacle with which they are thus confronted. To be able to bear one's own unflinching gaze throughout such thoroughgoing self-scrutiny, without resort to comforting delusions as to one's real motives and attributes, is no easy task in Nietzsche's view, and demands a greater strength of character than most individuals command. What makes such self-interrogation so difficult, he maintains, is that it is sure to bring to one's attention certain antisocial instincts of which it is part of the function of civilization to make one ashamed. Such potentially shame-inducing instincts include, for instance, an instinctive human delight in cruelty, of which Nietzsche writes at some length in *The Genealogy of Morals*, before remarking:

> Entertaining, as I do, these thoughts, I am, let me say in parenthesis, fundamentally opposed to helping our pessimists to new water for the discordant and groaning mills of their disgust with life; on the contrary, it should be shown specifically that, at a time when mankind was not yet ashamed of its cruelty, life in the world was brighter than it is nowadays when there are pessimists. (GM II, 7)

As such, and unlike those "pessimists" from whose revulsion at life he emphatically distances himself, Nietzsche aims to recover in mankind "the joy and innocence of the animal" (GM II, 7) and hence to counteract the domesticating process by which mankind has been taught to be ashamed of its instincts.

However uncomfortable one might find his apparent celebration of mankind's violent and aggressive proclivities, Nietzsche maintains that the suppression of such instincts has made of modern man a "tame domestic animal" (GM II, 6) in whom there is nothing left to revere. By learning to be ashamed of its natural instincts, Nietzsche maintains, mankind has become not only less threatening and less dangerous, but also less awe-inspiring and less impressive. Along with increased security from the threat of others, the process by which mankind has become civilized has, according to Nietzsche, brought with it a pernicious diminution of human majesty and grandeur. One may perhaps have less to fear from one who has become ashamed of their natural instincts, but there is also less that might be thought impressive about such a being—or such, at least, is Nietzsche's view. Herein lies the great danger which Nietzsche takes to confront the culture of his day—that the potential for individual greatness may have been entirely compromised by the disciplining of mankind's savage and turbulent impulses, and hence that "in losing the fear of man, we have also lost the hope in man" (GM I, 12).

Moreover, according to Nietzsche, it is in order to make people less threatening to one another that they have been encouraged to be ashamed of their natural instincts—particularly those aggressively self-assertive impulses the unbridled indulgence of which puts the weak at risk of subjugation by the strong. For Nietzsche, then, it is those who would otherwise be vulnerable to domination by more powerful individuals that benefit most from the shame which mankind has come to experience in connection with its instincts. Indeed, Nietzsche maintains that the institution of morality originates in the collective effort by the weak to shame the strong into being reluctant to act on their tyrannical impulses. In Nietzsche's view, moral prohibitions against cruelty and exploitation are merely ideological instruments by which the weak majority seek to influence and constrain the actions of the strong minority. As such, claims Nietzsche, those feelings of self-reproach which attend the consciousness of one's violently anti-social instincts are the result of a process of indoctrination to which the weak have resorted for the sake of their own self-preservation. Hence it is Nietzsche's view that morality serves the agenda of those who would naturally be prey to the predatory instincts of the strong, and that it does so by encouraging the belief that the instinctive desire to oppress and subdue is something of which to be ashamed.

To be ashamed of such instincts is, however, entirely contrary to nature according to Nietzsche, who asserts that "[o]ne should *unlearn the shame* that would like to deny and lie away one's natural instincts" (WP Bk 2, §327, 179). For Nietzsche, human beings are naturally host to various unruly and belligerent drives which incite them to forceful assertions of will. Were it not for the corrupting influence of certain historical developments, he maintains, individuals would not be ashamed of their domineering instincts, nor would they think it incumbent upon themselves to check their behaviour by renouncing the instinctive drive to impose one's will upon others. However, with the emergence of moral ideologies which forbid against acting on such ruthlessly egoistic impulses, humankind has, in Nietzsche's view, become estranged from its natural drives, experiencing them as malign alien forces to be resisted. As such, Nietzsche claims, individuals have come to exist in an unhealthy state of denial and repression, troubled by natural impulses of which they are ashamed and upon which they are therefore reluctant to act.

This is the allegedly unnatural condition which Nietzsche proposes that humanity overcome. For Nietzsche, shame at one's natural instincts is a reactive force which undermines human potential by inhibiting those vigorous expressions of will without which nothing truly great is achievable. Hence Nietzsche maintains that release from shame shall result in the liberation of energies currently suppressed in the name of morality. According to Nietzsche, those who are ashamed of their natural instincts are victims of an action-confining deception propagated for the sake of preserving weakness at the expense of excellence—a delusion from which it is necessary that humankind free itself in order to live fully.

SCHOPENHAUER AS NIETZSCHE'S "ANTIPODE"

In advocating the renunciation of shame and the affirmation of the will, Nietzsche is in profound disagreement with Schopenhauer, whom he calls his "great teacher" (GM, P) and his "first and only educator" (HH, II, P, I). As Cartwright remarks "Schopenhauer championed the denial of the will as the ultimate human accomplishment, and Nietzsche praised the will's affirmation as the ultimate" (Cartwright 1998, 117). What is more, Schopenhauer maintains that the affirmation of the will, although inherent to the human condition, is something of which individuals are rightly ashamed, whereas Nietzsche decries any such shame at one's natural and instinctive drives. All the same, Nietzsche is greatly indebted to Schopenhauer's conception of empirical phenomena as expressions of violent and irrational efforts of will, differing from his erstwhile mentor principally in terms of his longing to celebrate, rather than escape from, the tumultuous brutality of sensible reality.

According to Schopenhauer—who purports to endorse a Kantian distinction between appearances and things-in-themselves—the empirical domain is merely a phenomenal manifestation of an underlying reality which he characterizes as blind, insatiable will. Because nothing can satisfy its boundless appetite, Schopenhauer maintains that the will is destined to remain in a state of unfulfilled desire, perpetually yearning for and striving after a gratification which it cannot possibly attain. Moreover, since, for Schopenhauer, sensible experience is only the phenomenal appearance of such a primordial reality as qualified by the human subject's conditions of representation, the entire empirical world is a manifestation of ceaseless willing and endless torment.

To the extent that one's own existence represents an affirmation of the will, one is, for Schopenhauer, complicit in the savage drama of passion and suffering to which the empirical domain gives sensible expression. As such, Schopenhauer maintains that "our existence involves guilt" (Schopenhauer 1966b, 569) and that this is "the profound reason for the shame connected with the business of procreation" (Schopenhauer 1966a, 328). In Schopenhauer's view, sexual desire is perhaps the most vivid empirical manifestation of the primordial will to life insofar as it represents the instinct of a species to preserve its own existence and, at a more fundamental metaphysical level, the will's continued, self-torturing assertion of itself. Hence Schopenhauer holds that the conscience of humankind is naturally troubled by sexual desire and the procreative instinct, claiming that "the act by which the will affirms itself and man comes into existence is one of which all in their heart of hearts are ashamed" (Schopenhauer 1966b, 569). It is, moreover, because one is thereby implicitly conscious of one's complicity in the affirmation of the will, and the consequent perpetuation of suffering which this entails, that sexual desire is, in Schopenhauer's view, a cause of shame. Furthermore, according to Schopenhauer, the reason for such shame receives mythic expression in "the dogma of the Christian teaching that we all share the sin of Adam (which is obviously only the satisfaction of sexual passion) and through it are guilty of suffering and death" (Schopenhauer 1966a, 328).

His own atheism notwithstanding, Schopenhauer frequently compares his own commitment to the innate culpability of humankind with that contained in certain Christian doctrines. On more than one occasion he quotes approvingly from Calderón's *La Vida es Sueño*, "For man's greatest offence/ Is that he has been born," (Schopenhauer 1966a, 254) adding in one place that "[i]n that verse Calderón has merely expressed the Christian dogma of original sin" (Schopenhauer 1966b, 355). For Schopenhauer too, individuals are morally compromised from birth and are by nature disposed to further disgrace because of their innate tendency to affirm a morally corrupt will. Schopenhauer also takes himself to be in agreement with Christian teachings concerning the human need for deliverance from suffering and evil, and might almost be offering a summary of his own position when he writes:

> Christianity is the doctrine of the deep guilt of the human race by reason of its very existence, and of the heart's intense longing for salvation therefrom. That salvation, however, can be attained only by the heaviest sacrifices and by the denial of one's own self, hence by a complete reform of man's nature. (Schopenhauer 1966b, 625)

As such, Schopenhauer endorses what he takes to be something like the Christian position when he maintains that the miserable predicament in which humankind naturally finds itself is one from which it can only be saved through self-denial and passivity.

Nothing, it seems, could be further from Nietzsche's audacious challenge to embrace life in all its turbulent splendour, for which Nietzsche calls Schopenhauer his "antipode" (Nietzsche 1954, 670). As Berman remarks, much of Nietzsche's work is motivated by the concern that "life is being endangered by the moral perspective, which shows itself most distinctly in Schopenhauer's nihilistic philosophy" (Berman 1998, 189). If, as Nietzsche claims, "[a] nihilist is a man who judges of the world as it is that it ought not to be, and of the world as it ought to be that it does not exist" (WP Bk III, §585, 318) then Schopenhauer—according to whom a state of sheer nothingness would be an improvement upon matters as they stand—qualifies very certainly as a proponent of nihilism.

For Nietzsche, Schopenhauer—although he is to be credited for revealing life in its naked appetitive being—is mistaken for assuming to find fault with such a predicament. In particular, Nietzsche thinks Schopenhauer guilty of weakness for reacting with horror to the thought of those untamed, lawless impulses which lie at the core of human motivation and for shrinking in disgust from condoning humankind's instinctive drives. As such, Schopenhauer is, for Nietzsche, illustrative of the kind of attitude to be overcome in becoming liberated from shame, and becoming capable of living fully and without inhibition. Despite having seen through Christianity's false promise of salvation in an afterlife, Nietzsche maintains, Schopenhauer remains captive to Christian world-denial in his attempts to escape from the unrest of sensible reality and achieve solace in a state of dispassionate resignation, rather than bravely affirming reality and participating joyfully and wholeheartedly in all its exhilarating upheavals.

Although he credits him with having the stomach to expose human nature in its raw instinctive being, unembellished by reassuring humanistic dogma, Nietzsche is disparaging of Schopenhauer for reacting with shame and horror at his own findings, and for lacking the strength to embrace the fierce and powerful will that he had shown to underlie all empirical phenomena. For Nietzsche, Schopenhauer is more honest than most philosophers in his willingness to face disquieting truths about humankind, but he shows the limits of his resolve by judging our condition to put us in need of salvation rather than as something to be celebrated. In this respect, Nietzsche maintains, Schopenhauer's philosophy displays the corrupting influence of Christian culture, which teaches individuals to be ashamed of their natural instincts and to long to be free of the travails of sensible reality.

Schopenhauer also appears close to Christian thought in his espousal of an ethics of compassion. According to Schopenhauer, compassion, or the wish to relieve another's suffering, is the motive for all morally praiseworthy action. In seeking to illustrate the kind of morality which he advocates, Schopenhauer writes that "Christianity is nearest at hand, the ethics of which is entirely in the spirit we have mentioned, and leads not only to the highest degrees of charity and human kindness, but also to renunciation" (Schopenhauer 1966a, 386). The biographies of the Christian saints, such as St. Francis of Assisi, serve as examples of the moral life, according to Schopenhauer, for whom selflessness and a sympathetic concern for others' hardships are the marks of a virtuous character.

COMPASSION AND SHAMELESSNESS

In Nietzsche's view, however, compassion or "pity"—as Schopenhauer's German word "*mitleid*" may also be translated—is almost entirely without merit. He writes in *The Gay Science*, for instance, of "the nonsense about pity" (GS II, 99) in Schopenhauer's ethics. Moreover, Nietzsche has Zarathustra speak against the ignoble shamelessness of the compassionate when he writes:

> Truly, I do not like them, the compassionate who are happy in their compassion: they are too lacking in shame.
> If I must be compassionate I still do not want to be called compassionate; and if I am compassionate than it is preferably from a distance.
> And I should also prefer to cover my head and flee away before I am recognized: and thus I bid you do, my friends! (Z II, 25, "Of the Compassionate")

Given what Nietzsche has to say elsewhere in criticism of those who encourage individuals to be ashamed, it is quite remarkable to find him objecting to the compassionate for their lack of shame. What is more, Zarathustra declares that one who is noble in spirit "resolves to feel shame before all sufferers" (Z II, 25, "Of the Compassionate"), so that Nietzsche seems thereby to qualify his calls for individuals to live without shame.

It is not only the compassionate that are too lacking in shame according to Nietzsche, however. In the first of the *Untimely Meditations*, for instance, he denounces the positivist philosopher David Strauss for his "shameless philistine optimism" (DS, 6)—an unbecoming characteristic which Nietzsche alleges to be common amongst his contemporaries. For Nietzsche, Strauss—whose account of historical progress and advocacy of scientific materialism, as a replacement for Christianity, both bear comparison with Comte—exemplifies a complacent bourgeois triumphalism which had become commonplace in German culture following unification.

Strauss and his like are unworthy of Germany's great cultural inheritance, according to Nietzsche, who maintains that in thinking themselves qualified to judge the aesthetic merits of Mozart's or Beethoven's works, "all shame has been lost, on the part of the public as much as on that of [Strauss]" (DS, 5). What is more, Nietzsche writes of what he alleges to be the impudent reception in Germany of Wagner's *Tannhäuser* and *Lohengrin* as illustrating "the shamelessness which characterises German scholars no less than it does German journalists" (RWB, 8).

In each of these cases, Nietzsche maintains, his contemporaries are guilty of a presumptuous over-familiarity in their attitudes toward cultural achievements of monumental significance and are, as such, vulgar and lacking in taste, displaying a philistine lack of humility in the presence of something of inestimable value. Whereas such individuals are objectionably shameless, according to Nietzsche, he also remarks that "[n]o honourable man of our age can fail to feel ashamed when he sees how Schopenhauer seems to belong to it only by accident" (SE, 7), suggesting that a person of honour and distinction will be sufficiently discerning to experience shame at the vulgarity and poor taste of their contemporaries. For Nietzsche, in particular, his own contemporaries should feel ashamed of the fact that in a culture such as their own, a genius of Schopenhauer's standing is the exception rather than the rule.

In the third of his *Untimely Meditations*, "Schopenhauer as Educator," Nietzsche asserts that one cannot attain "the first consecration to culture" without having been impressed and inspired by some great individual, and that

the sign of that consecration is that one is ashamed of oneself without any accompanying feeling of distress, that one comes to hate one's own narrowness and shrivelled nature, that one has a feeling of sympathy for the genius who again and again drags himself up out of our dryness and apathy and the same feeling in anticipation for all those who are still struggling and evolving, with the profoundest conviction that almost everywhere we encounter nature pressing towards man and again and again failing to achieve him, yet everywhere succeeding in producing the most marvellous beginnings, individual traits and forms. (SE, 6)

This is in stark contrast to what Nietzsche calls "the arrogant self-satisfaction of our contemporaries," (SE, 2) representing instead the profound desire for greatness and the humbling consciousness of powerful natural forces striving to find fuller expression through individuals, thereby bringing humankind nearer to its as yet unmet potential. Importantly, however, the sense of shame which Nietzsche describes in this passage results not from disgust at an intrinsic human depravity, but rather from dissatisfaction with the gulf between humankind's enormous potential and the mediocrity of its present condition. As such, the shame in question is life-affirming rather than life-denying, inciting one to overcome present limitations rather than meekly retreat from the world. Clearly then, Nietzsche, is not hostile to shame in every sense of that term.

"THE UGLIEST MAN"

Nietzsche's hostility to the alleged shamelessness of the compassionate is vividly illustrated in book four of *Thus Spoke Zarathustra*, in Zarathustra's encounter with "the Ugliest Man." Drawn to investigate the source of a "cry of distress" Zarathustra finds himself in a "kingdom of death" where he happens upon "something . . . shaped like a man and yet hardly a man, something unutterable" (Z IV, 67, "The Ugliest Man"). At first, Zarathustra is ashamed to have set eyes upon such a being, which he soon identifies as "the murderer of God" and "the Ugliest Man." Upon recognizing this unfortunate, Zarathustra is initially overwhelmed by pity, and falls to the ground, only to recover his resolve and, having risen to his feet, is about to make his departure when the Ugliest Man asks him to remain. Complementing him for having overcome his sense of pity and regaining his footing, the Ugliest Man expresses gratitude for Zarathustra's shame and, in a deeply enigmatic passage, declares his contempt for the compassionate herd from which he has fled:

> But that you went past me, silent; that you blushed, I saw it well: by that I knew you for Zarathustra.
>   Anyone else would have thrown me his alms, his pity, in glance and speech. But for that—I am not enough of a beggar, you have divined that—for that I am too rich, rich in big things, in fearsome things, in the ugliest things, in the most unutterable things! Your shame, O Zarathustra, honoured me!
>   I escaped with difficulty from the importunate crowd of those who pity, that I might find the only one who today teaches "Pity is importunate"—you, O Zarathustra!—be it the pity of a god, be it human pity; pity is contrary to modesty. And unwillingness to help may be nobler than that virtue which comes running with help.
>   That however, pity, is called virtue itself with all little people—they lack reverence for great misfortune, great ugliness, great failure.
>   I look beyond all these, as a dog looks over the backs of swarming flocks of sheep. They are little, well-meaning, well-woolled, colourless people. (Z IV, 67, "The Ugliest Man")

Despite his apparently unenviable condition, then, the Ugliest Man is appalled by those who pity him, and denounces their intrusiveness and triviality. Much as Nietzsche in his *Untimely Meditations* bemoans the shameless complacency and self-satisfaction of his contemporaries, the Ugliest Man shows disdain for the uncomprehending condescension of his. In both cases, a certain attitude and set of behaviours widely deemed "respectable" and "fitting" to bourgeois mores is criticized for its alleged shamelessness. Whether it is the most sublime cultural achievements or the unutterable predicament of the Ugliest Man, the outlook which Nietzsche has in mind trivializes great things by the presumptuous over-familiarity which it displays toward them. Hence the Ugliest Man is honoured by the shame which Zarathustra shows before him, and takes this as a sign of Zarathustra's distinction.

Unlike the crowd of mediocrities from which the Ugliest Man has fled, Zarathustra recognizes, and is humbled by, the magnitude of the awesome tragedy manifested in the person of this "murderer of God." According to the Ugliest Man, moreover, those who give him alms and are shameless in their pitying philanthropy are like flocks of sheep and allow their ethical standards to be determined by the interests of the weak. As such, claims the Ugliest Man, theirs is the morality of the weak, as preached in the New Testament by he that declared "I am the truth." Like Nietzsche himself, the Ugliest Man deems Christianity to be the expression of a frail and squeamish temperament which cannot bear to face the hard and violent realities of life and must delude itself with comforting illusions instead. Moreover, the Ugliest Man further acts as Nietzsche's spokesperson in lamenting the enfeebling influence which he claims Christianity to have had over human affairs.

However, whereas Nietzsche elsewhere criticizes Christianity for encouraging one to be ashamed of one's natural instincts, it is the alleged shamelessness of Christian thought and practice which he has the Ugliest Man condemn. Hence the Ugliest Man declares that it is because "[h]is pity knew no shame" (Z IV, 67, "The Ugliest Man") that the Christian god could not be allowed to live. Christian shamelessness is also the target of Nietzsche's criticism when the Ugliest Man states:

> This immodest man has long made the cock's comb of the little people rise up in pride—he who taught "I—am the truth." Was an immodest man ever answered more politely? But you, O Zarathustra, passed him by and said: "No! No! Thrice No!" (Z IV, 67, "The Ugliest Man")

According to the Ugliest Man then, Christianity appeals to the conceited self-righteousness of those who lack the power to assert their will and are resentful of those who do. As such, for Nietzsche, the shamelessness of Christianity is, like that for which he criticizes his contemporaries in the *Untimely Meditations*, the expression of a life-denying mode of thought. In Nietzsche's view, "the first consecration to culture" involves shame, but not distress, at the limits of one's manifestation of those creative forces of which all sensible phenomena are the expression, and a profound longing to better facilitate, through one's own being, ever greater expressions of such natural powers. The shamelessness which Nietzsche claims to identify in Christianity, the compassionate, and his own contemporaries evinces a naïve sense of superiority over nature and one's own natural drives, indicating a misplaced pride in a moral ideology that masks the self-preserving agenda of those who are naturally vulnerable to the whims of the powerful, and need therefore to shame them into an unthreatening, but uninspiring docility. Hence the shamelessness to which Nietzsche takes exception is a feature of what he maintains is a culture made sickly and tepid as the result of an insidious strategy of self-preservation by which the "herd" or "slave-type" has come to determine society's standards of what is admirable. For Nietzsche then, to be without shame is deplorable when this represents the cultural influence of a life-denying slave ideology.

SHAME IN ANCIENT GREEK CULTURE

A concern with the topic of shame is apparent throughout Nietzsche's literary career, prior even to the publication of *The Birth of Tragedy* in 1872 and up to his posthumous work, *The Will to Power*. As perhaps befits his early classical studies, some of Nietzsche's earliest remarks concerning shame are made in the context of a discussion of ancient Greek culture. For instance, in "The Greek State"—the preface to a book never completed—Nietzsche describes the ancient Greek citizen's shame at the fact of their culture resting upon the exploitation of labour, including slavery. Although aware of their cultural greatness, Nietzsche claims, the ancient Greeks also knew that such achievements were only possible because of a class hierarchy which relieved a privileged group of certain economic pressures, thereby setting them free to enjoy various luxuries, including art products. In a passage reminiscent of Marx, Nietzsche describes the ancient Greek citizen's uncomfortable knowledge that

> [c]ulture, which is chiefly a real need for art, rests upon a terrible basis: the latter however makes itself known in the twilight sensation of shame. In order that there may be a broad, deep, and fruitful soil for the development of art, the enormous majority must, in the service of a minority, be slavishly subjected to life's struggles to a greater degree than their own wants necessitate. At their cost, through the surplus of their labour, that privileged class is to be relieved from the struggle for existence, in order to create and to satisfy a new world of want. (GSt, 6)

Hence, according to Nietzsche, shame attaches to the awareness of the hierarchical socioeconomic conditions without which, he maintains, artistic culture would not be possible. Far from advocating the revolutionary over-throw of such conditions, however, Nietzsche instead suggests that they be recognized as media necessary for the expression of certain great efforts of impersonal will. Sounding much like Schopenhauer, Nietzsche compares the shame of artistic culture with that involved in procreation and claims that both kinds of shame-inducing phenomena represent the activity of forces of will operating behind all individual consciousness and personality. Hence, according to Nietzsche:

> [t]hat feeling by which the process of procreation is considered as something shamefacedly to be hidden, although by it man serves a higher purpose than his individual preservation, the same feeling veiled also the origin of the great works of art, in spite of the fact that through them a higher form of existence is inaugurated, just as through the other act comes a new generation. The feeling of shame seems therefore to occur where man is merely a tool of manifestations of will infinitely greater than he is permitted to consider himself in the isolated shape of the individual. (GSt, 6)

As such, Nietzsche maintains, one experiences shame when one finds oneself reduced to the status of an instrument, channelling natural forces for ends one has not chosen and compelled to facilitate primordial drives far more power-ful than oneself.

According to Speirs, Nietzsche held shame to be occasioned by "the sub-ordination of human beings to any kind of impersonal process which oper-ated with no regard for the individuals who were the continent instruments of its realisation" (Speirs 2013, 6). Such brute processes seem to rob one of any supposed claim to dignity as an autonomous rational individual, but are, in Nietzsche's view, absolutely necessary to the development of healthy and vigorous forms of cultural life. In later works, such as *The Genealogy of Mor-als* and *The Gay Science*, where he more explicitly challenges his audience not to be ashamed of their natural instincts, Nietzsche urges that such forces be harnessed rather than resisted and claims that to stifle their expression is to impede the development of life and culture.

Their shame aside, however, Nietzsche maintains that the ancient Greeks at least acknowledged the cultural necessity of cruelty and suffering, and did not attempt to deceive themselves about either the condition of the exploited or the possibility of a flourishing artistic culture in the absence of great social inequality. In this regard, claims Nietzsche, the ancients were far stronger than the moderns, who find it necessary to concoct ideologies which declare all humans to be equal and promise liberation for the oppressed classes. Such movements as democracy, socialism, and liberalism are, in Nietzsche's view, testaments to the inability of the moderns to accept and live with the shameful conditions upon which culture is founded, and to their demand for pleasing fictions to alleviate the painful consciousness of the suffering which must be endured in order for life to flourish.

It is, in any case, noteworthy that the shame which Nietzsche describes in connection with the ancient Greeks was, in his view, part of the greatness of their culture. For Nietzsche, whereas the ancient Greeks felt humbled by those violent and creative natural impulses the cultural expression of which was mediated by their own historical activity, the moderns need to repress all consciousness of any such primordial forces at work within themselves. Moreover, Nietzsche maintains, what was, for the ancient Greeks an awesome and sublime natural power before which they felt utterly insignificant but which they longed to embrace, is, for the moderns, a source of disgrace by which they are appalled. As such, according to Nietzsche, the shame experienced by the ancient Greeks was life-affirming, whereas that of the moderns is life-denying. Unlike the moderns, Nietzsche claims, the ancient Greeks felt privileged to act as vessels for the expression of powerful natural forces of which they were in awe. It was not disgust at instinctive drives of which they had been persuaded to disapprove that prompted the shame which the ancient Greeks felt, according to Nietzsche, but rather a sense of wonder in the presence of something overwhelmingly vast and powerful. This is the sense of shame which Nietzsche criticizes his contemporaries for lacking. In Nietzsche's view, his contemporaries were at fault for their shameless unwillingness to acknowledge their indebtedness to primordial energies which they longed to suppress, and for the ill-befitting pride which they took in their own bourgeois values.

SHAME IN THE BIRTH OF TRAGEDY

Nietzsche's admiration for the culture of ancient Greece is perhaps nowhere more evident, nor his study of the sophistication of classical Greek shame more extended, than in *The Birth of Tragedy*. According to this early work, Greek tragedy is the greatest cultural expression of antagonistic creative forces that have never been in a more perfect balance than in ancient Greece. These competing forces—which Nietzsche calls the "Apollonian" and the "Dionysian"—lie at the heart of all creative activity and it is the balance of power between them that determines the basic character of a culture. Whereas Apollo represents order, proportion, harmony, restraint, and reason, Dionysus is the figure of excess, abandon, vigour, spontaneity, and passion. What distinguishes the ancient Greeks, according to Nietzsche, is that they were able to embrace Dionysian energies without being engulfed and destroyed by them. Because of its firmly established Apollonian element, ancient Greek culture could absorb and safely give expression to powerful instinctive drives without risking the destructive self-abandonment that would otherwise result from the Bacchanalian indulgence of uninhibited Dionysian revelry. For Nietzsche then, complete exposure to the Dionysian is too much for the human mind to bear, and Apollonian forces are therefore required to preserve a sense of rational order in the face of a bewildering and incomprehensible chaos of violent instinctive energies. Were the Dionysian to have gained supremacy over the Apollonian, then classical Greek culture would have degenerated into a frenzied cacophony of unrest.

In Nietzsche's view, however, European culture has, under the influence of Platonic and Christian thought, fallen afoul of the opposite danger by insulating itself too much from the Dionysian and thereby restricting its own access to such life-affirming instinctive energies. According to Nietzsche, it is in large measure by enabling one to think in terms of discrete individuals that the Apollonian offers psychological protection against the turbulent confusion of unrefined Dionysian energies. Hence Nietzsche describes Apollo as the "apotheosis" (BT, 4, "Preface to Richard Wagner") of the principle of individuation and as "the glorious divine image of the *principium individuationis*" (BT, 1, "Preface to Richard Wagner"). For Nietzsche, Apollonian influences introduce conceptual distinctions and relations into the mind's dealings with nature, thereby permitting rational understanding to gain some purchase on sensible reality by articulating it into discrete and conceptually identifiable particulars. Such an individuating function is also operative in distinguishing oneself from others and accounting for one's sense of oneself as a discrete individual. Furthermore, since he associates them with the suspension of the principle of individuation, Nietzsche regards Dionysian forces as inviting submission to, and the loss of oneself within, impersonal manifestations of will. As such, Apollonian forces in classical Greek culture made it possible for ancient Greeks to experience Dionysian energies without abandoning their self-identities.

Moreover, one of the most important means available to the ancient Greeks for thus preserving one's sense of individual selfhood was provided by the phenomenon of shame. As Nietzsche describes in an aphorism from *Daybreak*, the experience of shame involves a pronounced self-focus and a sense of being radically separate from others:

> *Centre*—The feeling "I am the mid-point of the world!" arises very strongly if one is suddenly overcome with shame; and then one stands there as though confused in the midst of a surging sea and feels dazzled as though by a great eye which gazes upon us and through us from all sides. (D IV, 352)

Such egocentric experiences provide a powerful antidote to the lure of self-abandonment in the Dionysian throng. Nietzsche describes shame, in particular as "[t]he drive *to conceal something*" and "a protective drive" (KGW 7, 239). For Nietzsche, shame has a valuable function therefore in protecting one's sense of integrated selfhood from dissolution under the weight of undiluted Dionysian forces.

All the same, Nietzsche at least came to maintain that the psychological defence mechanisms by which individuals are protected from complete submergence in the Dionysian tumult of instinctive forces are only illusions necessary for personhood and culture. As Janaway remarks, Nietzsche ultimately holds that "personhood is not ontologically basic" and that "each human being is constituted by a plurality of subpersonal drives and affective states" (Janaway 1998, 36). It is also Nietzsche's view, however, that these are not truths which one can permit oneself to admit without dissemblance. As such, the sense of selfhood which it is the function of shame to protect against Dionysian excess is only a psychologically necessary illusion, according to Nietzsche, albeit one without which the greatest cultural achievements of ancient Greece would not have been possible.

Notwithstanding their dependence on such pleasing illusions, however, the ancient Greeks were nonetheless, according to Nietzsche, able to countenance and bear far more of Dionysian reality than any society which has succeeded them. Unlike that of Christianity, the shame of ancient Greek culture was, in Nietzsche's view, life-affirming, insofar as it was utilized to achieve the greatest psychologically admissible proximity to Dionysian influences while ensuring against the mental collapse that would have prevented their expression in artistic accomplishments of the first rank. By contrast, Nietzsche maintains, Christian shame aims to eradicate the influence of the Dionysian, leaving one estranged from one's natural instinctive drives. Moreover, in priding itself on what are in fact ideological illusions involving denial of violent realities too uncomfortable for the weak to confront, Christian culture is also shameless in its life-denying attitude, according to Nietzsche. Hence what distinguish classical Greek and Christian cultures, with respect to shame and shamelessness, are, in Nietzsche's view, their respective attitudes toward the affirmation of life. For Nietzsche, ancient Greek culture has a far healthier and more life-affirming relationship with shame than does Christianity, and he therefore advocates, as part of a campaign of cultural re-invigoration, the overcoming of such shame as Christian doctrine allegedly encourages one to feel at one's natural instinctive drives so that these might again be freed and productively utilized in the creation of works of sublime genius.

CONCLUSION

In Nietzsche's view then, it is not shame as such that one should strive to be without, but rather the feeling of being ashamed by one's deepest instinctive drives. This aspect of Nietzsche's thinking with respect to shame is vividly illustrated in the following enigmatic aphorism from *Daybreak*:

> *Shame*—Here stands the handsome steed and paws the ground: it snorts, longs for the gallop and loves him who usually rides him—but oh shame! His rider cannot mount up on to his back today, he is weary.—This is the shame of the wearied philosopher before his own philosophy. (D 5, 487)

Nietzsche may be understood here to compare his own life-affirming philosophy with a "handsome steed" and to represent the debilitating consequences of modernity in the figure of a weary rider who lacks the energy to participate in the liberating adventure of Nietzsche's challenge to be without shame. He portrays the life-inhibiting consequences of shame in terms of "the philosopher's" lethargic unwillingness to participate in the adventure of a philosophy by which instinctive energies may be unleashed and embraced.

For Nietzsche, it is the task of his own philosophy to liberate individuals from such stultifying attitudes, thereby allowing them to affirm life unashamedly. In particular, Nietzsche wants for his audience to rise to the challenge of being able to withstand their own self-scrutiny without the need of comforting illusions. This requires, moreover, that they should be able to acknowledge their instinctive being, without shame. To be thus unashamed of one's instincts is compatible, however, with having a sense of shame in terms of a due humility before something sublime and awe-inspiring. According to Nietzsche, the ancient Greeks were without shame of the first kind but not the second, whereas the reverse was true of his own contemporaries. As Schneider helpfully summarizes Nietzsche's approach, "[o]ne needs a sense of shame, but one needs not to be ashamed" (Schneider 1977, 23). Only thus is it possible, in Nietzsche's view, to live in full recognition and appreciation of those same life-affirming influences which found their greatest cultural expression in ancient Greece, but have since been a cause for denial.

ACKNOWLEDGMENTS

I am very grateful to Mark Alfano and Matthew Bennett for having provided feedback on earlier drafts of this chapter. I would also like to thank the University of Sheffield and the Universidad Popular Autónoma del Estado de Puebla for providing a supportive academic community during the completion of this chapter.

NOTE

1. Although there are important discussions (in philosophy, psychology, and sociology, amongst other disciplines) concerning the difference between guilt and shame, Nietzsche does not himself explicitly draw any distinction between the two. This is not to deny that later work on the distinction may be used to identify an implicit difference between guilt and shame in Nietzsche's work, although this is a topic to be addressed in a separate essay from the present.

REFERENCES

Berman, David. 1998. "Schopenhauer and Nietzsche: Honest Atheism, Dishonest Pessimism." In *Willing and Nothingness: Schopenhauer as Nietzsche's Educator*, edited by Christopher Janaway, 178–95. Oxford, England: Clarendon Press.

Calderón de la Barca, Pedro. 1994. *La Vida es Sueño*. Madrid, Spain: Castalia.

Cartwright, David E. 1998. "Nietzsche's Use and Abuse of Schopenhauer's Moral Philosophy for Life." In *Willing and Nothingness: Schopenhauer as Nietzsche's Educator*, edited by Christopher Janaway, 116–50. Oxford, England: Clarendon Press.

Janaway, Christopher. 1998. "Schopenhauer as Nietzsche's Educator." In *Willing and Nothingness: Schopenhauer as Nietzsche's Educator*, edited by Christopher Janaway, 13–36. Oxford, England: Clarendon Press.

Nietzsche, Friedrich. (1871) 1911. "The Greek State" (GSt). In *Early Greek Philosophy. Volume II, The Complete Works of Friedrich Nietzsche*, edited by Oscar Levy, translated by Maximilian A. Mügge, 1–19. London, England: George Allen and Ltd.

———. 1968. *The Will to Power* (WP). Edited by Walter Kaufmann. Translated by Walter Kaufmann and R. J. Hollingdale. New York, NY: Vintage Books; Random House, Inc.

———. (1883) 1969. *Thus Spoke Zarathustra* (Z). Translated by R. J. Hollingdale. London, England: Penguin.

———. (1882) 1974. *The Gay Science* (GS). Translated by Walter Kaufmann. New York, NY: Random House.

———. 1975. *Kritische Gesamtausgabe Briefwechsel* (KGW). Edited by G. Colli and M. Montinari. 24 Vols. Berlin, Germany: Walter de Gruyter.

———. (1872) 1993. *The Birth of Tragedy* (BT). Translated by Shaun Whiteside. London, England: Penguin.

———. (1878) 1996. *Human, All Too Human* (HH). Translated by R. J. Hollingdale. Cambridge, England: Cambridge University Press.

———. (1876) 1997. "Schopenhauer as Educator" (SE). In *Untimely Meditations*, translated by R. J. Hollingdale, 125–94. Cambridge, England: Cambridge University Press.

————. (1876) 1997. "David Strauss: The Confessor and the Writer" (DS). In *Untimely Meditations*, translated by R. J. Hollingdale, 1–55. Cambridge, England: Cambridge University Press.

————. (1876) 1997. "Richard Wagner in Bayreuth" (RWB). In *Untimely Meditations*, translated by R. J. Hollingdale, 195–254. Cambridge, England: Cambridge University Press.

————. (1881) 1997. *Daybreak* (D). Translated by R. J. Hollingdale. Cambridge, England: Cambridge University Press.

————. (1887) 2003. *The Genealogy of Morals* (GM). Translated by Horace B. Samuel. Mineola, New York, NY: Dover Press.

Schneider, Carl D. 1977. "'The Reddened Cheek' Nietzsche on Shame." *Philosophy Today* 21, no. 1: 21–31.

Schopenhauer, Arthur. (1818/19) 1966a. *The World as Will and Representation*. Vol. 1. Translated by E. F. J. Payne. New York, NY: Dover Publications.

————. (1844) 1966a. *The World as Will and Representation*. Vol. 2. Translated by E. F. J. Payne. New York, NY: Dover Publications.

Speirs, Ronald. 2013. "Nietzsche's 'Thier Mit Rothen Backen': The Birth of Tragedy out of the Spirit of Shame." *German Life and Letters* 66, no. 1: 1–21.

Chapter 7

Shame and Moral Learning in Coetzee's *Disgrace*

Alba Montes Sánchez

Numerous attempts have been made at making sense of various conflict-ing claims and intuitions regarding the moral significance of shame. One of the main issues is how to square the classic and widely defended claim that shame is morally constructive and contributes to moral learning (see Aristotle 2014; Burnyeat 1980; Rawls 1999; Williams 2008; Deonna, Rodogno, and Teroni 2011) with the psychological finding that it can damage self-esteem and lead to antisocial behaviors, including violence (Gilligan 2003; Tangney and Dearing 2004; Thomason 2014). In this chapter, through a reading of J. M. Coetzee's *Disgrace* (Coetzee 1999), I argue that these aspects are not necessarily in contradiction. On the one hand, I agree with those who defend that a susceptibility to shame in all its varieties is ethically valuable because it is a powerful guard against moral solipsism (Williams 2008; Thomason 2014). On the other hand, I argue that, in some circumstances, ethics demands that one's self-identity be damaged (or even fully dismantled), and shame can help do this, as Coetzee shows in his novel. Both these claims are compat-ible with recognizing that shame often has an ambiguous impact in our moral lives: All varieties of shame share a basic structure that reveals our vulner-ability and interdependence, but this revelation can pull us both in virtuous and vicious directions, depending on other factors. This becomes clear in a reading of *Disgrace* that pays attention to the emotional and moral life of its main character, specifically, the main character's experience of bypassed narcissistic shame, survivor shame and moral shame.

DISGRACE AND THE SOCIAL SELF-CONSCIOUS STRUCTURE OF SHAME

J. M. Coetzee's *Disgrace* deals with the question of how to be a white man in post-apartheid South Africa, the position this puts one in (which in principle is the position of a privileged oppressor), and also with the issues of whether redemption, forgiveness, and reconciliation are possible in such a context (see, for example, Kossew 2003; Saunders 2005; Zembylas 2008; van Heerden 2010; Pippin 2010; Bewes 2010). Coetzee, however, doesn't address these issues from a sociological or political point of view, but instead from the point of view of individual ethics and interpersonal relations, investigating how someone like the main character, David Lurie, relates to himself, to others, and the world.[1] David is a white fifty-two-year-old university professor in Cape Town, South Africa, in the post-apartheid period. After an abusive affair with a colored student that cost him his job, he takes refuge at his daughter Lucy's farm in the Eastern Cape, where both are victims of a violent burglary in the course of which he is half burned and she is gang-raped. These traumatic experiences trigger in David a process of self-transformation, where shame, disgrace, and humiliation play a central role (Kissack and Titlestad 2003; Kossew 2003).

Before I proceed, let me say a word on the distinction between shame and disgrace. As van Heerden (2010, 47) argues, this distinction is central to understanding the novel. When I talk about shame, I refer to an emotion,[2] which belongs to the subjective realm of first-personal experience. Being evaluative states, emotions have normative, sociocultural, and political dimensions that go beyond subjective experience; but in what follows, I reserve the term "shame" for the experienced emotion. I also agree with the received view that shame is an emotion of negative self-assessment (Taylor 1985), where the subject experiences herself as degraded or inferior. I follow Zahavi (2014) in his Sartrean characterization of shame as an emotion of *social* self-consciousness (see Montes Sánchez 2015): in shame, you don't experience yourself as an experiencer, as the subject for whom experiences are given, as one does when simply contemplating the world without focusing on oneself at all. In shame, you experience yourself as the object of someone else's perception, you become an object for the other. You don't relate to yourself as the one who looks, but as the one who is being looked at. In shame and other emotions of social self-consciousness, we relate to ourselves from the perspective of engagement with others. This does not mean that others have to actually be present or that one needs to imagine a specific audience. It means that we focus on the dimension of ourselves that can be perceived from the outside and engaged with.

Disgrace is intimately connected to shame, but it is not an emotion. It is an attribution made by others, a third-person judgment. It is a social verdict that one's actions or traits are shameful and one ought to feel ashamed of them. The relation between disgrace and shame would then be analogous to that which obtains between legal guilt and the feeling of guilt (see van Heerden 2010). Disgrace therefore belongs to the social realm of third-person attribution of flaws, and not (like shame) to the subjective realm of first-person experience. Throughout the novel, Coetzee explores the relations between the realms of self-evaluation and social evaluation, between shame and disgrace.

The first scene where this relationship explicitly comes to the fore is in David's university hearing for sexually harassing his student, Melanie Isaacs. David makes a guilty plea for his charges, but refuses to show any contrition and repentance (51–58). To him, this is a legal plea, a "secular plea," which means he admits his guilt as a fact—the fact that he has broken a public norm—but it entails no moral self-assessment, nor any expression of his emotions. Before the hearing committee, which is supposed to evaluate David's case and send their recommendations for disciplinary measures to the Dean, David accepts the external, objective consequences of his actions (legal guilt and social disgrace), but he rejects all attempts to force him to endorse the moral judgment behind them and to publicly display regret or repentance, taking these as obscene assaults on his privacy.

Here van Heerden (2010, 47) thinks that Coetzee is opening up the possibility that David's disgrace is imposed by society on the basis of morally specious values, and that David is justified in resisting shame (for a similar view, see Kissack and Titlestad 2003). In my view, however, this reading establishes a simplistic connection between both ideas: If the committee is wrong, then David must be right, and vice versa. This reading presents David as a moral pioneer (Calhoun 2004, 129–32), as someone who actively criticizes narrow-minded social conventions and opens up new moral ground or upholds better values in the face of bigotry (Hutchinson 2011, 105–107). In my view, this is not at all what Coetzee is doing. He shows that *both* David *and* the committee are wrong. The committee is wrong in demanding a public display of repentance, and David is wrong in his defiant shamelessness, which, as I will argue below, betrays a type of shame. This is so because the conditions of moral appropriateness that apply to *feeling ashamed* of oneself and to *shaming someone* are completely different. There are good reasons to argue that feeling ashamed of oneself can often be appropriate, while *shaming* others never is, especially when performed by institutions, because it constitutes an offense against the human dignity of the shamed individual (see Nussbaum 2006, ch. 5).

As for the committee, a piece of historical-contextual evidence can help explain Coetzee's criticisms of them. Most analyses of the novel (including van

Heerden 2010, 49; Saunders 2005) agree that the committee is a literary stand-in for the Truth and Reconciliation Commission (TRC) that was functioning in South Africa at the time of the novel's publication. The TRC was a court-like body of restorative justice, which was established in order to deal with the crimes of apartheid after its end in 1994. Like the University's disciplinary commission in *Disgrace*, it was not a court of law and had no legal powers; its mission was to gather public testimonies of victims and perpetrators with a view toward establishing what actually happened and reconciling both sides so that the relations among members of the society could be restored. In it, perpetrators were asked to tell the truth, express repentance and ask for amnesty, which was sometimes granted. According to most analyses of *Disgrace*, Coetzee used the disciplinary hearing scene to harshly criticize the TRC, and specifically the idea that reconciliation and forgiveness can be achieved in such an institutional setting (Saunders 2005; Charos 2009). Indeed, the whole novel contains a disheartening meditation on whether forgiveness and reconciliation between racial groups can ever be achieved after apartheid.

This reading offers indirect support for my claim that what Coetzee criticizes about the bigots in the committee is not their moral condemnation of David's actions: His actions are disgraceful and deserve condemnation, just like the crimes of apartheid. What Coetzee questions is the implication that a public display of repentance can mitigate David's offense. Coetzee suggests here that forgiveness is a private matter between victim and perpetrator, and a public institution is not the right addressee for an apology, nor can it grant forgiveness in the name of the victim. Therefore, it seems to follow that when such an institution demands a display of repentance and contrition, it is imposing a shaming penalty; it is engaging in publicly shaming the perpetrator (Coetzee 1999, 54, 56, 58).

As Nussbaum (2005, 227–38) argues, shaming penalties are extremely problematic for various reasons, the main one being that institutional shaming is always potentially humiliating, it constitutes an attack on the dignity of the shamed individual, and it therefore violates the core principles of decent democratic liberal institutions. In such cases, it can still be appropriate for a society to consider David's actions disgraceful and blameworthy, and it can be appropriate for him to feel ashamed of himself, even though it is not appropriate for an institution to shame him or for them to offer forgiveness in the name of the victims at the price of abasement.

Van Heerden is right in proposing that this scene needs to be understood in terms of the distinction between shame and disgrace, but we need a third element: shaming—the act of publicly exposing someone to be scorned. Shaming is more likely to cause humiliation rather than shame. Humiliation involves a sense of being *unjustly* put down and diminished, it involves an attack or a slight by another, which is perceived to affect one's social status negatively (Nussbaum 2006, 203–204; Deonna, Rodogno, and Teroni 2011, 118). The crucial difference is that in humiliation the subject, while acknowledging the social impact of the other's evaluation, strongly resists it and doesn't incorporate it into her self-evaluation (Gilbert 1998). In shame, however, the subject accepts that the evaluation is correct in some sense, or that the other has some power to define her (cf. Calhoun 2004).

In my view, at his University hearing, David is publicly shamed and feels humiliated. This is one of the sides of his defiance. And if one agrees with Nussbaum, he is justified and right in opposing his shaming. However, he is not justified in resisting shame about his behavior to Melanie Isaacs, as van Heerden suggests. David's moral problem is precisely that he tries to conflate his disgrace with his shaming, and to get rid of both (and the potential shame attached to them) with one stroke. He tries to dismiss all social evaluations and indictments at the same time, and to resist incorporating any in his self-evaluation. But as I go on to show in the next section, this is extremely difficult to do and morally wrong. In my view, his disgrace is appropriate, even though his shaming is not.

NARCISSISTIC SHAME AND BYPASSED SHAME

Van Heerden's reading and mine are at odds on another crucial point: He says that David does not feel ashamed about his dealings with Melanie Isaacs (van Heerden 2010, 47). I argue throughout this chapter that David feels deep shame about many things, *including* his dealings with Melanie. How are two such interpretations possible? In line with van Heerden's reading, David declares that he is not ashamed nor does he regret what he did (56, 58). But those statements are nuanced by other information. For example, near the end of the novel, in a conversation with his ex-wife Rosalind, David asserts that he had rejected the committee's demands to issue a public apology in order to defend his freedom of speech—his right to be silent. Rosalind replies: "That sounds very grand. But you were always a great self-deceiver, David. A great deceiver and a great self-deceiver. *Are you sure it wasn't just a case of being caught with your pants down?*" (188, emphasis added). In my view, Rosalind is exactly right: It *was* a case of being caught with his pants down, of being caught red-handed in his shameful act, and as I show below, there are clear signs of this from the beginning.

Here we encounter the adult version of what Nussbaum (2006, 173–202) calls primitive or narcissistic shame, a type of shame that is often bypassed. In Nussbaum's psychoanalytic object relations account, primitive shame is the first type of shame that appears in development, as a consequence of the thwarting of the infant's omnipotent narcissistic desires. In this account

(Nussbaum 2006, 184–85), the infant finds itself oscillating between two extreme states: a state of complete contentment and satisfaction, and a state of utter privation and vulnerability, where it depends absolutely on a caretaker to satisfy its needs. The latter is what produces the sense of inadequacy that lies at the heart of primitive shame. Primitive shame thus responds to a sense of failure to attain an ego-ideal, to attain a sense of completeness or perfection that one has already judged that one rightly ought to have. As Nussbaum (2006, 184–85, 188–203) emphasizes, this infantile type of shame keeps exerting a pervasive influence even later in life, and many adult manifestations of shame, of both a pathological and non-pathological nature, still have this narcissistic structure despite the involvement of more complex social elements.

When I refer to "narcissistic shame" in this chapter, I mean to refer to an adult experience that is rooted in a narcissistic kind of relation to others, which is ultimately traceable to infantile primitive shame: In adult narcissistic shame, the ashamed self is only concerned about others as sources for one's own pleasure or pain, and not insofar as they are their own subjects with their own feelings. In being socially self-conscious and feeling exposed to the evaluations of others, the ashamed self is exclusively preoccupied with obtaining what (s)he wants from them.

Nussbaum also remarks that primitive shame is often connected to aggression against those who fail to minister to the subject's needs (186). However, very soon in development this tendency becomes not only motivated by frustration, but also by an urge to hide or ignore shame, because acknowledging it implies acknowledging a feeling of inadequacy or inferiority. We therefore possess a range of psychological mechanisms to bypass this type of shame: denying it and transforming it into less uncomfortable feelings (see, for example, Lewis 1971; Scheff 1997; Pattison 2000). One of these mechanisms is the so-called shame-anger connection, or shame-rage: a defensive, often violent, angry reaction against the person who uncovers one's shame (see, for example, Tangney 2005). This bypassing mechanism is clearly at play in David's defensive attitude at the disciplinary hearing, where he tries to deflect his own shame by attacking his shamers.

But David's narcissistic shame predates the public exposure of his affair with Melanie and goes much deeper than that. It is a result of his increasing difficulties to sustain the identity he aspires to, his self-image, which from the start is subjected to intense pressure and begins to crack. He goes to tremendous lengths to avoid the shame that this causes him. The identity that David self-ascribes to is the epitome of male white privilege in a colonial context. He has always seen himself as an intellectual, a professor with a good social standing, a sexually attractive man: pretty much like his hero Lord Byron. But in the context of post-apartheid South Africa, this sort of masculinity, which is at the heart of an abusive relation to the world and others, cannot be sustained, and both David and the reader become witnesses to its decline on all fronts: sex appeal, physical strength, power, dominance, intellectual superiority, his role as a father, and so on (see Kossew 2003; Boehmer 2002; Charos 2009; Pippin 2010; Bewes 2010).

David feels insignificant as an intellectual and mediocre as a teacher (3), as well as terribly insecure as a father (61, 76, 79). As for his sexual life, his relations to women are shown to be objectifying, narcissistic, and self-absorbed. It is no coincidence that all the women he chooses as sexual partners are much younger than him and colored—they represent the epitome of the oppressed in a colonial context. Furthermore, David often behaves like a stalker, violating his partners' dignity and privacy: He secretly follows the prostitute he frequents, Soraya, and hires a detective to find out her home address and phone number (all the while fantasizing that they have a special relationship that he needs to salvage). He obtains Melanie's personal details from the University records instead of asking her. He calls her, goes to her house uninvited, and forces himself on her, describing their sexual encounter as "not rape, not quite that, but undesired nevertheless, undesired to the core" (25).

However, there is a difference between being a selfish womanizer, which we are told he has always been (7), and being the "not quite" rapist we encounter in the novel. The difference for David is aging, and his inability to handle his loss of sex appeal. He sees himself as a declining Casanova, and he is afraid and ashamed of growing old and becoming unattractive. He imagines the conversations of young prostitutes shuddering with disgust at the spectacle of old clients like himself (8). He imagines Melanie taking a bath to cleanse herself of her contact with him after he has "not quite" raped her and, more importantly, he also appears to feel revolted at what he has just done when he wishes to "slide into a bath of his own" (25).

These thoughts are unequivocal signs of shame, as are also the desperate idealizations he resorts to in order to repair his self-image and keep these shaming ideas at bay, like pretending that Soraya sees him as more than a customer, or pretending he has a Byronic poetic sensibility that entitles him to use Melanie as a "muse," regardless of what she wants. These are all subterfuges to block from view what these women actually think and feel about him. He desperately clings to his false self-image of Byronic masculinity; he produces fantastic self-narrations to sustain it and he avoids listening to those who question it.

David's reactions at the disciplinary hearing are, thus, clear examples of bypassed narcissistic shame. His attempt to excuse himself by saying "I became a servant of Eros" (52) is paradigmatic. Through his excuse, he tries to isolate desire from judgment, evade responsibility by claiming he was in the grip of an insurmountable force (a god!),[3] and establish his intellectual superiority through a scholarly reference that places him, in his own eyes, in kinship with his hero Lord Byron. Through arrogance, he tries to build a barrier between himself and the committee, to place himself above them, so that their eyes and opinions won't have the power to shame him.

During the whole hearing he is desperately trying to hide from everybody, especially from himself, the real problem: that he has abused his privileged position as a white man imbued with professorial authority and has become a predator because he is terrified of having to acknowledge his decline, because he needs to reaffirm himself. He clings to his self-image as a Byronic seducer, in a desperate attempt to escape being described as a harasser. He attacks the committee in order to reaffirm himself and bypass his shame.

At the beginning of *Disgrace* we therefore find some clear examples of narcissistic shame, and its bypassing through anger and arrogance. If we ask about its moral significance, it seems obvious that the self-assessment involved in this shame is not moral: David is ashamed of his crumbling charm, of not being a Byron. This kind of shame has all the antisocial and immoral consequences that Tangney and Dearing (2004), among others, describe and deplore: David lies and attacks, and doesn't do anything to repair the damage he has done. But even this type of shame has one important virtue: it is still socially self-conscious, and so it forces the narcissistic David to keep others in mind to a certain extent, thus hindering him from indulgently falling into utter moral solipsism (see Thomason 2014, 21–22). It forces David time and again to confront himself; it prevents him from getting too self-indulgent in his justificatory narratives, which get wilder and harder to be confirmed by others, and therefore more fragile, making it clear that such a strategy won't work in the long run. Nevertheless, at this point it can be hard to see how shame can break the cycle of narcissism and antisocial behavior, instead of fueling it. So how is the cycle broken for David?

SURVIVOR SHAME AND MORAL SHAME

The two other varieties of shame that feature prominently in *Disgrace* are, I contend, survivor shame and moral shame. As I interpret the novel, for David these varieties are intimately connected, such that survivor shame paves the way for moral shame, because trauma radically changes his attitude to others. I am not proposing that moral shame and survivor shame always need to be connected in this way (even though survivor shame carries a moral component) or that we all need trauma to break out of narcissism—this is clearly not the case, but because of the type of person he is, this is how things are for David.

What I mean by moral shame is relatively straightforward: shame involving a self-evaluation in terms of moral values or considerations, which includes a proper concern for others. In moral shame, others figure as subjects with dignity that deserve respect and consideration: one cares about them for their own sake, not as mere instruments of pleasure or pain to the self. As Gómez Ramos (2005,

25–26) remarks in a Levinasian spirit, this type of shame does not come from focusing on one's own shortcomings and insufficiencies, but from confronting the suffering and the fragility of the other, which reveals my responsibility and the ambiguity of my position. The socially self-conscious structure of shame thus becomes a full-fledged moral emotion when it is accompanied by this openness to the vulnerability of the other: feeling the look of the other on me teaches me that I can harm the other, as when one feels ashamed, for example, of betraying a friend, or of having been tempted to do so.

Survivor shame is more complex and difficult to make sense of. It refers to the feelings of intense self-reproach and inadequacy frequently reported by survivors of traumatic events, like severe abuses or catastrophes. Indeed, shame features among the diagnostic criteria for post-traumatic stress disorder, or PTSD (American Psychiatric Association 2013). As Leys (2009) remarks, when psychoanalysts started paying attention to this phenomenon, they interpreted it as survivor *guilt*, not shame. Some argue that the two emotions are not as different as they are usually considered to be, and that guilt is a species of shame (Ortony 1987; see also Williams 2008).

In my view, the term "shame" is preferable, because it covers wider ground, and it better describes some of the feelings of inadequacy that are part of this phenomenon. In any case, psychoanalytic accounts of guilt and shame describe them as very closely related emotions, both caused by the introjection of an external authority figure, which becomes an internal "criticizing agency," the superego, that judges and censors the ego (see Wollheim 1999, section 3; Velleman 2003). Independently of this terminological choice, the challenge in accounting for this phenomenon is to square the intuition that such feelings are irrational (why should innocent victims reproach themselves for what befell them?) with the testimony of victims that assign them some moral significance (see, for example, Agamben 1999; Velleman 2003; Fessler 2007; Hutchinson 2008; Leys 2009; Maibom 2010; Guenther 2012; Corbí 2012; Montes Sánchez and Zahavi 2018).

One of the most famous, awe-inspiring, and illuminating survivor voices is Primo Levi's (1989). In the last volume of his Auschwitz trilogy, trying to grapple with the apparent contradiction between the irrationality and the moral significance of survivor shame and guilt, he explains that these feelings can have several sources: the state of real degradation in which the prisoners were forced to live (75); the prisoner's failure to fight or rebel against their oppressors (76); their failures of solidarity to other prisoners (78); the suspicion that they might have survived in the place of a worthier person (81–82); and what he calls "the shame of the world": the shame of knowing that humanity is capable of horrors such as Auschwitz (85).

Examples of all of these sources can be found in testimonies of many other atrocities besides the Nazi Holocaust. From a quick look at this list, two things are worth noting: First, the list covers episodes of several different emotions, including not only fear, disgust, humiliation, and irrational shame and guilt, but also instances of justified moral shame and guilt.[4] Second, temporality is crucial: the emotions felt while being abused are very different from survivor emotions (Budden 2009; Welz 2011; Montes Sánchez and Zahavi 2018). Therefore, in previous work, Zahavi and I have proposed to conceive this type of shame not as an isolated mental state, but as a temporally extended process unfolding over time (Montes Sánchez and Zahavi 2018; also see Goldie 2012, 56), involving rational and irrational, moral and non-moral elements. Such moral elements are, in my view, what show David the way to moral shame.

When David takes refuge at his daughter Lucy's farm in the Eastern Cape after losing his job, he tries to cling to his Byronic image of colonial masculinity, telling justificatory stories about his disgrace[5] and trying to pretend he is a misunderstood artist. Then, his daughter's home is burglarized by three black men, who also set David on fire and gang-rape Lucy. After this attack, a remarkable change takes place in David: he becomes sensitive to the suffering of others. Shortly after the attack, while his neighbor Bev Shaw changes David's bandages, Bev's husband makes a remark spontaneously assuming that David would also help them if they, the Shaws, were in distress (Coetzee 1999, 106–107, 102). Upon reflecting in silence, David skeptically asks himself if this assumption is true, with the suspicion that he is the kind of person who would have remained unmoved by his neighbors' suffering. This is the first time that David feels (moral) shame at being selfish and makes no attempt at masking it. In imagining the look of the other on him, he focuses on their suffering, and not on his own narcissistic desires.

From this moment on, we see a whole new range of causes of shame enter the picture. Until now, David was primarily ashamed of not being a Byron. The failures that preoccupy him now are of a different kind, and his attitude toward them is also different. This is expressed with particular poignancy in his response to Lucy about her rape, after she tells him that he does not understand what happened to her:

> "On the contrary, I understand all too well," he says. "I will pronounce the word we have avoided hitherto. You were raped. Multiply. By three men."
> "And?"
> "You were in fear of your life. You were afraid that after you had been used you would be killed. Disposed of. Because you were nothing to them."
> "And?" Her voice is now a whisper.
> "And I did nothing. I did not save you."
> That is his own confession . . . . (157)

That was indeed his confession: the first naked, truthful admission of his powerlessness and fragility. We are told that since the attack, David has had nightmares where Lucy cries out to him for help. And here it becomes unambiguously clear that he is tormented by the thought of having failed his daughter. The difference with his previous attitudes is clear: David is very much concerned about the harm *she* has endured, and he makes no attempt to hide his failures. His narcissism and his bypassing strategies seem to be gone. It is still possible to detect here a slightly more narcissistic element of shame about his failure to conform to the ideal of traditional masculinity (the powerful, protective father), but the other is framed as a suffering being, not as a mere instrument of pleasure or self-reaffirmation.

In my view, in this passage we find survivor shame and guilt. Lucy replies to David's confession that he could not have been expected to rescue her; there was nothing he could have done about it. She exonerates him from guilt, but this is no consolation, because at the same time she confirms his shame-inducing powerlessness. His formulation is not that he *was not able* to save her, but that he *did not* do so: he is implying that he *ought to have been able* to. This passage (and others in the novel) justifies the reading that David is experiencing something akin to what Levi described: he is ashamed of the degradation he experienced during the burglary, of his powerlessness in the face of the attackers, and of not having helped Lucy; he is ashamed of her having endured a worse fate than his.

But the parallels between Levi and David end here. David is not a Holocaust survivor, his experience is very different from Levi's, and his efforts to grapple with it lead him through a very different path.[6] The crucial dissimilarity between their experiences of harm is that both did not perceive the violence they endured as being arbitrary, indiscriminate, or undeserved in the same way. Therefore, David's experience of survivor shame teaches him a moral lesson that Levi didn't need.

There are two main reasons why David does not perceive the violence he suffered as arbitrary in the way Levi did. First, as a white middle-class family in post-apartheid South Africa, the Luries were on the privileged side of a brutally racist colonial regime: there are good historical and political reasons for black people to have wanted to take revenge on people like them, as both father and daughter explicitly recognize (112, 133, 156, 158–60). As far as we know (and nothing in the novel suggests otherwise), neither of them had been actively involved in the crimes of apartheid. However, David's predatory attitude toward women, especially "exotic" ones (8), and the smug sense of superiority he constantly exhibits, betray his complicity with the colonial regime and its underlying worldview—his belonging to and identifying with the oppressing white ruling class. This is the blurry moral territory of individual complicity with colonial or national wrongs that is a favorite ground for Coetzee's literary exploration. David often tries to shove off this sense of historical responsibility while Lucy openly expresses it (158) (on this point, see Kossew, 2003; Charos 2009).

There is another sense in which the attack (unlike the atrocities suffered by Levi) was not indiscriminate. The kinds of violence suffered by the father and the daughter are also different in non-arbitrary ways. Their places are not interchangeable; it could never have been David instead of Lucy who was raped. Of course men can also be victims of rape, but in his efforts to process his trauma, David clearly considers it a gender-specific crime. This is evidenced by his clumsy attempts to understand Lucy, which reveal both his newfound sensitivity to the suffering of others and the limits of such sensitivity. When David tries to talk to Lucy, he is often reminded that he was locked up in the bathroom on his own during the rape, that he was not there, that he does not know what happened. He tries to imagine what Lucy underwent, and discovers that he can easily identify with the rapists: as Coetzee puts it, David can "inhabit them, fill them with the ghost of himself;" but David further questions, *"Does he have it in him to be the woman?"* (160, emphasis added). Thus, David starts to take seriously the possibility that his view of the world is too narrow, and therefore often mistaken or inadequate.

Although David never openly compares his daughter's rape and Melanie's "not quite" rape by him, Coetzee connects them narratively, and there are signs that the connection is playing some inchoate role in David's mind. The ease with which he can stand in the rapists' shoes and his apology to Melanie's father are indications that he sees himself as the cause of a sort of harm he never thought about or tried to understand before. At one point, in an attempt to convince Lucy to report her rape to the police (she decides to only report the burglary), unable to interpret her exasperated silence, he says:

> "Can I guess?" he says. "Are you trying to remind me of something?"
> "Am I trying to remind you of what?"
> "Of *what women undergo at the hands of men.*" (111, emphasis added)

These words contain no explicit comparison to Melanie, but they indicate that he is not completely oblivious of the parallel (cf. Attridge 2000; Kissack and Titlestad 2003). Admittedly, they do not mean that he takes, or that we as readers should take, what he did to Melanie and what the rapists did to Lucy on a perfectly equal footing (there is, among other things, the difference between exercising privilege and taking revenge). And being able to imagine oneself committing a crime does not make one actually guilty of that crime. But realizing that he is able to identify with the rapists and not with the victim has a strong effect on David.

Spurred by survivor shame (shame that others undeservedly endured a worse fate), he comes face to face with the limits of his empathy and imagination, and realizes that his sensibilities have always been closed to the feelings of others, that he can't stand where oppressed victims stand. Coetzee shows us that in some circumstances (like post-apartheid South Africa), some subject positions (the white male colonizer) are inherently predatory and abusive, and come with a host of mechanisms to shut out the suffering inflicted on others. Having always belonged to the class of the privileged oppressors, David feels an almost insurmountable imaginative resistance to putting himself in the position of the abused. At the same time, he can no longer ignore such suffering, because he is partly experiencing it himself. Thus, he only comes to understand his own responsibility for the harm suffered by others when he finds himself in the place of the victim, but in the ambiguous manner of, in a sense, being and not being the victim at the same time.[7] For the first time, David grapples—in an incomplete and unsatisfactory way—with gender and race divides, and he thinks about his place in the power relations at play in them.

The shame that emerges is no longer a shame of *not* being a Byron, but a shame of being one. It is shame informed by moral considerations and a concern for others as other subjects (not mere objects of pleasure). Survivor shame, because of its social self-conscious structure, makes David sensitive to his own vulnerability and that of others—to the vulnerability that comes from interdependence. This sensitivity is also expressed in his attitude toward the sick abandoned dogs that are euthanized at the charity clinic that Bev runs, in his efforts to give them a dignified incineration to "safeguard their honour" (Coetzee 1999, 146; cf. also Gaita 2011), and it paves the way for the moral shame of a perpetrator, for the shame connected with understanding himself as an abuser and a rapist.

In starting to pay attention to and care about the suffering of others, not because they accuse him and point fingers at him, but simply because they look at him, showing their wounds, David also starts to understand that his disgrace is deserved, that there might be good reasons for a society to proscribe certain forms of behavior and to demand that one feels ashamed of certain things. Shame replaces humiliation and David comes to accept his disgrace as deserved. This is, in my view, what leads him to offer an apology to the Isaacs family (cf. Kissack and Titlestad 2003).[8]

MORAL SHAME AND THE CONTINUED THREAT OF NARCISSISM

Coetzee, however, is careful not to suggest that narcissism can ever disappear, that a full redemption is ever possible. When David tries to act on his moral shame and guilt by offering reparation and seeking forgiveness, the shame of powerlessness and passivity tempts him again into narcissistic bypassing and self-deception: he doesn't want to be a dog, he wants to be a Byron. This tension between virtue and vice is found in the scene where David pays a visit to Melanie Isaacs' family (ch. 19), where he expresses genuine regret, but he refuses to entirely step down from his position of white privilege, and secretly maintains his objectifying and preying attitude toward women (specifically Melanie's younger sister).

At the end of the dinner offered to David by Melanie's family as a sign of Christian mercy, David tells Melanie's father that he is sorry for the way things turned out and asks for his pardon. He then kneels in front Melanie's mother and younger sister (who elicits in him the same kind of riotous desire). These are the gestures and words of guilt and moral shame, of someone who confesses and regrets the harm he has caused by being the person that they were. But narcissism shows its face too. In front of the Isaacs family, David depicts his affair with Melanie without any acknowledgment of the power relations he abused, and he attributes the problems to his clumsiness ("I lack the lyrical," 171). Mr. Isaacs, who clearly enjoys having David at his mercy to humiliate him, and at the same time proudly relishes in his own show of Christian generosity toward his enemies, ends up thinking that David's apology was instrumentally directed at regaining his position at the university.

The problem is that, in finally offering the apology that the committee had demanded, David again misses the target: he doesn't address the victim, but her father. The whole conversation happens between the two men, and in it they treat Melanie as an object of their property, as a pawn in their fight for power and status. Nobody shows their wounds, their vulnerability, to the other, and David reverts to pride, to male white privilege and face-saving fantasies to try to keep at bay the humiliation inflicted by Mr. Isaacs. So, there is no possible forgiveness or reconciliation. Face to face with a suffering other, David might have been better able to admit the social verdict of disgrace as deserved, but not in the context of a fight for status.

After the dinner, the humiliations pile up (he finds his house ransacked, Melanie's boyfriend violently prevents him from seeing her) and he ends up hiring, from the street, an extremely young black prostitute, who performs oral sex on him in his car. This helps him shake his intense shame and humiliation, but the thought that ends this utterly disturbing episode is revelatory: "So this is all it takes!, he thinks. How could I ever have forgotten it?" (194). How could he have forgotten that sexually abusing a young black woman can bring relief to his crushed pride, that all his acts of abuse stem from a desperate desire to be again the master he can no longer be, in a society that is still predominantly misogynistic and racist.

There is a feeling of deep shame running through this passage, and particularly in this sentence. Once again, it is connected to his abusive sexual relationships with colored women, but it has a different form compared to the one we saw at the beginning of the novel. The trigger is again shame of his failing masculinity: of not being able to stand up to Melanie's cocky boyfriend. In order to alleviate that shame and to be the dominating white male again, he needs to subjugate someone fragile and oppressed, someone whose character-istics (female, young, black) permit him to revert to the position of the pow-erful colonizer. But the passage ends with the deeper shame that "This is all it takes." "This"—as soon as he feels vulnerable and weak, hurt in his pride, his narcissistic shame kicks in, and he is driven to reassert his superiority by hurting others and reenacting colonial and patriarchal attitudes.

Is he too old to learn, as he insists again and again throughout the novel? The answer is both yes and no. After assaulting Melanie at her house, he did feel ashamed and disgusted with himself. What has changed, however, is that his excuses and bypassing strategies are now entirely unavailable to him. There is much more self-awareness here, a much more lucid perception of who he is and what he is doing. He is back to his old vices, but he sees them in a completely different light, as desperate maneuvers to maintain a version of himself that is deeply flawed. Time and suffering have turned David's shame into the device for lucidity that, according to Morgan (2008), it can be in the right circumstances.

Several authors have interpreted what David learns throughout the novel as a newfound sensitivity that is necessary (not sufficient) for moral understand-ing (Crary 2010): an openness to the suffering of others (Zembylas 2008) and a capacity to recognize them in their singularity (Attridge 2000, 117). This openness comes hand in hand with a much clearer perception of himself, with a greater degree of self-awareness. He is much more lucid, much less self-deceiving, and more respectful of alterity. This state of mind is what Attridge (2000) calls "grace." But there is no redemption here. Can there be any for a colonizer in post-apartheid South-Africa? *Disgrace* does not give much hope for this: David ends as a thoroughly defeated social outcast, with no means for self-reconstruction. For a redemptive reconstruction might require a different context, and it certainly requires different emotional resources. It cannot be accomplished by shame alone, and the result would be in various ways a very different kind of person.

WHAT IS MORAL ABOUT SHAME, ACCORDING TO COETZEE

The process whereby David comes to acknowledge his abusive approach to the world and others (a process of ethical learning) cannot be understood without the role of his feelings of shame and guilt, and the interplay between external judgments and David's self-assessment. David goes from narcissism to a proper sensibility toward others, from "I was a servant of Eros" to the realization of the ease of destructive pride that his privilege affords him. His opening up to others goes hand in hand with a diminishing self-deceit, and a growing clarity about himself. His trajectory seems to indicate that moral shame is an achievement that requires a proper openness to others. But contrary to Aristotle's account of shame as the semi-virtue of the learner (Aristotle 1991, bk. 2; cf. Burnyeat 1980), the moral shame that David discovers has much more to do with connectedness and recognition than with one's understanding of norms or standards.

It's the shame that comes not from focusing on one's own shortcomings, but from confronting the suffering of others, which reveal my responsibility and the ambiguity of my position (Gómez Ramos 2005, 25–26). As Coetzee shows, disgrace—the mere existence of external standards and third-person verdicts that some things deserve shame—is not sufficient on its own to motivate individuals to act morally, for it can easily fuel a narcissistic fight for higher status. The standards of disgrace can only be a guide to virtue when one is also sensitive to and cares about the suffering of others (sometimes one is indeed justified in resisting disgrace, even though David wasn't). Nonetheless, as Coetzee also shows, the fact that we learn to look at the world in non-narcissistic ways does not mean that we can leave narcissism behind and make it entirely disappear from our outlook.

This conclusion seems to suggest that we can clearly distinguish between moral and immoral varieties of shame, based on whether shame is informed by a proper openness to others or by narcissistic concerns, but the picture is a bit more nuanced. David's initial narcissistic shame might not be ethically constructive, but by pressing him once and again to confront who he is, it has a crucial role in his final lucid self-understanding. Coetzee shows in this novel that some subject positions can be inherently immoral, and shame (including narcissistic shame) can help dismantle them.

Shame brings home to David time and again the precariousness of his assumptions, his own fragility, his failings, the danger of becoming too convinced and secure of one particular picture of himself. It brings his character into focus and pushes him to realize how much of his problems in his relations to others are actually his responsibility; they stem from the way he confronts the world and others. Shame on its own does not bring this openness, but as I have shown in this chapter, it can enhance lucidity and act as a guard against moral solipsism.

ACKNOWLEDGMENTS

I wish to thank Antonio Gómez Ramos, Dan Zahavi, Lisa Guenter, Carlos Thiebaut, and José Medina for their comments on preliminary versions. I am also extremely grateful to my anonymous reviewer for extensive comments on this chapter.

NOTES

1. Bewes (2010) argues that shame in Coetzee's work goes far beyond the depiction and analysis of the individual emotions of his characters. According to Bewes, in a postcolonial context, and given Coetzee's own position in it as a white South African raised during apartheid, shame becomes an "event" indissolubly linked to writing, to pursuing an aesthetic endeavor. I agree with him that, in order to fully understand the role of shame in Coetzee's oeuvre, it is necessary to go beyond the emotions of his characters. This, however, is not my endeavor here: my chapter remains focused on showing the potential in engaging with literature as a philosopher of emotion by drawing some lessons about shame from a discussion of a fictional character's emotions. A full discussion of Bewes' work would require far more space than I have here. Suffice it to say here that I strongly disagree with his claim that shame is not an ethical response (see, especially Bewes 2010, 28–39), but this might be due to our different interpretations of the meaning of "ethical."

2. Or an affective experience: I want to leave room for "occurrent" shame, episodic shame caused by a particular situation, and "standing" shame, which is a very strong and reliable disposition to feel shame in any circumstances that reveal a certain character flaw, in line with one's own background cares and concerns (see Helm 2017, ch. 7).

3. He even does this later on, talking to his daughter: "'My case rests on the rights of desire,' he says. 'On the god who makes even the small birds quiver.' . . . *I was a servant of Eros*: that is what he wants to say, but does he have the effrontery? *It was a god who acted through me*. What vanity! Yet not a lie, not entirely" (89). Notice David's ambivalent judgment of his own justification.

4. One may argue that the intensity of survivor shame is disproportionate to the moral transgressions, given the circumstances. I would agree with this, but proportionality is only one of several dimensions of appropriateness (see D'Arms and Jacobson 2000).

5. See 2n above.

6. Of course, *Disgrace* is a fictional story and David is a fictional character. The *writer* (Coetzee) here is not a victim of extreme abuse trying to make sense of his experience and communicate it (like Levi), but a man linked by many identity traits with the oppressing side of a brutal regime trying to formulate an adequate individual call to collective responsibility for the atrocities perpetrated during apartheid.

7. I do not want to suggest that it is necessary for anyone in a position of privilege to undergo such aggressions in order to learn to listen to the oppressed other. And I am certainly *not* suggesting that exerting violence against anyone is the right solution to anything. It is not. All I am trying to do here is describe the process through which David's sensibilities change in the novel.

8. Kissack and Titlestad (2003) describe David's transformation as a growing humility that comes from suffering. I think their reading is too weak, because it doesn't acknowledge that Melanie Isaacs was raped, and does not give an adequate account of the gender and power dimensions implied.

REFERENCES

Agamben, Giorgio. 1999. *Remnants of Auschwitz*. New York, NY: Zone Books.

American Psychiatric Association. 2013. *Diagnostic and Statistical Manual of Mental Disorders*. 5th edition. Washington, DC: American Psychiatric Publishing. http://dsm.psychiatryonline.org/.

Aristotle. 1991. *On Rhetoric: A Theory of Civic Discourse*. Edited by George Alexander Kennedy. Oxford, England: Oxford University Press.

———. 2014. *Nicomachean Ethics*. Edited by C. D. C. Reeve. Indianapolis, IN: Hackett Publishing.

Attridge, Derek. 2000. "Age of Bronze, State of Grace: Music and Dogs in Coetzee's 'Disgrace.'" *NOVEL: A Forum on Fiction* 34, no. 1: 98–121. https://doi.org/10.2307/1346141.

Bewes, Timothy. 2010. *The Event of Postcolonial Shame*. Princeton, NJ: Princeton University Press.

Boehmer, Elleke. 2002. "Not Saying Sorry, Not Speaking Pain: Gender Implications in Disgrace." *Interventions* 4, no. 3: 342–51. https://doi.org/10.1080/1369801022000013770.

Budden, Ashwin. 2009. "The Role of Shame in Posttraumatic Stress Disorder: A Proposal for a Socio-Emotional Model for DSM-V." *Social Science and Medicine* 69, no. 7: 1032–39. https://doi.org/10.1016/j.socscimed.2009.07.032.

Burnyeat, Myles. 1980. "Aristotle on Learning to Be Good." In *Essays on Aristotle's Ethics*, edited by Amélie Rorty, 69–92. Berkeley, CA: University of California Press.

Calhoun, Cheshire. 2004. "An Apology for Moral Shame." *Journal of Political Philosophy* 12, no. 2: 127–46. https://doi.org/10.1111/j.1467-9760.2004.00194.x.

Charos, Caitlin. 2009. "States of Shame: South African Writing after Apartheid." *Safundi* 10, no. 3: 273–304. https://doi.org/10.1080/17533170903020890.

Coetzee, J. M. 1999. *Disgrace*. London, England: Vintage.

Corbí, Josep E. 2012. *Morality, Self Knowledge, and Human Suffering, An Essay on The Loss of Confidence in the World. Routledge Studies in Contemporary Philosophy*. New York, NY: Taylor and Francis.

Crary, Alice. 2010. "J. M. Coetzee, Moral Thinker." In *J. M. Coetzee and Ethics: Philosophical Perspectives on Literature*, edited by Anton Leist and Peter Singer, 249–68. New York, NY: Columbia University Press.

D'Arms, Justin and Daniel Jacobson. 2000. "The Moralistic Fallacy: On the 'Appropriateness' of Emotions." *Philosophy and Phenomenological Research* 61, no. 1: 65–90. https://doi.org/10.2307/2653403.

Deonna, Julien, Raffaele Rodogno, and Fabrice Teroni. 2011. *In Defense of Shame: The Faces of an Emotion*. New York, NY: Oxford University Press.

Fessler, Daniel M. T. 2007. "From Appeasement to Conformity: Evolutionary and Cultural Perspectives on Shame, Competition, and Cooperation." In *The Self-Conscious Emotions: Theory and Research*, edited by Jessica L. Tracy, Richard W. Robins, and June Price Tangney, 174–193. New York, NY: Guilford Press.

Gaita, Raimond. 2011. *The Philosopher's Dog*. Melbourne, Australia: The Text Publishing Company.

Gilbert, Paul. 1998. "What Is Shame? Some Core Issues and Controversies." In *Shame: Interpersonal Behavior, Psychopathology, and Culture*, edited by Paul Gilbert and Bernice Andrews, 3–38. New York, NY: Oxford University Press.

Gilligan, James. 2003. "Shame, Guilt, and Violence." *Social Research: An International Quarterly* 70, no. 4: 1149–80.

Goldie, Peter. 2012. *The Mess Inside: Narrative, Emotion, and the Mind*. Oxford, England: Oxford University Press.

Gómez Ramos, Antonio. 2005. "Cuerpo, Dolor y Verdad. A Propósito de un Relato de J. M. Coetzee." In *Nadie Sabe lo Que Puede un Cuerpo: Variaciones Sobre el Cuerpo y Sus Destinos*, edited by Natividad Corral, 13–28. Madrid, Spain: Talasa Ediciones.

Guenther, Lisa. 2012. "Resisting Agamben: The Biopolitics of Shame and Humiliation." *Philosophy and Social Criticism* 38, no. 1: 59–79. https://doi.org/10.1177/0 191453711421604.

Heerden, Adriaan van. 2010. "Disgrace, Desire, and the Dark Side of the New South Africa." In *J. M. Coetzee and Ethics: Philosophical Perspectives on Literature*, edited by Anton Leist and Peter Singer, 43–63. New York, NY: Columbia University Press.

Helm, Bennett W. 2017. *Communities of Respect: Grounding Responsibility, Authority, and Dignity*. Oxford, England/New York, NY: Oxford University Press.

Hutchinson, Phil. 2008. *Shame and Philosophy: An Investigation in the Philosophy of Emotions and Ethics*. 1st edition. New York, NY: Palgrave Macmillan.

———. 2011. "Facing Atrocity: Shame and Its Absence." *Passions In Context: International Journal for the History and Theory of Emotions* 2, no. 1: 93–117. https://www.passionsincontext.de/index.php/?id=775&L=1.

Kissack, Mike and Michael Titlestad. 2003. "Humility in a Godless World: Shame, Defiance and Dignity in Coetzee's Disgrace." *The Journal of Commonwealth Literature* 38, no. 3: 135–47. https://doi.org/10.1177/00219894030383008.

Kossew, Sue. 2003. "The Politics of Shame and Redemption in J. M. Coetzee's 'Disgrace.'" *Research in African Literatures* 34, no. 2: 155–62.

Levi, Primo. 1989. *The Drowned and the Saved*. Translated by Raymond Rosenthal. London, England: Abacus.

Lewis, Helen B. 1971. *Shame and Guilt in Neurosis*. New York, NY: International Universities Press Inc.

Leys, Ruth. 2009. *From Guilt to Shame: Auschwitz and After*. Princeton, NJ: Princeton University Press.

Maibom, Heidi L. 2010. "The Descent of Shame." *Philosophy and Phenomenological Research* 80, no. 3: 566–94. https://doi.org/10.1111/j.1933-1592.2010.00341.x.

Montes Sánchez, Alba. 2015. "Shame and the Internalized Other." *Etica e Politica/ Ethics and Politics* XVII, no. 2: 180–99.

Montes Sánchez, Alba and Dan Zahavi. 2018. "Unravelling the Meaning of Survivor Shame." In *Emotions and Mass Atrocity: Philosophical and Theoretical Explorations*, edited by Thomas Brudholm and Johannes Lang, 162–84. Cambridge, England: Cambridge University Press.

Morgan, Michael L. 2008. *On Shame*. New York, NY: Routledge.

Nussbaum, Martha C. 2006. *Hiding from Humanity: Disgust, Shame, and the Law.* New edition. Princeton, NJ/Oxford, England: Princeton University Press.

Ortony, Andrew. 1987. "Is Guilt an Emotion?" *Cognition and Emotion* 1, no. 3: 283–98. https://doi.org/10.1080/02699938708408052.

Pattison, Stephen. 2000. *Shame: Theory, Therapy, Theology.* Cambridge, England: Cambridge University Press.

Pippin, Robert. 2010. "The Paradoxes of Power in the Early Novels of J. M. Coetzee." In *J. M. Coetzee and Ethics: Philosophical Perspectives on Literature*, edited by Anton Leist and Peter Singer, 19–42. New York, NY: Columbia University Press.

Rawls, John. 1999. *A Theory of Justice.* Cambridge, MA: Belknap Press of Harvard University Press.

Saunders, Rebecca. 2005. "Disgrace in the Time of a Truth Commission." *Parallax* 11, no. 3: 99–106. https://doi.org/10.1080/13534640500134003.

Scheff, Thomas J. 1997. *Emotions, the Social Bond, and Human Reality: Part/Whole Analysis.* Cambridge, England: Cambridge University Press.

Tangney, June Price. 2005. "The Self-Conscious Emotions: Shame, Guilt, Embarrassment and Pride." In *Handbook of Cognition and Emotion*, edited by Tim Dagleish and Mick J. Power, 541–68. Chichester, England: John Wiley and Sons, Ltd. http://onlinelibrary.wiley.com/doi/10.1002/0470013494.ch26/summary.

Tangney, June Price and Ronda L. Dearing. 2004. *Shame and Guilt.* New York, NY: Guilford Press.

Taylor, Gabriele. 1985. *Pride, Shame, and Guilt: Emotions of Self-Assessment.* Oxford, England: Clarendon Press.

Thomason, Krista K. 2014. "Shame, Violence, and Morality." *Philosophy and Phenomenological Research* 91, no. 1: 1–24. https://doi.org/10.1111/phpr.12110.

Velleman, J. David. 2003. "Don't Worry, Feel Guilty." *Royal Institute of Philosophy Supplements* 52: 235–48. https://doi.org/10.1017/S1358246100007992.

Welz, Claudia. 2011. "Shame and the Hiding Self." *Passions In Context: International Journal for the History and Theory of Emotions* 2, no. 1: 67–92. https://www.passionsincontext.de/index.php/?id=774&L=1.

Williams, Bernard. 2008. *Shame and Necessity.* 2nd edition. Berkeley, CA: University of California Press.

Wollheim, Richard. 1999. *On the Emotions.* New Haven, CT: Yale University Press.

Zahavi, Dan. 2014. *Self and Other: Exploring Subjectivity, Empathy, and Shame.* Oxford, England: Oxford University Press.

Zembylas, Michalinos. 2008. "Bearing Witness to the Ethics and Politics of Suffering: J. M. Coetzee's Disgrace, Inconsolable Mourning, and the Task of Educators." *Studies in Philosophy and Education* 28, no. 3: 223–37. https://doi.org/10.1007/s11217-008-9108-0.

Body Shaming in the Era of Social Media

Lisa Cassidy

This chapter examines body shaming in the current social media atmosphere of Facebook, Twitter, YouTube, Instagram, "Am I hot?" apps, and the like. I will attend to how body shaming is practiced and experienced online versus how it is in real life (popularly abbreviated as IRL) in order to make three foundational observations: First, body shaming generally involves a triangular relation between the body shamer, the one who is body shamed, and the consuming viewer, which reflects the dynamics of how values are negotiated among members of an honor group (a group of individuals bound by an honor code of shared expectations). Second, not everyone in this shame triangle is subject to shame reversals (which is when the body shamer is publicly shamed in return for initially shaming someone else). Third, although it might appear at first that body shaming is never justified, I make the normative argument that body shaming (online and in real life) can be justified when certain conditions are met. Along the way, this chapter also sketches several cases of body shaming. The overarching point of this chapter is not to endorse thoughtlessly and hurtfully shaming each other, but to make the observation about how body shaming is used in negotiating values among community members. This chapter also sketches several cases of body shaming, and provides a case study at the end that focuses especially on the ongoing body shaming of professional athlete Serena Williams.

BODY SHAMING ONLINE AND IN REAL LIFE

It is not a coincidence that body-shaming stories typically feature women or minorities being body shamed for failing to meet preposterous standards. Both online and in real life, the unrelenting message is, *"Be young, skinny, and beautiful or else!"* For example, in July of 2016 Playboy model Dani Mathers secretly photographed a naked seventy-year-old woman changing in the locker room of their gym and posted it to Snapchat with the caption, "If I can't unsee this than you can't either." This was accompanied with a selfie of Mathers being disgusted by the sight of this anonymous woman's body. (Mathers maintains that her post was always meant to be a private conversation with a friend, and that the public post was accidental.) Mathers had more than a million and a half followers on Facebook, Twitter, and Instagram combined at the time (Kirkova 2016). The backlash (what I will call a *shame reversal*) against Mathers was immediate; she was denounced online and on television as a cyberbully and body shamer, and the gym where the incident happened publicly banned her for life. Eventually, Mathers was convicted of a misdemeanor for invasion of privacy, and was ordered to clean graffiti for thirty days (Fox News 2017). Mathers apologized for her actions, but also appeared to see herself as a victim. Mathers pronounced on *Good Morning America*: "To hide out at my mother's house at age 30 because of something I've done—it just felt really low" (McCarthy 2017).

While the Mathers case could only happen in the age of social media, similar real-life examples of body shaming abound. People are body shamed for who they are (e.g., when African-American women are told that the style of their natural hair is inappropriate for a workplace setting); how they are dressed (e.g., when school girls wearing perfectly ordinary clothes are accused of being too "distracting"); or what they are doing (e.g., when breastfeeding mothers are told to leave public spaces). Although I offer the above as examples of body shaming in real life today, all of them might also take place online, or perhaps be hybrids (by also being documented online as they occur in real life). In addition, we cannot stress enough how much each of these examples of shaming are contextually dependent upon our time and place. We can easily imagine that other people in other places or times might be confused as to why these occasions could possibly be causes for shaming, just as we would be surprised to learn that the exposure of a Victorian lady's ankles was once shameful.

Alas, almost everyone is vulnerable to the negative judgments of body shaming. Vulnerability to shame over our bodies is part of what makes us human, according to Velleman (2005) and Dolezal (2017), because it speaks to our yearning to have a connection to other humans. Bonnie Mann has noticed how enmeshed body shame is with gender in her idea of "ubiquitous" shame, which is the "shame-*status* that attaches to the very fact of existing as a girl or woman, or of having a female body, which is captured so powerfully in such common phrases as "like a girl" and "such a pussy" (Mann 2018, 403). Body shaming, both online and in real life, begins with a perception of certain "facts" about human bodies (our own or other people's). These seeming facts are then compared against cultural standards about how such a body ought to be, to look, or to behave.[1] When the body in question seems to fail or flout these standards, such as beauty standards in the Mathers case, it is often subjected to body shaming.

Of course, it is not only older women who are the victims of body shaming. Our society is simultaneously patriarchal and imbued with white supremacy. As with women's bodies, the bodies of nonwhites have always been the object of crushing regulation (e.g., slavery), and have been seen as shameful. So, in main-stream US culture today, just about any of us who fails to abide by the strict honor code of what Gail Weiss calls the "normative body"—of being a straight, white, physically fit, able-bodied man—may be particularly vulnerable to the condemnations (such as body shaming) of the "honor group." According to Wiess, "These [racist, sexist, able-bodied societies] are never separate societies, each enforcing its own brand of discrimination and oppression, but one society in which the shame of having a nonnormative body is magnified with each bodily norm that one is seen as transgressing" (Weiss 2018, 544). This is the first and most important commonality between body shaming in real life and online.

Philosopher Gabriele Taylor's (1985) monograph, *Pride, Shame, and Guilt: Emotions of Self-Assessment*, gives an excellent scaffolding for understanding shame. Taylor is relevant to my analysis because aspects of bodily appearance *are* ascribed moral content; embodiment discourse is a way of negotiating the values for in- and out-members of an honor group. Taylor identifies shame as a moral emotion, an emotional experience fundamentally concerned with the moral regulation of oneself. She also posits that shame can only be profoundly felt by individuals who live in a shame culture, in which the members share a common honor code.[2] We feel shame when we lose our honor *vis-à-vis* the group's honor code, by failing to uphold its expectations, and the emotion of shame arises as a result of failing to retain one's identity as a member of the honor group (either publicly or simply before oneself).[3] In this discussion of shame, Taylor first turns to Jean-Paul Sartre's famous account of shame, in which he posits that shame is a bilateral relation between the audience (the looker) and the one who is shamed (the looked-upon). Sartre goes so far as to call the shameful knowledge of the other a kind of "rape by looking" (Schneider 1977, 120).[4] Yet, as Taylor correctly notes, we sometimes feel shame without any audience (58). So, shame must instead involve a more complicated relation between the self, an actual or metaphorical audience, and the self's recent awareness of itself as being seen or being caught-out in an unflattering light (60–61). Furthermore, when we feel shame, we see ourselves as being perceived as doing things we didn't think of ourselves as doing, or as being understood as the kind of people we didn't think we were. Thus, shame is a failure to be ourselves as we thought we were or ought to be—"It follows that for any individual a breakdown of his various expectations must involve his total loss of value in his own eyes" (56).

Taylor's idea of moral shame is that it involves a triangular relation between the (a) self, (b) a hypothetical audience, and (c) the self-made-conscious-awareness-of-one's-perceived-failures. For body shaming in the era of online social media, this triangular relation is re-cast in the following way: (1) "The body shamer"—the one who ascribes shame by speaking or writing (or tweeting, Instagraming, or Snapchating, etc.) that another person's body is shameful and beyond the pale; (2) "the body shamed"—the shamed person who is on the receiving end of the negative attention and is frequently called the "victim" of body shaming (i.e., the person whose body is the object of the body shamer's ascription of shame); and (3) "the audience of shame"—the consuming viewer of social media who witness body shaming through their readings, viewings, likings, and re-tweetings of social media. We can thus understand the Mathers scandal in the following way: the social media, commercial mass media, and their individual consumers form an honor group. When Mathers (the body shamer) shamed her victim (of body shaming) for the amusement of her consuming public (the consuming viewers of social media), what was at stake for like-minded members of the group was the upholding of the honor code to maintain certain bodily standards.[5] Thus, seeing body shaming in the era of social media as a triangular, rather than a Sartrean bilateral relation, stays true to Taylor's insight that shame only makes sense in a shame culture, in which a strict adherence to a shared honor code is expected and rigidly enforced. It also stays true to the idea that experiences of shame can effectively put at a distance one's understanding of oneself from how one may be negatively understood by others.

Furthermore, given Taylor's account of shame in real life, that body shaming online and in real life shares this triangular structure should not be surprising since occasions of body shaming are recognized in virtue of the common term "body shame," which indicates the employment of the same conceptual scheme in both online and in real-life body shaming. The term was initially an aspect of our real-life lexicon, and it has been popularized online.[6] Thus, when used online, the term has a resonance that allows shamers, the subjects of shaming, and the consuming audience of that shame to participate in a dialogue that we can all recognize as a conversation about "body shaming."[7] In doing so, the use of the common term "body shame" in social media raises our perception to the practice of body shaming in both forums.

BODY SHAMING ONLINE VERSUS IN REAL LIFE

Although body shaming online and in real life shares an essential triangular relation between the shamer, the body shamed, and the audience of shame, there are also some significant differences. First, it is worth reflecting on the perplexingly simultaneous intimacy and anonymity of online experiences. On the one hand, anyone who has a smart phone can attempt to make instantaneous contact with literally half of the world, the half which has access to the internet. So, we have the potential to reach prime ministers, presidents, celebrities, rebel hacktivists, and all manner of ordinary folk all over the globe with a few clicks. On the other hand, because many online interactions are essentially anonymous, we have no idea whom we are reaching, or who is reaching out to us. We might also talk of a "virtual honor group"—virtual because it is online, but also because its anonymity might make membership in such a group particularly ephemeral. Online body shaming can, therefore, be contrasted with body shaming in real life because the body shamed in real life is immediately aware of the shaming and has no choice but to respond publicly to that body shaming through the contextually unmistakable physical manifestations of shame (e.g., flushed face, pallor, sweat, and/or tears). These physical manifestations can be hidden or experienced privately when one is body shamed online—where we can cry alone, in front of the screen. Likewise, online body shaming makes it possible to be the body shamed *but not even know it* (this appears to be the case with Mathers' victim, until the L. A. P. D. alerted her). In such instances, body shaming serves to caution members of the honor group as a demand that their bodies conform to the honor code (*we must never age or wrinkle!*), and possibly extends as far as cautioning a wider viewing public, who may also have some allegiance to the honor code.

Another difference between body shaming online and body shaming in real life has to do with exactly who does the body shaming (the body shamer) and that person's relationship to the one being body shamed (the body shamed). In body shaming online, the relation between the body shamed and the self-made-conscious-awareness-of-one's-perceived-failures is externalized outside the self (the body shamed) in virtue of a disparaging representation of the body shamed that is made public via some social media by the body shamer, whereas Taylor's point about traditional cases of shame is to show that moral shame emerges internally, as a result of the self's struggle with being made aware of a disparaging understanding of itself. Thus, in the case of body shaming online, Taylor's internal self dismay at being caught in an unflattering light (the true source of moral shame for Taylor) becomes brazenly exterior to the self in the form of an online post, tweet, or some other digital representation.

A final distinction is that shame reversals are never directed at the audience in cases of online body shaming. Shame reversals happen when the body shamed (or sympathetic allies) try to reverse or redirect shame at those who initiated it. This is usually phrased in terms of "shaming the shamer" or "calling out" the shamer to create a "backlash." This reversal of shame, however, never seems to be directed at consuming viewers themselves. No one (neither the shamer nor the body shamed) seems to ever shame the audience of shame (i.e., the consumers of online social media) about its consumption of articles, interviews, video, or tweets that are intended to shame others' bodies. The viewers seem to escape shame reversals because they are the consuming public that journalists, bloggers, trolls, retailers, etc. (the likely body shamers of online body shaming) rely on for their bread and butter in this online "knowledge economy." Furthermore, both the perpetrator of online body shaming and the body shamed may be included as members of the consuming audience of shame, but not vice versa. As part of the consuming audience of shame, the body shamer and body shamed lose their individual identities and are treated as mere members of the larger audience. So, it appears, the customer is always right and is never made to feel ashamed.

WHEN MIGHT BODY SHAMING BE JUSTIFIED?

At this point, one might be tempted to draw the conclusion that body shaming—be it online or in real life—is never justified, repudiating the practice entirely with several supporting reasons: First, body shaming hurts the victim of shaming by reducing the person's body to an object of publicly shared ridicule, and thus degrading someone's entire personhood. Second, body shaming causes emotional pain to all others whose bodies resemble the shamed one, making these others fear similar shaming from the other members of the honor group. Third, body shaming might cause anguish in the allies of those who are body shamed: people who do not share the shamed body's traits, but feel an alliance with those who have been body shamed. Finally, one might say that body shaming today is typical of the tacky, hate-filled, consumer-oriented discourse that has apparently replaced meaningful, civic conversation between fellow citizens about issues that actually matter: *Ergo, responsible, ethical people would never engage in body shaming, be it browsing the tabloid headlines at the supermarket checkout or online in the pages of Reddit!*

While I am sympathetic to these arguments, I reject their conclusion. If we summarily dismiss all body shaming as the provenance of abhorrent jerks that needlessly hurt the innocent and their allies, I think we will ironically miss opportunities to have conversations that matter—conversations about human bodies, and what they mean for us, and how our agency relates to our embodiment. In other words, body shaming practices are part of how members of a society negotiate their honor codes. I propose that body shaming, both online and in real life, is justified *if and only if* the shamed body (1) symbolizes values antithetical to human well-being and (2) exists as a result of the agent's own doing. I defend each of these conditions in the context of the shared, but nevertheless contestable, honor codes that Americans today use to regulate their bodies and behaviors. (And while I think these conditions apply to both body shaming online and body shaming in real life, my focus here will continue to be on online body shaming.)

First, body shaming someone is justified if and only if the shamed body symbolizes values antithetical to human well-being. To make sense of this claim, we first have to accept the background assumption that human bodies can and do symbolize values. The question of what kinds of bodies are symbols of which specific values is, of course, a wonderfully diverse matter that is entirely dependent on one's time and place—it's part of how an honor group maintains and reinforces shared values. Art is the most obvious venue for treating the body as symbolic of a culture's values. Consider, for example, American photographer Carrie Mae Weems' work, which interrogates the twin values of whiteness and femininity in a racist, sexist society by photographing black women—sometimes carefully posed in "historic" settings, sometimes captured with seeming spontaneity at kitchen tables. Her subjects are invariably depicted as resilient, strong, and fully human (Weems 2017).

Assuming, then, that bodies can and do symbolize values, we can ask whose bodies now symbolize which values for us, according to our honor codes. The case of Serena Williams is illustrative. Serena Williams (b. 1981) is a superior tennis player. Nonetheless, for her entire career, much of the conversation about Williams (from professional journalists to anonymous tweeters) has focused on her body, rather than her tennis (Rankine 2015). For her body shamers (e.g., the Twitter user who attributed Williams' Wimbledon wins to her having the body of a man; the professional coaches who decry "bulking up" for fear of their athletes looking too masculine (Rothenberg 2015); and the viewer who complains that Williams has "aggressive looking" nipples (Brennan 2016)), Williams' body symbolizes power, and they shame her body not only for symbolizing too much power, but also for symbolizing the power that is not under their control.

Williams is not docile, she is not dainty, she is not white, and her body is not what we expect women's bodies to be like, especially as they are displayed in public settings (see, for example, Patricia Hill Collins' (2005) work on slavery's intersecting sexual, racial, and political legacies). It is indisputable that Williams' body symbolizes that same value—*power*—for her fans and those who would reverse shame her body shamers. In the eyes of her supporters, Williams' power is thrilling precisely because it is under her control alone. We praise her grace and speed (and muscles), and we admire the tenacity and willpower it takes to do what she does. Her body symbolizes the power that is in every woman's potential, but Williams has actualized that power in her own unique way.

Is the value of *power* antithetical to *human well-being*? Of course not. Thus, body shaming Williams would not be justified under my condition (1) that ascriptions of body shame are justified if and only if the shamed body symbolizes values antithetical to human well-being. It is extremely important to note, though, that the kind of power that Williams' body symbolizes is absolutely antithetical to, and challenges, other values that some in the United States seems to still hold dear—namely, patriarchy and white supremacy. Serena Williams violates the dominant culture's honor code for women to be thin, to be white, and to be physically vulnerable (the code of a patriarchal, misogynistic, white-supremacist American society). Williams is a celebrated female athlete who continues to defy the expectations of this group and is hence body shamed for that defiance.

In contrast to the body shaming directed at Williams, we can easily think of a case of someone being body shamed online or in real life for reasons that are justified according to condition (1). For example, imagine a man who had Nazi swastikas tattooed on his face. He might be popular in some tenebrous corners of the internet, but he also might be widely body shamed for his appearance. The swastika certainly symbolizes values antithetical to human well-being: anti-Semitism, white power, and genocide. If one were to reject this person as a Facebook friend, retweet an image of his tattooed face with disparaging captions, or ridicule him as a LinkedIn applicant for employment, I think all of these body shaming acts would be justified. His face quite literally symbolizes values that are antithetical to human well-being. This hypothetical case is in fact very close to Byron Widner's actual story. Widner is a former racist thug, and co-founder of "one of the most notorious and violent racist skinhead outfits in the country" (Wood 2011). Widner's white power facial tattoos were removed with surgeries that were paid for by a donation from a Southern Poverty Law Center benefactor, documented in the 2011, MSNBC film, *Erasing Hate* (Wood 2011).

One might object that Widner's body literally has symbols of political values on it, and to shame him is justified because one is shaming his politics, not his face. This, the objection continues, is different from considering how someone's body in-itself is said to symbolize a value. However, I don't think there is a stable dividing line between the body-proper on the one hand, and our symbolic bodily adornments or enhancements, on the other. One enduring lesson from Donna Haraway's work (1991) is that there is no authentic, natural human body wholly separated from artificial human technologies or cultural inscriptions. In the same vein, one cannot really distinguish between the *symbols of Widner's tattooed face* and *Widner's tattooed face*, or (as in Williams' case) the "naturally" athletic body—whatever that might be—and the professionally trained, modern athlete's body. Bodies, be they natural, artificial, or cyborg, are interpreted as place-holders for values. The condition I am defending here is that bodies which convey life-denying values (such as Widner's tattooed face) are justifiably called shameful.

My second condition was that ascriptions of body shame online and in real life are justified if and only if the shamed body also exists as a result of the agent's own doing. This condition also helps to differentiate cases such as Byron Widner's from cases like Serena Williams'. Widner chose to tattoo his face with these symbols, and while Williams certainly did choose to be an athlete, she did not choose to be an African-American woman, competing in a racist and sexist society with its strict honor codes. Many aspects of our bodies are well beyond our individual agency, and members of our honor-group ought to recognize this by rejecting unjustified body shaming.[8]

We might also consider another case, one in which someone is body shamed on social media for being "fat." For instance, body builder Diana Andrews Instagramed to her 17,000 followers a photo of another woman on a gym treadmill with the caption "love handles," and a follow-up note that implied that the woman was busy ordering burgers (Godden 2017). Is Andrews justified in body shaming this woman? According to my proposal, we have to first determine what values the overweight body symbolizes, and whether or not those values are antithetical to human well-being. We also have to ask ourselves if the shamed body exists as a result of the agent's own doing. For Andrews' victim, we would begin with trying to settle what the overweight body symbolizes (for members of the same honor group) today, then determine if those values are antithetical to human well-being. Next, we would contemplate the victim's possible genetic predisposition for obesity, as well as personal food-history, character development, and present-day commitments to wellness. We would have to determine all this just from seeing a single snapshot of a woman, from behind, on a treadmill! And, all these queries must be framed in terms of an honor group's shared honor code—it is a challenge I will leave to you, the readers. My own sympathies, quite obviously, lie with the victim in this case.

ON SHAME REVERSALS

This chapter so far has observed body shaming in the era of social media, and then posited that there are two conditions that define justified body shaming, both online and in real life. I want to conclude with some general reflections on how we ought to respond to body shaming in the era of social media, and on how one ought to show solidarity with, and support for, the person who has been unjustly body shamed without losing one's own ethical footing in the process.

Ethically responsible consumers of social media ought to take umbrage with body shaming that is not justified. Prescient philosopher of technology Neil Postman (1985) wrote in *Amusing Ourselves to Death: Public Discourse in the Age of Show Business*:

Americans no longer talk to each other, they entertain each other. They do not exchange ideas, they exchange images. They do not argue with propositions; they argue with good looks, celebrities and commercials. (92–93)

This is even more true now than when he wrote it. Perhaps I am too nostalgic for a by-gone age of public discourse, when civic-minded people would debate the issues of the day in town halls, editorial pages, and barbershops. But assuming that Postman is right, and meaningful discussion has been reduced to just a hash and rehash of competing images, we ought to combat unjustified body shaming with superior images and snazzier memes (as per author J. K. Rowling's defense of Serena Williams—a tweet of Williams looking glamorous in an evening gown in reply to a tweet that Williams "looks like a man").

Is it possible to make viewing consumers of body shaming feel ashamed of *their* online engagement? Journalist Jon Ronson documents how seemingly righteous cases of shame reversal can mutate into extreme virtual vigilante justice (2015), and his work strikes me as a muted attempt to reverse shame upon viewing consumers. But it remains to be seen if the consuming public would ever really experience such a shame reversal. Internet safety advocate Sue Scheff has endorsed taking a deeply cautious approach to online engagement, lest one find oneself either the victim of online shaming *or* online shame reversal: "The Internet is unforgiving. Before texting, tweeting, emails, posting, or sharing anything, consider how you'd feel if your words or images went viral . . . You should have zero expectation of privacy when it comes to cyberspace" (2017, 127).

I think the more nuanced ethical challenge is how to engage in social media without getting swept up in the vitriol, which seems to be a hazard for otherwise well-meaning people who are trying to shame the shamers. To return to the earlier example, Serena Williams has been feistily defended by those who would reverse that body shaming to shame the shamers for being sexist and racist. Unfortunately, the consuming viewers in this triangular shame relation, those people who click articles, forward them to friends and colleagues, post comments on their Facebook pages, retweet, like, chat, and debate about Williams' body and/or about her ongoing body shaming, anonymously escape any critical attention.

While it seems trite, an increasingly popular option for those who are only the audience of shame in the social-media-body-shame-triangle is to take short sabbaticals from technology for one's own well-being, and to reconnect with others and the natural world. Sherry Turkle's books, *Alone Together: Why We Expect More from Technology and Less from Each Other* (2011) and *Reclaiming Conversation: The Power of Talk in a Digital Age* (2016), are just two examples of calls to action, demanding that we as friends, colleagues, families, lovers, parents, children, educators, and students do better to mindfully engage with others (with digital devices off) because of the documented negative consequences of failing to do so. In other words, we need to reconnect with those smaller groups that one truly cherishes. Another suggestion is to become life-affirming consumers of social media by guardedly spending our time online with those who share life-affirming values and attitudes about bodies, such as at the site thisisbeauty.org, an online campaign that is "a source of inspiration and support for those on their journey towards a life of self-love and self-celebration," itself a tight-knit honor group with its own honor codes for online engagement.

Novelist Margaret Atwood (2006) has said in an interview with Bill Moyers, "Everything that we do, and every piece of technology we make, is an extension of either a fear or a desire, and those human fears and human desires really have not changed." Specifically, for this chapter, the desire for one's body to be loved and admired and the converse fear or anger that one's body is seen as repellant and shameful are universals, such that if Atwood is right, they are also unchanging. For almost all of human history our social circles would have consisted of a few hundred people, at most. If we were body shamed, justly or unjustly, that shame would burn before the people in our lives, but definitely not before the entire world. The novelty of social media and online life, and the honor groups found there, is that we are now exposed to thousands or potentially millions who can shower us with love or confirm our worst fears—to belittle us with shame. The challenge is how to recognize differences in bodies, online and in real life, in ways that do not reduce the other to being broken, to being someone who is a victim of "unbounded shame" where only suicide seems an option (Mann 2018) because the respect of the honor group is forever lost (Taylor 1985). Yet, I conclude in defense of *justified* body shaming. Some differences of embodiment don't simply call for recognition, but in fact demand to be shamed. It will not do to acquiesce to naive relativism about values for fear of seeming "too judgmental." We cannot like, friend, or retweet support for Nazism if we are to be part of the honor group that should really matter—the group of ethical human beings.

CASE STUDY: THE ONGOING BODY SHAMING OF SERENA WILLIAMS

Serena Williams (b. 1981) is, quite simply, one of the very best professional athletes of all time. Among the accomplishments listed on her Wikipedia page: "She is the only tennis player in history (man or woman) to have won singles titles at least six times in three of the four Grand Slam tournaments, and the only player ever to have won two of the four Majors seven times each (seven Wimbledon titles and seven Australian Open titles). She is also the only tennis player to have won 10 Grand Slam singles titles in two separate decades" (Wikipedia Contributors 2017). In addition to her accomplishments on the courts, Williams is also a fashion entrepreneur, paid spokesperson, media personality, and noted philanthropist.

When Serena Williams and her older sister Venus, both professional tennis players, made their debut in the international tennis scene in the 1990s. The novelty of two, young African-American sisters playing their way up from dilapidated courts in Los Angeles to Grand Slam tournaments was sensational. But a good deal of the attention paid to the pair, from the very start, focused on their *bodies* (and hair) rather than their tennis (see Drucker 2009 and Dillman 1999). For example, Serena Williams' body was the object of "professional" scrutiny from sports journalists, such as Jason Whitlock, who compared her to livestock in the *Kansas City Star*: "Seriously, how else can Serena fill out her size 16 shorts without grazing at her stall between matches?" (Whitlock 2009).

By the summer of 2015, when the *New York Times* ran a front-page article, "Tennis's Top Women Balance Body Image with Ambition" by Ben Rothenberg (2015), Serena Williams was no longer just Vensus' little sister or a decent competitor, but in fact the dominant women's tennis player. Rothenberg spotlighted Williams' muscular physique, and then segued to the fact that "body-image issues among female tennis players persist, compelling many players to avoid bulking up" (Rothenberg 2015). Journalists and social media users had an immediate reaction to the article. In "Stop Body Shaming Serena Williams," *Salon* writer Mary Elizabeth Williams wrote, "The implications were clear—Williams treads a lonely path. And if you've ever dared to go deeper into some online sports conversations or God forbid the replies on Twitter, you'll see a consistent level of far worse observations, a deluge of flat-out mockery for Williams' body" (Williams 2015). Ten days after the *New York Times* article, retired professional athlete and activist Kareem Abdul-Jabbar wrote in *Time Magazine*, "The bigger issue here is the public pressure regarding femininity, especially among our athletes. It's a misogynist[ic] idea that is detrimental to professional women athletes and to all the young girls who look up to these women" (Abdul-Jabbar 2015). *The New York Times'* "Public Editor" blog published a response acknowledging the challenges with Rothenberg's article (Sullivan 2015).

In addition to this journalistic conversation, anonymous Twitter users took to the platform in the summer of 2015 to comment on Serena William's body after her Wimbledon win. One Twitter user (@diegtristan8) posted the comment, "Ironic then that the main reason for [Williams'] success is that she is built like a man." To this, famed *Harry Potter* author J. K. Rowling (@jk_rowling) replied on Twitter with a picture of Serena Williams in a glamorous, form-fitting red dress, and the comment, "'[S]he is built like a man.' Yeah, my husband looks just like this in a dress. You're an idiot."

At the end of 2015, *Sports Illustrated* named Serena Williams "Sportsperson of the Year." This event itself caused a minor media uproar, as fewer than 1 percent of the magazine's 600,000 online voters (who have no actual role in the naming of the award's recipient) chose her. Nearly half of them preferred that the Triple Crown winning *horse* be named Sportsperson of the Year (Murphy 2015). Williams was the first woman in thirty years to win the award, and the first woman of African-American descent (Stone 2015).[9] In a gracious acceptance speech, Williams thanked the magazine but also acknowledged the racism, sexism, and ageism that have challenged her, quoting sections from Maya Angelou's 1978 poem "Still I Rise."

During 2015 Serena Williams continued to position herself, as well as be positioned by others, as a uniquely *embodied* person. The annual Pirelli calendar in which she was featured (which usually features scantily clad models cavorting with Italian tires) was reconceived as an "art item" and photographed by noted celebrity photographer Annie Leibowitz, who said: "I wanted the pictures to show the women exactly as they are, with no pretense" (quoted in Groden 2015). Serena Williams' shot is mostly nude except for black underpants, her back is to the viewer with her hands on a draped wall, her legs are posed in a slight lunge, and the wind is blowing her long hair. The image is striking, particularly because it contrasts with the traditional calendar girl, and shows off Williams' dynamic physique.

And as if to atone for its earlier article, *The New York Times* again profiled Williams in the summer of 2015, in late August, on its weekend magazine cover-story, "The Meaning of Serena Williams" (Rankine 2015). In her introduction, acclaimed poet Claudia Rankine outlines Williams' prodigious achievements on the court and then contrasts them with an exploration of what it must be like to be Williams:

> Imagine that you have to contend with critiques of your body that perpetuate racist notions that black women are hypermasculine and unattractive. Imagine being asked to comment at a news conference before a tournament because the president of the Russian Tennis Federation, Shamil Tarpischev, has described you and your sister as "brothers" who are "scary" to look at. Imagine. (Rankine 2015)

The summer of 2016 seemed to be a repeat of the previous summer for Serena Williams, in social media and on the tennis courts. At Wimbledon, instead of getting attention for winning matches (she eventually won Wimbledon, again), Williams won attention for her nipples, which were visible during the chilly English summer in her completely suitable white tennis dress. According to a headline in *The Sun*, "Shocked Wimbledon fans slam BBC after it shows Serena Williams' 'distracting' nipples." Tennis fans complained on Twitter that it was too difficult to watch her quarter final match because Williams' nipples were visible (Jones 2016). The article in the *Daily*

Mail, however, noted the body shaming of Williams in its title, "Serena Williams's Outraged Fans Defend Her as She is Body Shamed on Twitter." This article includes a review of the Twittersphere's denouncement of Williams' nipples. Soifra Brennan's article, however, focuses on how "her outraged fans have leapt to the champion's defense calling for the body-shamers to 'grow up' and accusing them of treating her like a piece of meat" (Brennan 2016). Finally, Perez Hilton, a professional celebrity blogger, craftily tried to play both sides of the "nipple controversy" with his headline, "Serena Williams' Nipples Are The Real Stars Of Wimbledon This Year—But Only Because Twitter Won't Stop Body-Shaming Her For Them!" (Hilton 2016).[10]

The above case study documents a year's worth of journalistic and social media responses to Serena Williams's body. Her sporting achievements make her remarkable. But it seems that no one—professional journalists, fellow athletes, anonymous twitter users, best-selling novelists, celebrity bloggers, photographers, poets—can resist remarking on Serena Williams' body *and/or* remarking on those who make remarks about her body. It also illustrates how Serena Williams has been body shamed for being too much of anything (too strong, too black, too masculine, too muscular, too sexual, and so on).

In Taylor's terms, Serena Williams violates the honor code for women (to be thin, to be white, and to be physically vulnerable) of one of the United States's honor groups (that of a patriarchal, misogynistic, white-supremacist, American society) (Taylor 1985). Williams is a celebrated female athlete who continues to defy the expectations of this group and is hence body shamed for that defiance. Williams has also been defended by those who would reverse that body shaming *to shame the shamers* for being sexist and racist. And as I noted earlier, unfortunately, the consuming viewers in this triangular shame relation, those people who click articles, forward them to friends and colleagues, post comments on their Facebook pages, retweet, like, chat, and debate about Williams' body and/or about her ongoing body shaming, anonymously escape any critical attention.

ACKNOWLEDGMENTS

This chapter was written with financial support from Ramapo College of New Jersey. Thank you to Bernard Roy for his insights and suggestions.

NOTES

1. We must take the idea that there even are "facts" about bodies with a large grain of salt. First, so many of our "facts" about bodies are really just highly

subjective, idiosyncratic judgments. For example, the same body might be seen as desirably voluptuous by one person, but just plain fat to another. In addition, we all take it for granted that bodily appearance is easily manipulated, not just online but also in real life (think of the billions that consumers spend on cosmetics and foundation garments).

2. Bernard Williams' *Shame and Necessity* (1993) provides a history of shame by focusing on ancient Greek literature and philosophy. Like Taylor, he seeks to revalue shame's role in our ethical lives. Williams argues that shame is an exposure that is a "loss of power" (220) for the individual who suffers it. Unlike modern morality's notion of guilt, however, the ancient Greek idea of shame has the subtlety to reckon with human action as neither fully voluntary nor fully compelled.

3. John Deigh has called shame the "self-protective emotion" that preserves one's sense of worth. Seeing it as such does two things: "First, that a liability to shame regulates conduct in that it inhibits one from doing certain things and, second, that experiences of shame are expressed by acts of concealment" (1983, 243).

4. According to Schneider, Sartre references Ovid's myth of Actaeon, who was a human who was caught spying on the immortal huntress Diana as she bathed. Actaeon was turned into a deer as punishment and then killed by his own pack of dogs. Renaissance artists were particularly fond of the myth (Schneider 1977, 120).

5. In an interview in the *L. A. Times*, City Attorney Mike Feuer has spoken on behalf of Mathers' victim. The woman was made aware of her online body shaming after being contacted by Los Angeles police, who were able to identify her with the help of gym employees. The restitution that Feuer negotiated for the victim was $60 so that the victim could purchase a new backpack: "Because the photograph depicted her in the shower, her backpack was hanging there, and it was a way people could identify her. She had to replace that with another backpack" (Morrison 2017). Feuer also pledged to protect the victim's identity, who feels "humiliated" by the episode, but was prepared to testify publicly about the ordeal.

6. According to Mark Peters, lexicographer Ben Zimmer defines "slut-shaming" as "publicly deriding women who engage in sexual activity the speaker considers taboo, usually to modify behavior by inducing guilt or assign blame." Zimmer traces its use to blog entries in 2006, with "slut-shamer" appearing the following year. The more general "body-shaming" began use in 2008 (Peters 2013). Currently, as *Slate* humorist Mark Peters points out, the hyphenation of just about any kind of shame, including patently ridiculous entries, such as "horse-shaming" (a horse photographed in a silly, un-equine pose) or "fedora-shaming" (for those whose love of the retro hat style is excessive). Here are some other body shaming headlines from recent news: "'Body Shaming': Plus Size Models Speak Out" (Murphy 2012); "The Skinny on Body Shaming" (France 2015); "Shame on the *Star Wars* Body Shamers" (Milne 2016). Though the term "body shaming" is new, the phenomenon of body shaming is certainly not new. Women, the disabled, sexual minorities, ethnic minorities, and others have long been subject to body shaming, even if they didn't have the term at their disposal in order to describe their experience.

7. See Fricker (2007) for a discussion of how minorities suffer epistemic injustice, the injustice of being wronged as knowers.

8. Forty years ago Greer Litton Fox wrote about how patriarchal society constructs the ideal of the nice girl (a woman who is "chaste, gentle, gracious, good, clean, nice, noncontroversial, and above suspicion and reproach"), in order to better control women (1977, 805). Today the idea that small, white women are precious, harmless dolls persists. For example, Colgate University was once placed on lockdown after someone spotted an African-American male student carrying a glue gun for an art project. Following that incident, fellow student Jenny Lundt highlighted her experience of feminine, white privilege by posting pictures of herself carrying a Samurai sword on campus: "People laughed- oh look at that harmless, ~ silly white girl ~ with a giant sword!!" (Krishna 2017).

9. The role of race and gender in the dehumanization of black, female athletes such as Williams can be read against the larger problem of dehumanization of others more generally. Philosopher David Livingstone Smith has defined dehumanization as "conceiving of people as subhuman creatures rather than as human beings" (2011, 26). He finds that the way our minds work seems to conspire against us, overly crediting superficial differences between groups with culturally enforced prejudice.

10. As to why we had a world-wide conversation about an athlete's visible nipples, I turn to historian Marilyn Yalom. In the concluding chapter of *A History of the Breast* (called "The Breast in Crisis"), Yalom speculates about this historical moment when the breast seems to be a cultural flashpoint: "The breast has been, and will continue to be, a marker of society's values. Over time, it has assumed and shed various cloaks of religions, erotic, domestic, political, psychological and commercial hues. Today it reflects a medical and global crisis. We are anxious about our breasts, just as we are anxious about the future of our world" (1997, 278).

REFERENCES

Abdul-Jabbar, Kareem. 2015. "Body Shaming Black Female Athletes is Not Just About Race." *Time Magazine.* Accessed July 20, 2018. http://time.com/3964758/body-shaming-black-female-athletes/.

Atwood, Margaret. 2006. "Interview with Margaret Atwood." *On Faith and Reason.* By Bill Moyers. Public Broadcasting System. Accessed June 6, 2018. https://www.youtube.com/watch?v=VMrz_ivl8jo.

Brennan, Siofra. 2016. "Serena Williams Body Shamed for Nipples on Twitter." *The Daily Mail.* Accessed July 7, 2018. http://www.dailymail.co.uk/femail/article-3678536/Serena-Williams-body-shamed-nipples-Twitter.html.

Collins, Patricia Hill. 2005. *Black Sexual Politics: African Americans, Gender, and the New Racism.* New York, NY: Routledge.

Deigh, John. 1983. "Shame and Self-Esteem: A Critique." *Ethics* 93, no. 2: 225–245.

Dillman, Lisa. 1999. "Venus Loses Beads, Then Unravels." *Los Angeles Times.* Accessed January 27, 2018. http://articles.latimes.com/1999/jan/27/sports/sp-2152.

Dolezal, Luna. 2017. "Shame, Vulnerability, and Belonging: Reconsidering Sartre's Account of Shame." *Human Studies* 40, no. 3: 421–38. https://doi.org/10.1007/s10746-017-9427-7.

Drucker, Joe. 2009. "What Happened at Indian Wells?" *ESPN.com*. Accessed March 11, 2018. http://www.espn.com/sports/tennis/columns/story?columnist=drucker _joel&id=3952939.

Fox, Greer Litton. 1977. "'Nice Girl': Social Control of Women through a Value Construct." *Signs: Journal of Women in Culture and Society* 2, no. 4: 804–17.

Fox News. 2017. "Playboy Model Dani Mathers Ordered to Clean Up LA Streets." *Fox News*. Accessed May 25, 2018. http://www.foxnews.com/entertainment/201 7/05/25/playboy-model-dani-mathers-ordered-to-clean-up-la-streets-for-posting-pi cture-nude-woman.html.

France, Lisa Rospers. 2015. "The Skinny on Body Shaming." *CNN*. Accessed June 11, 2018. http://www.cnn.com/2015/06/05/living/body-shaming-skinny-fat-feat/ index.html.

Fricker, Miranda. 2007. *Epistemic Injustice: Power and the Ethics of Knowing*. Oxford, England: Oxford University Press.

Godden, Maryse. 2017. "Bodybuilder Diana Andrews Slammed for 'Bodyshaming' Woman at the Gym." *The Sun*. Accessed March 14, 2018. https://www.thesun. co.uk/news/3081987/bodybuilder-diana-andrews-slammed-for-bodyshaming-wo man-at-the-gym-with-social-media-photos-mocking-her-love-handles/.

Grodden, Claire. 2015. "Amy Schumer and Serena Williams are Giving the Perilli Calendar a Makeover." *Fortune Magazine*. Accessed December 1, 2018. http://for tune.com/2015/12/01/schumer-serena-pirelli-calendar/.

Haraway, Donna. 1990. *Simians, Cyborgs, and Women: The Reinvention of Nature*. New York, NY: Routledge.

Hilton, Perez. 2016. "Serena Williams' Nipples Are the Real Stars of Wimbledon— But Only Because Twitter Won't Stop Body-Shaming Her for Them!" *PerezHilton.com*. Accessed July 7, 2018. http://perezhilton.com/2016-07-07-serena-will iams-wimbledon-2016-finals-nipple-controversy-twitter-tennis-body-shaming#. WS78UzOZPVp.

Jones, Lucy. 2016. "Shocked Wimbledon Fans Slam BBC After It Shows Serena Williams' 'Distracting' Nipples." *The Sun*. Accessed July 7, 2018. https://www.thesun. co.uk/news/1402901/angry-viewers-slam-bbc-as-serena-williams-flashes-her-nip ples-during-wimbo-quarter-final/.

Krishna, Rachael. 2017. "A Woman Went Viral After Posting This Facebook Status About Her White Privilege." *Buzzfeed*. Accessed May 16, 2018. https://www.buz zfeed.com/krishrach/a-woman-went-viral-after-posting-this-facebook-status-a bout?utm_term=.ix3wLBB2a4#.bh2XVQQ2ZM.

Mann, Bonnie. 2018. "Femininity, Shame, and Redemption." *Hypatia* 33, no. 3: 402–17.

McCarthy, Kelly. 2017. "Playboy Model Dani Mathers Apologizes for Body Shaming." *ABC News Good Morning America*. Accessed May 31, 2018. http:// abcnews.go.com/US/playboy-model-dani-mathers-apologizes-body-shaming-70/s tory?id=47730886.

Milne, Graham. 2016. "Shame on the Star Wars Body Shamers." *Huffington Post*. Accessed January 4, 2018. http://www.huffingtonpost.com/graham-milne/shame-o n-the-star-wars-body-shamers_b_8902648.html.

Morrison, Patt. 2017. "Patt Morrison Asks: Mike Feuer." *The Los Angeles Times*. Accessed June 7, 2018. http://www.latimes.com/opinion/op-ed/la-ol-patt-morriso n-mike-feuer-20170607-htmlstory.html.

Murphy, Chris. 2015. "Serena Williams vs. American Pharaoh: The Sports Illustrated Fallout." *CNN*. Accessed December 16, 2018. http://edition.cnn.com/2015/12/16/s port/winning-post-serena-williams-sports-illustrated/.

Murphy, Eliza. 2012. "'Body Shaming': Plus Sized Models Speak Out." *ABC News Good Morning America*. Accessed October 11, 2018. http://abcnews.go.com/blo gs/entertainment/2012/10/body-shaming-plus-size-models-speak-out/.

Peters, Mark. 2013. "Stop Calling All Criticism Shaming." *Slate Magazine*. Accessed October 20, 2018. http://www.slate.com/articles/life/the_good_word/2013/10/sto p_calling_all_criticism_shaming.html.

Postman, Neil. 1985. *Amusing Ourselves to Death: Public Discourse in the Age of Show Business*. New York, NY: Penguin Books.

Rankine, Claudia. 2015. "The Meaning of Serena Williams." *The New York Times Magazine*. Accessed August 25, 2018. https://www.nytimes.com/2015/08/30/ magazine/the-meaning-of-serena-williams.html.

Ronson, Jon. 2015. *So You've Been Publicly Shamed: A Journey Through the World Of Public Humiliation*. New York, NY: Penguin Books.

Rothenberg, Ben. 2015. "Tennis's Top Women Balance Body Image with Ambition." *The New York Times*. Accessed July 10, 2018. https://www.nytimes.com/2015/0 7/11/sports/tennis/tenniss-top-women-balance-body-image-with-quest-for-succ ess.html?_r=1.

Scheff, Sue (with Melissa Schorr). 2017. *Shame Nation: The Global Epidemic of Online Hate*. Naperville, IL: Sourcebooks.

Schneider, Carl D. 1977. *Shame, Exposure, and Privacy*. Boston, MA: Beacon Press.

Stone, Christian. 2015. "Why Serena Williams is SI's Sportsperson of the Year." *Sports Illustrated*. Accessed December 14, 2018. https://www.si.com/sportsperso n/2015/12/14/why-serena-williams-is-sportsperson-of-theyear.

Sullivan, Margaret. 2015. "Double Fault in Article on Serena Williams and Body Image?" *The New York Times Public Editor Blog*. Accessed July 13, 2018. https ://publiceditor.blogs.nytimes.com/2015/07/13/double-fault-in-article-on-serena-w illiams-and-body-image/.

Taylor, Gabriele. 1985. *Pride, Shame, and Guilt: Emotions of Self-Assessment*. New York, NY: Oxford University Press.

Turkle, Sherry. 2012. *Alone Together: Why We Expect More from Technology and Less from Each Other*. New York, NY: Basic Books.

———. 2016. *Reclaiming Conversation: The Power of Talk in a Digital Age*. New York, NY: Penguin Books.

Velleman, David J. 2005. *Self to Self: Selected Essays*. Cambridge, England: Cambridge University Press.

Weems, Carrie Mae. 2017. "Bodies of Work." *Carrie Mae Weems.net*. http://car-riemaeweems.net/work.html.

Weiss, Gail. 2018. "The Shame of Shamelessness." *Hypatia* 33, no. 3: 537–52.

Whitlock, Jason. 2009. "Serena Could Be the Best Ever But." *FoxSports.com.* Accessed July 9, 2018. http://web.archive.org/web/20090709162516/http://msn.fo xsports.com/tennis/story/9757816/Serena-could-be-the-best-ever,-but-.

Wikipedia Contributors. 2017. "Serena Williams." *Wikipedia.* Accessed May 3, 2018. https://en.wikipedia.org/wiki/Serena_Williams.

Williams, Bernard. 1993. *Shame and Necessity.* Berkeley, CA: University of California Press.

Williams, Mary Elizabeth. 2015. "Stop Body Shaming Serena Williams." *Salon. com.* Accessed July 13, 2018. https://www.salon.com/2015/07/13/stop_body_sh aming_serena_williams_its_time_to_break_this_absurd_and_insulting_habit_onc e_and_for_all/.

Wood, Laurie. 2011. "Leaving the Neo-Nazi Lifestyle, and the Tattoos, Behind." *Southern Poverty Law Center Intelligence Report.* Accessed November 15, 2018. https://www.splcenter.org/fighting-hate/intelligence-report/2011/leaving-neo-nazi-lifestyle-and-tattoos-behind.

Chapter 9

Shame and Its Political Consequences in the Age of Neoliberalism

Mikko Salmela

Thomas Scheff (1994; 2000) has for long argued that shame, especially in its unacknowledged and repressed forms, which he claims have increased in modern societies, is a powerful motive of hatred, political violence, and even war. Thus, he highlights the role of unacknowledged shame in political history as a key element on the French side, leading to the First World War, and on the German side, leading to the Second World War. In the latter context, Scheff makes a connection between Hitler's repressed, personal shame and the repressed, societal shame of the German people, which "began with Germany's defeat in World War I and culminated in the Great Depression, [providing] *both* outer and inner conditions for an explosion of humiliated fury. Repressed shame and rage were the link between Hitler and the masses" (Scheff 1994, 117).

The role especially of the shame of the middle class has been highlighted in other theorizing about the emergence of fascism and national socialism. Thus, Lipset (1963) argues that fascism was a movement of the propertied middle classes who used to support liberalism but turned away from it during the Great Depression, especially in Germany which suffered the most. Lipset does not recognize the role of shame explicitly in this middle-class conversion from liberalism to fascism. Even so, he writes that the supporters of fascism and national socialism were "those who for some reason or other had failed to make a success in their business or occupation, and those who had lost their social status or were in danger of losing it" (Lipset 1963, 178). Such loss of social status suggests the involvement of shame, as I will argue below.

Right-wing populism and radicalism are once again on the rise all over the Western world. If we accept Scheff's hypothesis about the contribution of wide-spread, unacknowledged shame to the emergence of fascism and national socialism between the two World Wars, an obvious question is if shame has had a similar influence on the rise of the contemporary "third wave" of right-wing populism since the 1990s. I claim in this chapter that it does, arguing that shame is a "master emotion" of contemporary neoliberal societies, and that its repression feeds anger, resentment, and hatred toward others who are identified in the politics and rhetoric of the populist right as "enemies" of the fragile self.

In order to defend this claim, we need to understand why people are prone to feel ashamed in contemporary neoliberal societies. This leads to a more theoretical question about the nature of shame and its neoliberal forms. Even if my aim is not to present a grand theory of all instances of shame, which is a traditional aim of philosophical investigation, I will say something about my understanding of this emotion. *In nuce*, I suggest in the first part of this chapter that typical instances of shame are both individual and social at the same time, as we judge ourselves in light of values that we endorse, knowing that there are others who share the same values by virtue of sharing a social identity of the same type. This *both* individual *and* social understanding of shame is essential for the thesis about the master emotion status of shame in contemporary neoliberal societies, which is presented in the second part of this chapter, and for an account of the political consequences of shame in these societies, which is presented in the third part.

SOCIAL IDENTITIES AND SHAME

My argument for both the individual and social nature of shame is founded on the idea that we share values by virtue of sharing with others social identities of the same type. Social identities are constituted in part by values, that is, conceptions of the good or valuable within the context of the particular identity. These values are shared by default with others who have the same social identity. A failure to live up to a value constitutive of a social identity therefore gives rise to shame that is felt through one's own eyes and through the eyes of relevant others who share the same social identity.[1] Moreover, these identities are social by virtue of their dependence on the recognition of others. If our salient social identity is not recognized by relevant others, this identity becomes precarious and liable to social erasure. This is painful to individuals whose salient social identities become stigmatized by shame.

Social identity theories in social psychology, and identity theories in sociology, argue that the self can be conceptualized in terms of different identities. Thus, these theories refer to William James (1890) who argued that there are as many "selves" as there are different positions that one holds in society, and different groups and social categories with which one affiliates. Identity theorists, such as Stryker (1980) and Burke (1980), distinguish between "role identities" (e.g., the role of a parent) and "social identities" (e.g., being an American). While social identity theorists, such as Hogg and Abrams (1988), typically talk of identities of the latter kind, I prefer "social identity" as a general term for both social and role identities, as the latter are inherently social as well.

Social identities come with culturally shared normative meanings of what it means to have a certain social identity and how to enact it successfully in different situations. These normative criteria are adopted and internalized together with the taking up of particular social identities, and with the more or less explicit awareness that the same normative meanings are binding for all who share the same social identity. Not all identities are social according to identity theorists for there are "person identities"—meanings attached to the self that define the individual as distinct from others—and even social identities involve an idiosyncratic component of what the particular identity means for the individual. Even so, social identities provide people important *shared self-conceptions* through which they evaluate their behavior. Satisfactory enactment of a social identity confirms and validates a person's status as having the relevant identity and reflects positively on his or her self-evaluation. Accordingly, people seek to enact their prominent and salient identities. The ability to successfully enact such identities, or the lack of this ability, exerts influence on a person's sense of self-meaning, feeling of self-worth, psychological well-being, and has emotional consequences.

Stryker (2004), and Stets and Burke (2005), offer several theoretical hypotheses of the influence of emotions on the enactment of identities and roles. Stryker suggests:

> [P]erformances that meet role expectations will produce positive affect (respect and liking) from others and self-esteem for the self; failure to meet role expectations will produce negative affect (anger and disappointment) from others and lowered self-esteem. When commitment is high, a greater discrepancy in failing to meet role expectations will result in a greater negative affective response. (Stryker 2004; quoted from Stets 2006, 207)

Stets and Burke (2005) have elaborated these hypotheses, suggesting that the source of the meanings of our identity (either the self or others), and the source of the disruptions to the meanings of our identity (either the self or others), are both relevant for the type of emotion felt. They observed that "when actors take responsibility for the identity disruption (an internal attribution), irrespective of whether standards of identity meanings are set by the actors or by others, the actors blame themselves for not being able to verify their identity standards" (quoted from Stets 2006, 211–12). The ensuing negative emotions are directed inward, and they include sadness, embarrassment, and shame—shame being prevalent when the identity is high in salience, prominence, and commitment.

As typical social scientists, Stets and Burke (2005) still associate shame primarily with a failure to meet the expectations or the identity meanings set by others rather than those set by the self. However, I believe this is a false dichotomy. Insofar as the expectations and normative meanings of social identities have been internalized by the self, they belong to the person's social identity irrespective of the source of those expectations and normative meanings, which are largely the same for everyone who share the same social identity. Indeed, the social psychologist Gecas (2000) remarked that most role and social identities have value components. As Gecas illustrates, "For example, physicians are expected to value life, ease suffering, show compassion; professors are expected to value knowledge and learning; and parents should love and care for their children" (Gecas 2000, 94). These values are shared *by default* by everyone who shares the relevant social identity (see also Salmela 2009). Individuals may have personal interpretations of what it requires to live up to the constitutive values of their shared identities; yet, insofar as those identities are central to their self-conception and feelings of self-worth, individuals feel ashamed if they fail to enact the meanings of their identities and they blame themselves for this failure.

Further still, when we fail to live up to the value constitutive of an important social identity, it is not merely a matter of negative appearance to others but something that undermines our having that relevant social identity, for individuals depend on each other for the recognition of their social identities. Many existing studies on recognition focus on struggles of recognition between social groups or categories that represent different forms of life or self-realization (e.g., Honneth 1996; Fraser and Honneth 2003). In these approaches, the internal relations of a social group or category whose members share a form of life or self-realization are usually understood to be characterized by solidarity that emerges from their joint struggle for recognition within the wider society on the one hand, and from their mutual recognition of each other as fellow members of the same social group or category on the other. However, forms of life and self-realization are also potential domains for struggles of recognition, especially if they operate on a competitive logic, for the recognition of others may depend on individual group members' ability to pursue the particular form of life or self-realization by living up to its constitutive values.[2] As in all other forms of denied recognition, according to Honneth (1996, 131–39), if others withhold their recognition from their fellow group members who fail in this pursuit, the resulting emotion is presumably shame.

A domain that exemplifies shame emerging from withheld social recognition is unemployment and its stigmatizing nature. Erving Goffman's description of this stigma is famous:

How hard and humiliating it is to bear the name of an unemployed man. When I go out, I cast down my eyes because I feel myself wholly inferior. When I go along the street, it seems to me that I can't be compared with an average citizen, that everybody is pointing at me with his finger. I instinctively avoid meeting any-one. Former acquaintances and friends of better times are no longer so cordial. They greet me indifferently when we meet. They no longer offer me a cigarette and their eyes seem to say, "You are not worth it, you don't work." (Goffman 1963, 27)

Here Goffman describes the stigma that emerges from losing the valued social identity of being employed. The others treat the person's loss of this social identity as a reason for withholding their recognition of this identity from him or her. The excerpt does not tell whether the stigma of denied recognition extends to the occupational identity of the unemployed person. However, it is likely that this social identity becomes precarious because it ceases to bring status, recognition, and honor to the person during unemployment. And even if the excerpt talks about humiliation, unemployment is widely associated with shame, especially if individuals blame themselves for their unemployment, and other financial or social losses, that are often associated with it (e.g., Walker 2014).

SHAME AS A MASTER EMOTION IN CONTEMPORARY NEOLIBERAL SOCIETIES

With retraction of the welfare state, the downsizing of the public sector, economic deregulation and privatization, and globalization, there are some reasons to assume that shame is particularly salient in contemporary Western societies that have adopted neoliberalism. With the adoption of neoliberalism, the principles of competition and market exchange have spread from the economy to domains of life that have been previously governed by informal and embedded ties, or reciprocal exchange, including social life, which has resulted in increased and expanded experiences of insecurity, vulnerability, and precariousness (e.g., Bauman 2001; Foucault 2008). In these social conditions, shame emerges as an emotion about actual or anticipated losses of valued social identities, for which individuals within a neoliberal ideology of individual responsibility blame themselves.

First of all, shame is involved in fear of *déclassement* that emerges in conditions of social uncertainty as an *anticipatory* emotion. This kind of fear is sometimes characterized as social anxiety, but still bears more resemblance to shame, as it is about the loss of social status—a shameful outcome—that is brought into presence in anticipation. Anticipatory shame may not be as intense as actual shame, but it resembles the latter in its unpleasant hedonic quality and negative implications for the self. This is because it signals an *expected* loss rather than a mere threat or possible loss or social exclusion (Neckel 1991; Barbalet and Demertzis 2013; Miceli and Castelfranchi 2015).

In general, the more insecure individuals feel about their ability to maintain their social status and standards of living, the more they come to anticipate the negative consequences that follow if they are incapable of doing so. Work has been an important source of respect, pride, and self-esteem for employees in both lower and middle classes, especially in those countries whose Protestant cultural heritage emphasizes the relevance of work and employment for social identity (Beck 2000; Sennett 2006; Hochschild 2016). In the bureaucratically structured organizations of modern Western-European capitalism, the occupational identities of workers—especially those of white males—were stable and permanent, based on skills and expertise that were developed over the years in their occupation, with the expectation of future rewards, and which were motivated by self-discipline at work and a commitment to work organization and occupational identity (Sennett 2006; Newman 1998).

In contemporary work life, by contrast, many traditional skills have become obsolete through automatization and other technological shifts, organizational structures are light and transient, the pressures to quickly produce results are intense, and work is organized into short-term projects with varying collaborators. These conditions make one's flexibility—one's capacity to adapt to new circumstances, challenges, and people—more important than any particular skill or ability, besides the skill to cooperate, whatever the circumstances: "An organization in which the contents are constantly shifting requires the mobile capacity to solve problems; getting deeply involved in any one problem would be dysfunctional, since projects end as abruptly as they begin. The problem analyzer who can move on, whose product is possibility, seems more attuned to the instabilities which rule the global marketplace" (Sennett 2006, 126).

Under these conditions, *potential ability* becomes valued, nurtured, and rewarded in the job market more than past achievements and accumulated experience, even though judgments about potential ability are much more subjective than judgments about achievements, especially as it is hard to imagine any other plausible ground for judgments of potential ability besides past achievements. For those evaluated as lacking potential to contribute in the job market, the situation is hard. As Sennett observes: "Potential ability focuses only on the self. The statement 'you lack potential' is much more devastating than 'you messed up.' It makes a more fundamental claim about who you are. It conveys uselessness in a more profound sense" (Sennett 2006, 123). These kinds of global negative evaluations of the self, which are associated with social practices that verify and reinforce the uselessness of people who are not perceived to be fitting to a new work life, are instrumental in experiences of shame among the rejected and those who fear rejection.

With the proliferation of individualized careers and risk, more and more employees have become "entrepreneurs of the self" (Foucault 2008, 226; see also Bröckling 2016)[3] who compete with each other for various resources and social recognition. Even those who maintain their jobs in spite of the ubiquitous changes feel the pressures of increased workload and flexibility that often come with reduced or stagnated salaries. Given the experience of work as an increasingly pitiless game of survival, employees "fear that, in spite of hard work and sacrifices, they are not able to maintain or attain the standard of living and social status they have previously enjoyed or which they aspire to" (Flecker et al. 2007, 41–42). Even people in relatively secure positions may feel threatened by changes in contemporary work life as they have witnessed the effects of downsizings, restructurings, and privatizations on others, and can expect the same fate sooner or later. These fears of social falling can affect all employees, not only low- or medium-skilled, blue-collar workers, whom these changes have so far affected most, but also skilled white-collar, middle-class employees who can anticipate being next in line.

In addition to unemployment, middle-class marginalization comes in the form of under- and semi-employment, in which one's income has to be gathered piecemeal from several sources (Sennett 2006). An alarming piece of evidence of precarization that cuts through the society is a recent finding that 47 percent of Americans would have trouble finding $400 to pay for an emergency; this standing financial insecurity is a secret source of shame for many middle-class Americans, as Neal Gabler points out in the title of his May 2016 cover story in *The Atlantic*: "The Secret Shame of Middle-Class Americans."

Along with fears of losing social status and established living standards come fears of becoming part of a stigmatized group, such as the unemployed, which is commonly regarded as shameful and stigmatizing (Walker 2014). The shamefulness of unemployment is exacerbated by several measures to which public (or privatized) unemployment agencies engage in order to return the unemployed to the workforce. The general change from "welfare" to "workfare" in Western societies from the 1990s onward has brought along activation policies that make the payment of unemployment benefits conditional on one's participation in workfare programs, as well as on an active job search. Being subjected to seemingly pointless job-seeking measures (such as obligatory participation in some vocational training courses) can be humiliating and shameful, especially as their implicit message is often that it is up to the individual to find a new job, whatever the circumstances. Another humiliating form of workfare is the requirement of an unemployed person to accept or apply for jobs even if they do not match his or her professional skills and competence, with sanctions on non-compliance. Policies of this kind are effective in weakening people's commitment to their chosen occupational identities as these are not respected by public unemployment agencies. Instead, those occupational identities become tagged with shame.

Even if working life is the most poignant venue of competition in contemporary neoliberal societies, it is not the only one. Bauman (2001) has argued that a new "life politics" has brought a spirit of consumerism and a pleasure principle to interpersonal relations that were previously governed by informal and embedded ties, or reciprocal exchange. Instead, these relations now come with implicit, inbuilt, "until-further-notice," and "withdrawal-at-will" clauses. Accordingly, it has become important for individuals to look after their exchange or market value, which becomes inseparable from experiences of personal worth and self-esteem. This value, as well as the adjacent self, however, is inherently precarious as it is dependent on one's success on the social market, and therefore liable to produce experiences of worthlessness, marginalization, dispensability, fear, and frustration (Mäkinen 2012). Importantly, the exchange value of different social roles and identities requires different skills and capacities: at work as an employee and a colleague, at home as a spouse, lover, and parent, as a friend and neighbor, in various hobbies, and so on, both on-line and off-line.

Consequently, the popularity of various work-related and lifestyle coaching services has increased immensely as individuals strive to become and remain valuable selves, both to themselves and to others, in different domains of life. The aim of coaching, rhetorically, is to become an autonomous self, which is a venerable ideal of classical liberalism. However, since the self is heavily involved in relations of market exchange, self-promotion becomes the consolidation of an already-commodified, entrepreneurial, neoliberal self (Mäkinen 2012; McGuigan 2014). Insofar as individuals perceive their value as depending on successful performances and self-presentation in several domains of life that operate on a competitive market logic, this value becomes highly contingent and volatile, which invokes more or less frequent instances of shame about the incapacity of "being the right kind of person" in different contexts.[4]

Shame is associated with a loss of self-esteem, either constitutively or causally (Deonna et al. 2012; Rawls 1971; yet see Deigh 1983 for a critical view). People who find themselves worthless or redundant in contemporary societies, for instance due to unemployment and/or lack of relevant social and cultural capital, may experience shame, especially if the constitutive values of their salient social identities derive from more affluent times or times of privilege, and are therefore unattainable or more difficult to obtain in their present situation. Loss of self-esteem is also more consequential if it is global rather than specific; that is, affecting several social identities of a person rather than only some of them (Cast and Burke 2002). Unfortunately, these losses to self-esteem often go together in contemporary market societies where financial resources are important for maintaining several social identities. In this way, economic uncertainty has the capacity of hampering the construction and maintenance of vital positive social identities and life projects, adding insult of self-esteem to material injuries (Bauman 1998). In general, the more domains of life in a society operate on the principles of competition and market exchange, the more chances there are for failing to live up to the constitutive values of one's salient social identities, and, consequently, for shame about this actual or anticipated incapacity.

The main reason for the expansion of shame in contemporary market societies is associated with the neoliberal citizenship regime, which places the responsibility for successes and failures on individual subjects, categorizing them as "successful" and "failed" citizens mainly on the basis of employment and income (Wacquant 2010; Tyler 2013). The successful, model citizens of Western-European, neoliberal societies embody the ideals of entrepreneurship: activity, autonomy, flexibility, and adaptability, and continually manage their "employability" with the help of practices such as lifelong learning or personal branding (Mäkinen 2017; Lem 2013). Accordingly, work, entrepreneurship, and various "activation" policies are offered as solutions to poverty and unemployment. Those who fail to embody or resist embodying these entrepreneurial ideals are regarded as surplus; "the useless and undeserving member[s] of the 'feral underclass'" (Tyler 2013, 186).

These unruly people are regulated and penalized by "the joint action of welfare-turned-workfare and an aggressive penal bureaucracy" that, according to Wacquant (2010, 197), "couple into a single organizational contraption to discipline the precarious fractions of the postindustrial working class." Shrinking welfare and expanding prisonfare become morally justified treatments of the unemployed and the poor in neoliberal societies as these are perceived to have chosen their wayward ways of life. Yet the targets of these measures in the United States that Wacquant (2009) characterizes as "a living laboratory of the neoliberal future" display class and ethnic selectiveness, as they include the unemployed, the homeless, and working poor of lower-class communities, as well as African Americans, who are a historically disadvantaged or marginalized group in American society.

While most people in postindustrial market societies have been able to keep their jobs in spite of economic turbulances and recessions, they cannot be sure that this will be the case also in the future, as I have argued above. Even those who have internalized the competitive ethos of neoliberalism face the threats of unemployment and social loss, because due to the precariousness of contemporary working life, staying employed is not entirely up to most of us. In this situation, the ideological assumption that individuals alone are responsible for their employment, regardless of job market conditions, helps the employed to maintain their optimism and to repress an unpleasant awareness of the precariousness of contemporary work life that undermines it. Berlant (2011) has characterized this kind of counterproductive optimism, in which something you desire is an obstacle to your flourishing, as "cruel." The cruelty reinforces the need to maintain a sharp boundary between "us," the winners (so far), and "them," the stigmatized losers who are blamed for their own condition (Bauman 1998). However, this sharp boundary may also feed shame insofar as in a neoliberal society anyone can become a member of a stigmatized group, such as that of being unemployed, through no fault of their own.

In sum, I have argued that contemporary Western neoliberal societies promote feelings of powerlessness, insecurity, worthlessness, as well as fears of losing one's status and established living standards, that give rise to actual or anticipatory shame, both in working life and in other domains of social life that have adopted a competitive market logic. Shame emerges as individuals accept responsibility for losses that they experience or anticipate in the context of their important social identities, and it is promoted by neoliberal citizenship regimes that blame individuals for such losses. Therefore, shame is a master emotion in such Western societies.

THE POLITICAL CONSEQUENCES OF SHAME IN CONTEMPORARY NEOLIBERAL SOCIETIES

If contemporary Western societies promote actual or anticipatory shame across borders, how does this increase of shame explain the emergence of populist parties and movements in recent years on both sides of the Atlantic? Right-wing populist parties have garnered significant support in Western, Eastern, Central, and Northern Europe, as well as in the United States. In contrast, left-wing populism has advanced in some, mainly Southern European, countries (such as Greece and Spain) that were most severely hit by the recent financial crisis and austerity policies that were designed to remedy it; although the success of socialist, anti-establishment, politicians, such as Jeremy Corbyn, in the United Kingdom, and Bernie Sanders, in the United States, can also be interpreted as an effect of left-wing populism. Even so, the preponderance of right-wing populism suggests that we may take it as a dominant type of populism in contemporary Western societies, while successful cases of left-wing populism appear as exceptions that need different type(s) of explanation.

One structural reason for the possibly dissimilar emotional dynamics in countries such as Greece and Spain is that the austerity cuts implemented in these countries were more radical and more noticeable than those in Western, Central, and Northern European countries. The fact that large segments of the population were affected by austerity cuts may have given rise to a common awareness, reinforced by left-wing populist slogans such as "We are the 99%," that individual citizens cannot be blamed for losing their jobs, homes, or prospects of a secure life, which were consequences of cuts to salaries, pensions, and public services (della Porta 2015; Gerbaudo 2017). In such conditions, people were more likely to self-identify as aggrieved by neoliberal policies and to direct blame at politics, politicians, and institutions that were perceived to be responsible for their situation instead of blaming themselves (Simiti 2016).

This is an important difference, for if others are blamed for demeaning and undeserved treatment rather than the self, the resulting emotion is humiliation rather than shame. Humiliation, similar to publicly acknowledged shame, has an emancipatory potential as these emotions allow individuals to identify and establish bonds with others who feel the same, and to transform their negative self-focused emotions into anger and indignation against others perceived to be responsible for their precarious situation. This kind of emotional dynamics, supported by tailored political rhetoric, can be seen among the supporters of left-wing populist parties and movements such as SYRIZA, *Indignados/Aganaktismenoi*, and Podemos in Greece and Spain (Salmela and von Scheve 2018). In contrast, citizens in countries less affected by the financial crisis, such as Western, Central, and Northern European countries, have faced the consequences of neoliberal globalization and their own vulnerability in more individualized terms, which contributed to each individual accepting more responsibility for his or her actual, or anticipated, losses, precarious condition, and ensuing shame.

In what follows, I identify an *emotional mechanism* of *ressentiment* involving shame behind the support of right-wing political populism.[5] In this account, I draw from Mikko Salmela and Christian von Scheve's (2017) recent article titled, "Emotional Roots of Right-Wing Political Populism."[6] This mechanism explains how feelings of fear, powerlessness, insecurity, worthlessness or shame—negative emotions that target the self—fuel *ressentiment* through which these emotions transform into anger, resentment, and hatred toward perceived "enemies" of the self and other outgroups, such as refugees, immigrants, the long-term unemployed, political and cultural elites, and the "mainstream" media. *Ressentiment* also contributes to emotional distancing from social identities that inflict shame and other negative emotions about the self, and instead promotes seeking meaning and self-esteem from other identities perceived to be stable and to some extent exclusive, such as nationality, ethnicity, religion, language, and traditional gender roles.

Ressentiment

Ressentiment figures in contemporary theorizing on the "third wave" of right-wing political populism as a general category of negative emotions—such as fear and insecurity, alienation and displacement, disappointment and distrust, and anger and frustration—that have been invoked to explain the support for these movements and parties (e.g., Betz 1994; Ignazi 2003; Berezin 2009). In these discussions, *ressentiment* is often treated as being coextensive with *resentment*, even if these are two different emotions. Resentment is generally understood as a long-term moral anger in response to being insulted, injured, or offended (e.g., Meltzer and Musolf 2002; Strawson 1974), whereas *ressentiment*, in philosophy, was introduced by Nietzsche ([1887] 2006), and elaborated by Scheler ([1915] 1994), who saw it as a complex emotion that emerges from the suppression of negative emotions such as envy, malice, or spite upon which one feels impotent to act. These emotions are therefore repressed and transmuted into resentment, hostility, or hatred toward the other or others who are portrayed as victimizers of the self. Even so, this process does not remove the powerlessness of *ressentiment* that remains part of the transmuted resentment, hostility, or hatred, in contrast to unmediated forms of these emotions.

Besides emotional change, *ressentiment* involves a value change or reversal. Scheler refers to Aesop's famous tale of a fox that renounces the value of grapes, deeming them "sour" instead, upon realizing that he is incapable of reaching them. Similarly, a person of *ressentiment* renounces his or her core value that the person is not able to live up to, deeming the value either worthless, or less valuable than other values that the person is capable of pursuing. A modern example might be the newly found value of harmonious family life in the countryside upon finding that one is incapable of building a successful business career in the city. Even so, a value change initiated by *ressentiment* is typically neither transparent nor complete, for it is motivated by a desire to avoid and repress negative emotions emerging from perceiving oneself as being a failure in terms of the former core value rather than by a sincere, reflexive endorsement of the new value. Therefore, the renounced value continues to influence the person's self-evaluations, contributing to feelings of inferiority and powerlessness that need to be repressed (see Scheler 1994; Aeschbach 2017).

Surprisingly, Scheler does not mention shame among the negative emotions that give rise to *ressentiment*. However, he talks about an "oppressive sense of inferiority" which results from constant comparisons with others, and argues that *ressentiment* is strongest in a society "where approximately equal rights (political and otherwise) or formal social equality, publicly recognized, go hand in hand with wide factual differences in power, property, and education" (Scheler 1994, 7–8). If shame belongs to emotions that emerge from an unfavorable comparison of oneself with others in a formally equal yet actually unequal society (such as contemporary Western societies), then it is part of the Schelerian account of *ressentiment* as well, although implicitly rather than explicitly.

More recently, psychoanalytically oriented, sociological theorists Scheff (1994; 2000) and Turner (2007) have described an emotional mechanism similar to *ressentiment* without, however, invoking this term. They argue that shame is often repressed due to its painfulness and negative implications for the self. However, repressed shame does not disappear, but instead persists, becomes more intensive, and transforms into anger, resentment, or hatred. The idea is that psychodynamic processes change both the emotion type (from shame to anger, resentment, or hatred) and its intentional object (from self to other), with the purpose of protecting the vulnerable self. This mechanism is similar to Scheler's *ressentiment* because the repression and transmutation of negative emotions, and a shift in their intentional directedness, are central to that concept as well.

Importantly, repression makes it difficult for the subject to recognize the social structures in which shame emerged. Therefore, "the structures that originally generated negative emotional arousal are frequently not the targets of external attributions," as Turner (2007, 521) remarks. Another reason for the invisibility of such structures are the ideologies, such as competitive individualism, that justify the unequal distribution of resources in different institutional domains. When these ideologies are taken for granted, the contribution of social structures to the shame-producing distribution of resources remains invisible. Turner remarks that once "shame is repressed, it can be manipulated by those with an interest in deflecting this anger onto chosen targets; typically, this manipulation involves the symbols of one social identity and juxtaposes this identity through narratives about the evils of another social category or social identity" (Turner 2007, 521–22).

Ressentiment can be seen in operation in the politics and rhetoric of right-wing populist parties that is carefully crafted (a) to contribute to the repression of shame and (b) to deflect shame-induced anger, resentment, and hatred away from the self and direct it instead toward the political and cultural establishment and various others, such as refugees, immigrants, the long-term unemployed, and ethnic, religious, or sexual minorities. This is why structural changes like globalization and economic liberalization—the actual causes of many of the events and processes that provoke individual shame—received little attention, until recently, from right-wing populists, who now seek to fight globalization by protectionism. Yet, this blaming of other countries and transnational organizations allows other aspects of contemporary capitalism to easily get off the hook or, paradoxically, to even receive support when figureheads such as Donald Trump are voted for.

Emotional Distancing

The idea of emotional distancing is that individuals distance themselves emotionally from those social identities that frequently evoke shame and other negative feelings, such as fear, powerlessness, worthlessness, and vulnerability. Shame-prone social identities become precarious, whereas other social identities that seem to be beyond shame become more attractive.[7] This process can be seen as part of *ressentiment*, especially of its value change or reversal, since social identities imply values, as I have argued above.

In contemporary capitalist societies, social identities that are based on resources allocated on the basis of competition are inherently shame-prone and therefore liable to alienation, particularly for people occupying precarious positions. These social identities include occupational identities, which used to be relatively stable and were thus building blocks of status, recognition, and honor, but have come under notable pressure over the recent years (Bauman 1998; Beck 2000; Hochschild 2016). This is true for occupational identities of low- and medium-skilled blue-collar workers, who have largely lost their trust in trade unions as protectors of their interests, as well as for white-collar workers, whose employers in both public and private sectors face pressures to cut expenditures. A further source of shame is the ideal of an entrepreneurial identity, with its demands of adaptability, flexibility, and lifelong learning, particularly in response to the growing reliance on advancing technologies, that many workers, especially in older generations, find difficult to meet. Indeed, in flexible labor markets where seamless working careers have become an exception, it makes little sense to develop strong emotional attachments to an occupational identity—even if employers encourage or even demand this in the age of emotional capitalism (Illouz 2007; Hochschild 1983).

Instead, social identities that do not involve competition such as nationality, ethnicity, language, religion, and gender become more and more attractive as sources of meaning, self-esteem, and efficacy at times in which other social identities are experienced to be insecure. There is some evidence that the increased salience of those social identities that right-wing populists seek to protect coincides with the precarization of other important identities that relate to work and occupation. Thus, Hochschild (2016) found that Tea Party and Trump supporters resented the preferential treatment of traditionally marginalized and disadvantaged groups, such as women, racial and ethnic minorities, the disabled, and sexual minorities, because they thought that work was the only fair criterion for distributing resources and benefits in society. This emphasis of work in the populist right narrative of distributive justice reveals the value of work for these people, even if it has ceased to be the key to prosperity, security, and honor for them, as Hochschild observed.[8] This is also a nice example of the way in which old values still "shine through" *ressentiment*-mediated new values by which individuals seek to avoid negative emotions associated with the old values.

The weakening of workers' mutual solidarity and of the power of their trade unions, in conjunction with the precariousness of occupational identities, hamper the mobilization of the traditional left. It also benefits the new populist right that attracts voters with allegedly "natural" and "stable" social identities such as ethnicity, nationality, gender, and sexuality. These identities are discursively framed as less contingent and less demanding than others based on a combination of efforts, dedication, and luck, such as having a continuous successful working career. These are also social identities in which solidarity and belonging with other group members can still be experienced in the framework of shared concerns, emotions, and meanings, unlike in the context of those social identities where individuals compete with one another.

Taking pride in the ascriptive aspects of one's identity, such as ethnicity, national culture, gender, or sexuality—what one already is or has in general—is less demanding and complicated than taking pride in what one has achieved, for the latter kind of pride requires constant efforts with increasingly uncertain chances of success in today's competitive societies. Insofar as there is competition at the group level as well, individuals can identify with their representatives such as national teams in sports who are competing for the entire group. Stable social categories may, therefore, become attractive as a kind of bedrock onto which one can fall back if the other, more contingently rewarding social identities fail to yield positive experiences in support of the self. This may explain the popularity of right-wing populism both among the "losers" and some "winners" of contemporary neoliberal capitalism, as well as the focus on issues of ethnicity, nationality, gender, and sexuality in recent political debates beween the right and the left. For those in disadvantaged positions, the appeal of stable social identities is obvious. But their appeal is also evident for those who profit from globalization and economic liberalization because they are aware of the precariousness of contemporary social life.

FINAL REMARKS

In this chapter, I have argued that shame about the inability to live up to the constitutive values of one's social identities is a master emotion of contemporary neoliberal societies, and an important underlying motivating factor in the emergence of a third wave of right-wing political populism in both Europe and the United States. There seems to be parallels between the effects of the Great Depression of the 1930s in Central Europe and the more recent global economic downturn of 2008, as both benefited nationalist, anti-immigrationist, authoritarian, protectionist right-wing parties, although the rise of right-wing political populism in contemporary neoliberal societies is a longer process that began in the 1990s (Mudde 2007). This makes sense as the development of neoliberalism in Western societies was a long process. It began with the economic policies of Margaret Thatcher and Ronald Reagan in the 1980s and was continued in the 1990s and 2000s by Democrats in the United States and Social Democrats in Europe (such as Bill Clinton, Tony Blair, and Gerhard Schröder), who willingly adopted the "third way" as a "modernized," social democracy fit for the new social, political, and economic landscape of contemporary capitalism.

The "third way" aimed at providing an alternative to both neoliberalism and traditional social democracy in an era of globalization, but its politics has been characterized rather as a capitulation to neoliberal globalization (see Hale et al. 2004). In consequence, what has emerged is an unprecedented convergence on economically liberal, market-oriented policies across the political spectrum in Western societies. However, the inherent shame-inducing tendencies of neoliberalism seem to render these societies, especially in times of crises, vulnerable to political turbulences, some of which pose a threat to the fundamental values of those societies: respect for human dignity and human rights, freedom, democracy, equality, and the rule of law. I believe that politicians and other decision-makers in Western societies, the advocates of neoliberalism included, neglect these signs of warning at their peril if they let neoliberalism run rampant, hoping that people become more resilient to experiences of shame and other negative emotions when they learn to live with competition in all domains of life. Such hope is groundless because market-based relationships cannot replace ethical relations founded on mutual recognition.

NOTES

1. My view of shame resembles that of Deonna et al. (2012) who argue that shame is felt in response to our incapacity to live up to or even minimally exemplify in behavior our core value or values. My point is that many of our core values are shared with others by virtue of sharing social identities whose constituents are those values.

2. Honneth (1996) characterizes forms of life and self-realization in civil society as communities of value.

3. Foucault presents the idea of *homo economicus* as an entrepreneur of himself in the context of arguing that neoliberalism is about "the application of the economic grid to social phenomena . . . it involves extending the economic model of supply and demand and of investment-costs-profit so as to make it a model of social relations and of existence itself, a form of relationship of the individual to himself, time, those around him, the group, and the family" (Foucault 2008, 239, 242).

4. It is possible that shame is involved in all social interactions in which individuals perceive their value as depending on successful performances and self-presentation in salient social roles and identities. However, there may be important cultural differences in the experience of shame in these situations. There is evidence that in East Asian cultures with interdependent construals of the self, shame is an important social emotion that signals the disruption of the social bond and motivates restoration of this bond in accordance with culturally established ways, whereas in Western cultures, with their independent construals of the self, shame is framed and felt as deviant, despised, and socially undesirable, and therefore an inexpressible emotion, as it is associated with weakness, inferiority, low status, defeat, and other unenviable attributes of the self (e.g., Ha 1995; Markus and Kitayama 1991). Due to its social unacceptability, there are generally less established means of regulating shame in the latter cultures, which render the effects of shame on the self more devastating than in those cultures that offer socially established means of regulating shame. These effects may have been exacerbated by the rise of neoliberalism in Western cultures, which place responsibility for losses, failures, and the lack of success on the individual, whatever the circumstances.

5. See Elster 1999 for the notion of "emotional mechanism."

6. In Salmela and von Scheve 2017, we treat *ressentiment* and emotional distancing as separate mechanisms. However, we now see emotional distancing as part of *ressentiment*, as presented in this article.

7. Theoretical support for the argument of emotional distancing from shame-prone social roles and identities comes from identity theories (Stryker 2004; Stets and Burke 2005). Stryker (2004) argues that intense emotions result when structural or interactional barriers prevent the enactment of highly positive identities or the denial of highly negative identities, and these emotions influence commitment to the affected identities such that "the more intense the emotional responses to identity affirmation or denial, the greater will be its impact on commitment" (14). Stets and Burke (2005) observe, in reference to shame, that "When the self is evaluated as responsible for the identity disruption, the negative emotion is directed against the self" (quoted from Stets 2006, 214). People try to change the meanings of situations in which their identity is not verified in social interaction. However, if this is impossible, the theory predicts that their identity standards and identities will change.

8. In contrast to right-wing populism, left-wing populist parties have sought to politically and discursively strengthen and reinforce precarious identities. Relating to occupational identities, they support increases in minimum wage, the unionization of workers, and bans of zero-hour contracts, reduced working hours, paid family and sick leaves, paid vacation, etc. These policies aim at protecting precarious occupational identities of workers, as well as other identities whose successful maintenance depends on financial resources raised from work. Moreover, the political left, including the populist left, has in general engaged more thoroughly and substantially in identity politics for the recognition and esteem of various marginalized identities, such as racial, gender, and ethnic identities, seeking to transform the shame frequently associated with these identities into pride. This is likely to have contributed to the acceptance of shame-prone identities that have become fragile and precarious only over the past years, such as certain occupational identities, amongst the left (see Salmela and von Scheve 2018).

REFERENCES

Aeschbach, Sébastien. 2017. *Ressentiment: An Anatomy*. Thèse de doctorat: Universite Genève 2017, no. L: 909. DOI: 10.13097/archive-ouverte/unige:103621.

Barbalet, Jack and Nicolas Demertzis. 2013. "Collective Fear and Societal Change." In *Emotions in Politics*, edited by N. Demertzis, 166–85. Basingstoke, England: Palgrave Macmillan.

Bauman, Zygmunt. 1998. *Work, Consumerism, and the New Poor*. Buckingham, England: Open University Press.

———. 2001. *The Individualized Society*. Cambridge, England: Polity Press.

Beck, Ulrich. 2000. *The Brave New World of Work*. Cambridge, England: Polity Press.

Berezin, Mabel. 2009. *Illberal Politics in Neoliberal Times*. Cambridge, England: Cambridge University Press.

Berlant, Lauren. 2011. *Cruel Optimism*. Durham, NC/London, England: Duke University Press.

Betz, Hans-Georg. 1994. *Radical Right-Wing Populism in Western Europe*. London, England: Macmillan.

Bröckling, Ulrich. 2016. *The Entrepreneurial Self. Fabricating a New Type of Subject*. London, England: Sage.

Burke, Peter. 1980. "The Self: Measurement Implications from a Symbolic Interactionist Perspective." *Social Psychological Quarterly* 43: 18–29.

Cast, Alicia D. and Peter Burke. 2002. "A Theory of Self-Esteem." *Social Forces* 80: 1041–68.

Deigh, John. 1983. "Shame and Self-Esteem: A Critique." *Ethics* 93: 225–45.

della Porta, Donatella. 2015. *Social Movements in Times of Austerity*. Cambridge, England: Polity Press.

Deonna, Julien, Raffaelle Rodogno, and Fabrice Teroni. 2012. *In Defense of Shame*. Oxford, England: Oxford University Press.

Elster, Jon. 1999. *Alchemies of the Mind: Rationality and the Emotions*. Cambridge, England: Cambridge University Press.

Flecker, Jörg, Gudrun Hentges, and Gabrielle Balazs. 2007. "Potentials of Political Subjectivity and the Various Approaches to the Extreme Right: Findings of the Qualitative Research." In *Changing Working Life and the Appeal of the Extreme Right*, edited by J. Flecker, 35–62. Aldershot, England: Ashgate.

Foucault, Michel. 2008. *The Birth of Biopolitics: Lectures at the Collège de France 1978–79*. Translated by Graham Burchell. New York, NY: Palgrave Macmillan.

Fraser, Nancy and Axel Honneth. 2003. *Redistribution or Recognition: A Political-Philosophical Exchange*. London, England: Verso.

Gabler, Neal. 2016. "The Secret Shame of Middle-Class Americans." *The Atlantic*. Accessed June 12, 2016. https://www.theatlantic.com/magazine/archive/2016/05/my-secret-shame/476415/.

Gecas, Victor. 2000. "Value Identities, Self-Motives, and Social Movements." In *Self, Identity, and Social Movements*, edited by S. Stryker, T. J. Owens, and R. W. White, 93–109. Minneapolis, MN/London, England: University of Minneapolis Press.

Gerbaudo, Paulo. 2017. *The Mask and the Flag: Populism, Citizenism, and Global Protest*. Oxford, England: Oxford University Press.

Goffman, Erving. 1963. *Stigma*. London, England: Penguin.

Ha, Francis Inki. 1995. "Shame in Asian and Western Cultures." *The American Behavioral Scientist* 38, no. 8: 1114–31.

Hale, Sarah, Will Leggett, and Luke Martell, eds. 2004. *The Third Way and Beyond: Criticisms, Futures, and Alternatives*. Manchester, England: Manchester University Press.

Hochschild, Arlie R. 2016. *Strangers in Their Own Land. Anger and Mourning on the American Right*. New York, NY/London, England: The New Press.

———. 1983. *The Managed Heart: Commercialization of Human Feeling*. Berkeley, CA: University of California Press.

Hogg, Michael A. and Dominic Abrams. 1988. *Social Identifications: A Social Psychology of Intergroup Relations and Group Processes*. London, England/ New York, NY: Routledge.

Honneth, Axel. 1996. *The Struggle for Recognition. The Moral Grammar of Social Conflicts*, translated by Joel Anderson. Cambridge, MA: MIT Press.

Ignazi, Piero. 2003. "The Development of the Extreme Right at the End of the Century." In *Right-Wing Extremism in the Twenty-First Century*, edited by P. H. Merkl and L. Weinberg, 143–58. London, England: Frank Cass.

Illouz, Eva. 2007. *Cold Intimacies. The Making of Emotional Capitalism*. London, England: Polity Press.

James, William. 1890. *Principles of Psychology*. New York, NY: Holt Rinehart and Winston.

Lem, Winnie. 2013. "Citizenship, Migration and Formations of Class in Urban France." *Dialectical Anthropology* 37: 443–61.

Lipset, Stuart M. 1963. *Political Man*. Garden City, NY: Anchor Books.

Mäkinen, Katariina. 2012. *Becoming Valuable Selves*. Tampere, Finland: University of Tampere.

———. 2017. "Struggles of Citizenship and Class." *Sociological Review* 65: 218–34.

Markus, Hazel Rose and Shinobu Kitayama. 1991. "Culture and the Self: Implications for Cognition, Emotion, and Motivation." *Psychological Review* 98, no. 2: 224–53.

McGuigan, Jim. 2014. "The Neoliberal Self." *Culture Unbound* 6: 223–40.

Meltzer, Bernard N. and Gil Richard Musolf. 2002. "Resentment and Ressentiment." *Sociological Inquiry* 72: 240–55.

Miceli, Maria and Cristiano Castelfranchi. 2015. *Expectancy and Emotion*. Oxford, England: Oxford University Press.

Mudde, Cas. 2007. *Populist Radical Right Parties in Europe*. Cambridge, England: Cambridge University Press.

Neckel, Sighard. 1991. *Status und Scham: zur symbolischen Reproduktion sozialer Ungleichheit*. Frankfurt and Main, Germany: Campus Verlag.

Newman, Katherine S. 1998. *Falling From Grace: Downward Mobility In The Age Of Affluence*. New York, NY: Free Press.

Nietzsche, Friedrich. (1887) 2006. *On the Genealogy of Morality*. Translated by Carol Diethe. Cambridge, England: Cambridge University Press. All citations to the reprint edition.

Rawls, John. 1971. *A Theory of Justice*. Oxford, England: Clarendon Press.

Salmela, Mikko. 2009. "Authenticity and Occupational Emotions." In *Emotions, Ethics, and Authenticity*, edited by M. Salmela and V. Mayer, 133–51. *Consciousness and Emotion Book Series*. Amsterdam, Netherlands: John Benjamins.

Salmela, Mikko and Christian von Scheve. 2017. "Emotional Roots of Right-Wing Political Populism." *Social Science Information* 56, no. 4: 567–95.

———. 2018. "Emotional Dynamics of Right- and Left-Wing Political Populism." *Humanity and Society* 42, no. 4. DOI: http://journals.sagepub.com/doi/10.1177/0160597618802521.

Scheff, Thomas J. 1994. *Bloody Revenge. Emotions, Nationalism, and War*. Lincoln, NB: Authors Guild.

———. 2000. "Shame and the Social Bond: A Sociological Theory." *Sociological Theory* 84: 84–99.

Scheler, Max. (1915) 1994. *Ressentiment*. Translated by L. B. Coser and W. W. Holdheim. Milwaukee, WI: Marquette University Press.

Sennett, Richard. 2006. *The Culture of the New Capitalism*. New Haven, CT/London, England: Yale University Press.

Simiti, Marilena. 2016. "Rage and Protest: The Case of the Greek Indignant Movement." *Contention: The Multidisciplinary Journal of Social Protest* 3, no. 2: 33–50.

Stets, Jan. 2006. "Identity Theory and Emotions." In *Handbook of the Sociology of Emotions*, edited by J. Stets and J. Turner, 203–23. New York, NY: Springer.

Stets, Jan and Peter Burke. 2005. "New Directions in Identity Control Theory." *Advances in Group Processes* 21: 51–76.

Strawson, Peter. 1974. *Freedom and Resentment and Other Essays*. London, England: Methuen and Co Ltd.

Stryker, Sheldon. 1980. *Symbolic Interactionism: A Social Structural Version*. Menlo Park, CA: Benjamin/Cummings.

———. 2004. "Integrating Emotions into Identity Theory." *Advances in Group Processes* 21: 1–23.

Turner, Jonathan H. 2007. "Self, Emotions, and Extreme Violence: Extending Symbolic Interactionist Theorizing." *Symbolic Interaction* 30: 501–30.

Tyler, Imogen. 2013. *Revolting Subjects: Social Abjection and Resistance in Neoliberal Britain*. London, England/New York, NY: Zed Book.

Wacquant, Loïc. 2009. *Punishing the Poor*. Durham, NC: Duke University Press.

———. 2010. "Crafting the Neoliberal State: Workfare, Prisonfare, and Social Insecurity." *Sociological Forum* 25: 197–220.

Walker, Robert. 2014. *The Shame of Poverty*. New York, NY: Oxford University Press.

Chapter 10

Queering Shame

Julian Honkasalo

The political implications of shame and shaming have been widely discussed and debated within American, academic queer theory, not only in the context of queer responses to the AIDS crisis and queer critiques of heteronormativity, but also through the queer resistance to the politics of assimilation, military service, and the marriage institution (e.g., Bersani 1987; 1996; Warner 1999; Duggan 2003; Sedgwick 2003; Halberstam 2005; 2008; Muñoz 2009). Yet queer theorization of shame is often centered on a normative conception of anti-utopianism. The body of literature on queer anti-utopianism, anti-reproduction, and death is theoretically embedded in North American, academia centers, primarily on sexual desire (not gender transgression), and largely sidesteps forms of local resistance to biopolitics other than cruising for sex (Nirta 2017). Despite a rising number of theoretical, empirical, and autoethnographic studies in the field of transgender studies,[1] research on trans people's living conditions and experiences of shame is still largely missing from academic, philosophical discussions that take place outside the field of transgender studies. If and when shame is discussed in regard to transgender communities, it is often viewed as an experience related to an individual's gender dysphoria. Shame is thus often interpreted from a clinical point of view that isolates and reduces trans experiences of shame to individual psychology, rather than examining shame also as a political and relational phenomenon to be resisted by activism and community building.

Drawing on transgender and queer disability theorizing, a central aim of this chapter is to question and problematize cis-normativity, ableism, and whiteness as the main prisms through which gay shame has been interpreted in academic queer theory, and produce a more intersectional understanding of shame as a relational and political concept. Throughout the chapter, I examine how alliances between feminist queer disability (or crip) theory and transgender theory can expose intersecting forms of oppression as well as provide a richer understanding of strategies of community building as resistance to subordination. I proceed by first discussing shame, stigma, and AIDS activism in the context of cultural critic Lee Edelman's theorization of "queer negativity" and heterosexual "reproductive futurism." I will then contrast Edelman's conception of anti-futurism with José Muñoz's "queer utopianism" as well as Alison Kafer's and Eli Clare's notions of crip and trans futurity and community. I conclude by offering an interpretation of community building as a form of Foucauldian counter-power to biopolitics.

SUBVERSIVE SHAME AND THE CRITIQUE OF HETERONORMATIVE FUTURE

Lee Edelman's 1998 essay, "The Future is Kid Stuff: Queer Theory, Dis-identification, and the Death Drive," and his later book, *No Future: Queer Theory and the Death Drive* (2004), present one of the most powerful and yet controversial critiques of heteronormativity. Edelman utilizes the performative concept of "queer" to critique heterosexual, reproductive normativity and calls for an anti-social and anti-political turn in queer theory. According to Edelman, the "figural Child" or the child-as-future is the condition of possibility for heteronormative political, economic, social, and temporal order. In other words, American liberal democracy is conditioned upon an idealization of heterosexuality, which aims to secure the existence of future generations and future citizens. Edelman contends that this normative order of "reproductive futurism" is in fact based on the fantasy of achieving immortality through heterogenital reproduction:

> In its coercive universalization, the image of the Child, not to be confused with the lived experiences of any historical children, serves to regulate political discourse—to prescribe what will count as political discourse—by compelling such discourse to accede in advance to the reality of a collective future whose figurative status we are never permitted to acknowledge or address. (Edelman 2004, 11)

For Edelman, citizenship and "equal rights" are linked to sexual reproduction, leaving those who cannot, do not want to, or are expelled from participating in "reproductive futurism" as abject. As a response, Edelman calls for a queer negation of the social order, through a psychoanalytic embracement of the death drive. Queerness must therefore not just resist, but reject the very framework through which liberal democratic politics and the heteronormative social order receives its meaning: "[W]hat is queerest about us, queerest

within us, and queerest despite us is this willingness to insist intransitively—
to insist that the future stop here" (Edelman 2004, 31). In this type of theoretical arguing "queerness" is defined in opposition to "the future." Edelman's
theory is thus termed the "antisocial" or "antirelational" turn in queer theory
(Halberstam 2008).

Edelman's critique of heteronormativity must be placed in the historical
and geopolitical context of the tradition of thinkers such as Leo Bersani, who
in his 1987 essay, "Is the Rectum a Grave?" polemically and provocatively
spoke up against the Reagan administration's indifference and refusal to
take action at the peak of the 1980s AIDS-epidemic (Edelman 1998, 29).
According to the historian Sander Gilman, the shaming and stigmatization of
gay men as carriers and spreaders of HIV, the terming of AIDS as the "gay
plague,"[2] and the religious Right's myth according to which the AIDS-pan-
demic was God's punishment for sodomites, bears affinity with the common
anti-Semitic and Nazi narration of Jewish men as carriers of syphilis (Gilman
1991). For these reasons, Larry Kramer, one of the founders of the radical
HIV/AIDS activist group ACT UP,[3] compared the AIDS crisis to a holocaust:
"AIDS is our holocaust. Tens of thousands of our precious men are dying.
Soon it will be hundreds and thousands. AIDS is our holocaust and Reagan is
our Hitler. New York City is our Auschwitz" (Kramer 1995, 173).

As the AIDS crisis grew into a national epidemic in the United States,
urban gay and lesbian politics in the late 1980s and early 1990s became
shaped particularly in relation to the question of how to respond to shame,
shaming, stigma, illness, death, and, furthermore, the question of the relationship between the gay and lesbian community and the dominant American society (Gould 2002, 179). At the same time, AIDS became a pretext
for the mainstream heterosexual society and the mass media to discuss,
debate, and express opinions about the nature and morality of homosexual-
ity publicly. Bersani's question, "Should a homosexual be a good citizen?"
(Bersani 1995, 113), critiques assimilationist gay politics of his time and
claims that it fails to generate any real change to the existing social order
(Nirta 2017, 188–90). Hence, both Bersani and Edelman attempted to dis-
rupt the symbolic order of heteronormative reproductive futurism. As Edelman writes in his 1998 essay:

> Choosing to stand, as many of us do, outside the cycles of reproduction, choos-
> ing to stand, as we do, by the side of those living and dying each day with the
> complications of AIDS, we know the depiction of the societal lie that endlessly
> looks toward a future whose promise is always a day away. We can tell our-
> selves that with patience, with work, with generous contributions to lobbying
> groups, or generous participation in activist groups, or general doses of political
> savvy and electoral sophistication, the future will hold a place for us—a place

at the political table that won't have to come, as it were, at the cost of our place in the bed, or the bar, or the baths. But there are no *queers* in that future as there can be no future for queers. (Edelman 1998, 29; emphasis in the original)

Although Edelman does not discuss AIDS, activism, or shame in his 2004 book, *No Future*, his unique terminology, such as "negativity" and the figure of the "sinthomosexual,"[4] envisions (cis)male, gay, sexual praxis, precisely because of its disconnection with reproduction, as in itself subversive, coura-geous, and celebratory (Edelman 2004, 27; Edelman 2007, 471; cf. Bersani 1987, 222; Halberstam 2008). Hence, his work must be interpreted as a criti-cal response, not just to American, mainstream gay and lesbian politics, but also to the stigmatization, and active marginalization and subordination, of gay men. As Gould (2002) argues, by the 1990s ACT UP and other forms of militant queer organizations had contributed to the birth of a new, radical form of queerness. To be queer meant to be free of shame, no longer inter-ested in the acceptance by mainstream gay or straight society and finally, righteously furious about the AIDS crisis. Hence grief was turned into politi-cal rage (Gould 2002, 189–90).

FROM SHAME TO QUEER UTOPIANISM

Whereas queer theorists, such as Bersani (1987; 1996), Warner (1999), Sedgwick (2003), and Halberstam (2008) most notably, theorize the political potential of queering shame as opposed to taking on gay pride,[5] others, such as José Esteban Muñoz, challenge such a juxtaposition between shame and pride. In *Cruising Utopia—The Then and There of Queer Futurity* (2009), Muñoz argues that shame is a modality of emotional recognition and belong-ing. He regards Edelman's work as an important ethical critique of both heteronormativity as well as the de-radicalization of queerness. However, in stark opposition to Edelman, Muñoz argues that hope and critical utopianism are crucial for understanding the importance of queer political community building and the sustaining of communities (Muñoz 2009, 97). For Muñoz, queerness is an ideal that is visible in the horizon of the future, but not here yet. Overcoming entrapment in the present "here and now" through an imagi-nation of different and transgressive future collectivities is central to Muñoz's queer utopianism, particularly with respect to queer youths of color. Against Edelman, Muñoz states:

[A]ll children are not the privileged white babies to whom contemporary society caters . . . . Theories of queer temporality that fail to factor in the relational rel-evance of race and class merely reproduce a crypto-universal white gay man that is weirdly atemporal—which is to say a subject whose time is a restricted and restricting hollowed-out present free of the need for the challenge of imagining a futurity that exists beyond the self or the here and now. (Muñoz 2009, 94)

Muñoz draws on the 2003 murders of the black queer women, Shani Baraka (30) and her girlfriend Rayshon Holmes (31), as well as the black queer teen Sakia Gunn, all in Newark, New Jersey. In this way Muñoz draws attention away from white, gay, male cruising to the systemic violence faced by queer persons of color (Muñoz 2009, 94–95). Black and brown queer teens do not even get to live long enough to have the possibility of thinking about whether establishing a family is normative or subversive. Thus, the ability to choose anti-futurity is a privilege of urban, white, abled-bodied, (cis)gay men.

According to other critics of queer anti-futurism, by emphasizing negativity and the death drive as subversive, Edelman also compromises the radical potential of collective political agency for an individualistic account of queer. Jasbir K. Puar for instance criticizes American, academic queer theory for offering no understanding of the importance of black and brown queer resistances to Western hegemony and imperialism (Puar 2007, 211). According to Puar, the challenge for queer politics is not the rejection of reproductive futures, but instead "to understand how the biopolitics of regenerative capacity already demarcate racialized and sexualized statistical population aggregates as those in decay, destined for no future, based not upon whether they can produce children but on what capacities they can and cannot regenerate" (Puar 2007, 211).

Whereas Muñoz and Puar call for attention to the unquestioned whiteness of the queer subject in anti-futurist theorizations, queer disability and crip-theorists such as Robert McRuer (2017) and Alison Kafer (2013) call for a critical examination of how disability configures in theories of queer negativity and the anti-social turn. Kafer confronts Edelman by envisioning disability in time, and calls for thinking and imagining alternative "crip futures" (Kafer 2013, 25). She agrees with Edelman that, in the Western political tradition, heterosexual reproduction and the creation of fit future citizens has traditionally been the precondition for democratic citizenship. Whereas heterosexual marriage is valued as normal and celebratory, same sex marriage is conceived as a union of mere sexual desire without offspring. Hence, within the heteronormative and repronormative frameworks, queer people have no future (Kafer 2013, 32; see also McRuer 2017).

Inspired by both Muñoz and Puar, Kafer argues that Edelman's "queer negativity" presupposes a white, (cis)male, able-bodied subject, and neglects the histories and realities of disabled queers, black and brown people, and transgender people, whose lives have historically been conceived as degenerate, as passing on bad genetic heritage and as destined to no future

(Kafer 2013, 28–46). As eugenic ideology operated by enforcing aesthetic ideals of the psyche, body, and self by means of statistical standardization, state-funded projects of institutionalization and warehousing operated on the logic that these groups of people are genetically defect and unworthy of a future, not because they cannot reproduce but because if they reproduced, they would lead to the degeneration of the human race (Mitchell and Snyder 2006, 70–77). Kafer thus challenges Edelman's contention that a reproductive future is always already a heteronormative project. It is also anti-reproductive.

Some trans studies scholars, such as Caterina Nirta, take the argument further and contend that the problem with not only Edelman's "queer negativity," but also Muñoz's "queer utopianism" is that they both rely on a framework of futurity that is out of touch with the day-to-day, bodily, and material realities of persons who belong to transgender communities (Nirta 2017). Although the increased visibility of transgender persons in media and popular culture during the past five years has contributed to increased public awareness of these marginalized groups, the mass media representation often frames transgender persons through progressive narratives that associate equality with individual success whilst ignoring, in particular, the structural oppression that disproportionately limit the life chances and future perspectives of trans persons of color (Spade 2015; Gossett et al. 2017, xv–xxvi). In that sense, both "negativity" and "utopianism" are a form of luxury that not everyone can afford (Nirta 2017, 191). Imagination and utopianism alone are insufficient for addressing the daily experiences of shame, stigma, and marginalization by people who are disproportionately exposed to violence and oppression. Such people cannot afford to wait.[6]

SHAME AS A RELATIONAL AND
POLITICAL EXPERIENCE

Genderqueer, feminist, disability activist, and writer, Eli Clare, analyzes both shame and pride through lived, bodily experiences of multiple, intersecting forms of oppression. He characterizes shame as a raw bodily experience that fuels isolation. In his writings, such as the classic trans and queer disability studies text *Exile and Pride—Disability, Queerness, and Liberation* (1999), shame emerges as a complex experience rooted in a myriad of social norms that control, administer, and regulate the accessibility of space and the organization of time. In the essay "Resisting Shame—Making Our Bodies Home" (2010) Clare analyzes shame through autoethnographic descriptions of his love and passion for cycling in the Pacific Northwest as well as his experience of being a genderqueer person with cerebral palsy. He describes the joy of experiencing a synchronized continuity of his body and his bike: "I was inseparable from my bike, that pile of metal, rubber, and plastic; I was all pleasure and emotion" (Clare 2010, 8). However, this experience of joy and pleasure is interrupted as other members of the three-hundred-mile, group, cycling trip begin to ask Clare's partner questions about Clare's disability and telling him that Clare is very brave for taking part in the two-week trip. In this essay, "home" is a frequently occurring metaphor which denotes both the experience of bodily belonging and shame. Shame is characterized here as a response to ableist social norms.

What's wrong with me, *why won't they talk to me*? What's wrong with me? Wrong with me. Wrong." This too is home—this isolation, this desolation, this inconsolable sense of wrongness. (Clare 2010, 458; italics added for emphasis)

Clare's prose describes compulsory norms of ableism (see also McRuer 2006), classism, heteronormativity, and racism as structuring social relations. Oppression at worst "steals the body" from the person experiencing shame, leading to an "exile" both from one's own bodily sense of self as well as to a concrete exile from places where one can no longer live due to suffocating social norms or risks to safety, for instance. In Clare's writing bodily dysphoria and social anxiety are intertwined, and shame is inherently a relational and political experience. The metaphor of the body being stolen entails that the materiality and the felt sense of the body is relational and performative, rather than a static entity or object. How else could the felt sense of the body be "stolen"? The experience of shame that Clare describes in this context is so isolating that the body no longer feels "like a home." Shame is thus not simply a self-alienating, but also a world-alienating experience. Trans theorist Jay Prosser also describes shame as a state of not being at home in one's body: "[S]hame is a profound grappling with the self's location in the world—the feeling of being out of place, of not being at home in a given situation, combined with the desire to be at home." He continues by describing gender dysphoria–related shame as "existential": "Gender dysphoric shame develops not from what one does, but who one is" (Prosser 1998, 179).

In his writing, Clare acknowledges the influence of black feminism—the Combahee River Collective and Audre Lorde in particular—on his understanding of oppression and institutional power. In the 1977 "Combahee River Collective Statement," intersectionality is defined in the following way:

We are committed to struggling against racial, sexual, heterosexual, and class oppression, and see as our particular task the development of integrated analysis and practice based upon the fact that *the major systems of power are interlocking*. The synthesis of these oppressions creates the conditions of our lives. (CRCS, 15; italics added for emphasis)

The main idea is thus that multiple forms of interlocked oppressions generate overlapping modes of suffering (Taylor 2017, 4). Shame and isolation are some of them. Clare's intersectional analysis of queerness and disability, as well as his prosaic and poetic style of writing, distinguishes his theorization of shame and community from the theories of the anti-social turn in queer theory.

In order to grasp the political significance of Clare's description of the stolen body, it may be helpful to recall queer/crip feminist theorist Alison Kafer's "political/relational model of disability." Kafer in fact draws partly from Clare's work. She contrasts "the political/relational model of disability" with both the individualizing "medical model of disability," as well as the "social model of disability." According to the medical model, disability is conceptualized as a pathology, as something to be overcome or cured. This model thus often leaves systems of oppression intact (Kafer 2013, 7). The "social model of disability" on the other hand, is a critical response to the medical model and regards disability as being produced by social and political barriers that, for instance, restrict free movement and accessibility. Yet "the social model" often sidesteps or does not hold as theoretically significant the actual materiality of lived, bodily experiences of disability, including pain and shame. Kafer's "political/relational model of disability" entails that disability is a contested and contestable notion, "a site of questions rather than firm definitions," and furthermore that "disability is experienced in and through relationships; it does not occur in isolation" (Kafer 2013, 8–11; cf. Butler 2004, 39; see also Stryker, Currah, and Moore 2008).

Kafer's proposed "political/relational model of disability" is important and useful also for understanding the complexity of gendered experiences and expressions of shame. For instance, when the shame and isolation experienced by genderqueer and transgender persons is examined exclusively as a psychological symptom of bodily gender dysphoria, shame as a relational response to interlocking, ableist, cis-normative, and heteronormative systems of power is easily left intact.

It is important to note here that neither Kafer nor Clare opposes medical interventions as such. Rather, the point of their critiques are the ways in which such interventions are framed through discourses that propel normalization. In order to understand the complex power dynamics between medical experts, gate-keepers, and patients, and in order to locate points of tension, disruption, and resistance in the midst of normalizing power, both Kafer and Clare suggest that although the genealogies of disabled persons and trans persons, and the modes of biopolitical violence that disproportionately render these groups of people precarious, are not the same, their histories nevertheless bear a family resemblance (Clare 2017). There is a distant kinship in the patchwork and fragments of histories of lives rendered invisible, unintelligible, and unlivable. Thus Kafer contends:

[W]hat is needed, then, are critical attempts to trace the ways in which compulsory able-bodiedness/able-mindedness and compulsory heterosexuality *intertwine in the service of normativity*; to examine how terms such as "defective," "deviant," and "sick" have been used to justify discrimination towards people whose bodies, minds, desires, and practices differ from the unmarked norm; to speculate how norms of gendered behavior—proper masculinity and femininity—are based on *nondisabled bodies*; and to map potential points of connection among, and departure between, queer (and) disability activists. (Kafer 2013, 17; italics added for emphasis)

The implication of Kafer's and Clare's arguments then is that a nonintersectional discussion of shame that relies on identity-politics may conceal some of the genealogies of power that render various minorities and marginalized groups (such as disabled, transgender, poor, black, and elderly) as differently and disproportionately oppressed. It may also conceal multiple modes of suffering generated by shame. Consequently, the context-dependent differences in formulations and strategies of resistance to oppression and normalization risk becoming obscured. In contrast, analyzing the ways in which certain groups of people are controlled through disciplinary and biopolitical administering of their futures may at the same time reveal important strategies and points of resistance to biopolitics.

BUILDING A COMMUNITY, MAKING A HOME, AND RECLAIMING THE BODY

In Clare's writing, shame, as constitutive of the experience of estrangement from the body, is also intimately linked to insult and injury. He recalls the psychosomatic impact of hate speech and bullying, such as being called "retard, monkey, defect" in his childhood. The memories of verbal abuse are coupled with his memories as a survival of childhood sexual abuse. Clare writes that "[M]ore than once I wished to amputate my right arm so it would not shake. My shame was that bald [*sic*]" (Clare 2015, 151). At other times, his coping strategy to shame was an attempt to assimilate, to prove, to do the extraordinary, to become what he calls a "supercrip." And yet, he still did not receive justice and respect. The ethical and philosophical question for Clare then becomes whether or not one can respond to past and present insult by "listening to the body" (Clare 2015, 150–52). The question of how to not just cope with, but to resist shame is intertwined with the question of how to reclaim the stolen body in order to make it a home.

In his theorization of shame, Clare challenges and problematizes American progressive narratives and the ideal of the American dream that centers on individualism and identity, rather than social justice. For him, responding to shame does not mean overcoming or curing disability, or simply fixing what's "wrong." "The dominant story about disability should be about able-ism, not the inspirational supercrip crap, the believe it-or-not disability story" (Clare 2015, 3).

Inspired by Clare, feminist disability theorists, such as Kim Q. Hall, has termed the American, self-made-man discourse the "overcoming narrative" (Hall 2011, 3). Instead of just celebrating exceptional individuals who have accomplished great things in life *despite* disability, Clare argues for structural reform, including social and economic justice, such as universal healthcare, education, and accessible spaces. Resisting shame cannot and must not be the sole responsibility of isolated individuals because claiming an identity with pride is by itself not enough to resist structural forms of oppression, such as the uneven, biopolitical distribution of life chances. To this extent, Clare shares the premises of earlier, queer theoretical critiques of assimilationist politics, and attempts to become regarded as normal as possible at the cost of losing one's place *as* queer *and as* disabled in the future yet to come.

Like José Muñoz, Clare contends that shame can be resisted only by nourishing networks of belonging and by building minority communities that persist. Rather than theorizing shame in opposition to individual feelings of achievement and pride, or regarding shame as a negative concept with radical, subversive potential, both Clare and Muñoz conceptualize shame as importantly related to desire and the need to connect and to belong.[7] Clare's account of community thus shares a resemblance with Muñoz's utopian ideal of "queerness as collectivity" that "queerness is primarily about futurity and hope. That is to say that queerness is always in the horizon" (Muñoz 2009, 11). In Clare's writing too, community is in the horizon of an ethical way of life. He ends his essay, "Resisting Shame: Making Our Bodies Home," by stating the following:

> Let us figure out ways of naming bodily difference that fosters comfort and joy. Let us build a politics that holds space, safety, options, and shuts no one out. Let us pay attention to shame as an issue of health and wellness, community and family. Let us create the space to make our bodies home, filling our skin to its very edges. (Clare 2010, 465)

Clare's and Muñoz's responses to shame are thus very different from Edelman's notion of "no future" and the anti-social turn. Belonging is for Clare importantly related to memory and the search for a history that has been violently erased. History in this context is not limited to a personal story and a place to belong, but signifies also the histories of networks and communities, coupled with an envisioning of alternative futures (Clare 2017). Community-building and community development thus become important ways of articulating minority responses and resistances to isolation, stigma, shaming, violence, and oppression. According to Clare, communities offer at best a site for self-identification, self-determination, and the naming of bodily differences from within a framework of solidarity. Longing for a community is at the same time an articulation of the desire to belong and to find a home. In Clare's works, communities are depicted as relational networks and spaces that have the power to ease, perhaps even heal multiple modes of suffering. As he writes, in communities "[w]e get to lay down the exhausting work of explaining our bodies" (Clare 2010, 462).

The frequent use of the metaphor of the home is not entirely unproblematic though because it risks reinforcing, normalizing, and stabilizing migrational and territorial narratives of the home, familiar from colonialist discourse, whilst ignoring the permanent dislocation or exile of many queer and trans immigrants and refugees (Camminga 2091, 8). However, Clare also argues that communities are not just simple solutions to discrimination. Rather, they are points of departure from which to begin a movement.

As communities often have internal tensions, demarcations, and norms regulating who gets to belong and who does not, communities are not immune to power hierarchies and discrimination (462–63). Historically, although offering a refuge for many trans men and genderqueer butches, many American lesbian communities were exclusive toward what they perceived as "transsexuals" in contrast to gender transgressing queers. In addition, feminist spaces have excluded trans women and queer femmes (Lev 2007; Stone 1993; Stryker 2017, 129–38). Similarly, various, American, white, urban, trans, activist communities have ignored racialized, structural oppression and violence as disproportionately distributed across the poor, the working class, as well as black and brown bodies (Rivera 1973; Bailey 2013; Spade 2013; Ellison et al. 2017; Gossett et al. 2018).

Finally, building communities and acting collectively in order to reduce isolation and oppression has also shown to strengthen the connection between heightened visibility and heightened risk of violence, particularly for queer and trans persons of color (Boellstorff et al. 2014; Gossett et al. 2018). As B. Camminga states, "Transgender phenomena become visible in moments where there is an attempt to control what is perceived as transgressive behavior—an attempt to maintain normative boundaries, binary gender, and social hierarchy" (Camminga 2019, 4).[8]

CONCLUSION

The depiction of the trans community as existing on the hinges between a past that has been violently erased or neglected and a future not yet here is familiar already in early 1970s trans revolutionary speeches by members of the Street Transvestite Action Revolutionaries (STAR), such as Sylvia Rivera and Marsha P. Johnson, as well as early 1990s transgender liberation texts, such as Leslie Feinberg's *Transgender Liberation: A Movement Whose Time has Come* (1992).

I have argued above that the ways in which certain groups of people are controlled through disciplinary and biopolitical administering of temporality, reveals at the same time strategies and points of resistance to biopolitics. Based on my critical reading of Edelman's queer negativity as a response to the AIDS crisis, coupled with my analysis of Muñoz's, Kafer's, and Clare's notions of queer and crip futures, I contend that shame as a political experience is often rooted in (1) the disciplinary power over temporality and (2) biopolitical control over futurity. In the context of the refusal of HIV/AIDS-related health care for gay men, indefinite waiting and being caught in a temporal standstill are constitutive of disciplinary power over the temporality of the subject (Edelman 1998). For trans persons and disabled persons, compulsory sterilization as well as suspension of assisted reproductive technologies are a form of biopower over the population, and operates through an intervention into a reproductive future, that is, temporality at the level of the population (Kafer 2013). Hence power over temporality operates both at the level of the subject and the population, rendering queer, trans and crip persons disproportionately vulnerable to discrimination, violence, and death.

In this context, Clare's conception of community building can be thought of together with Foucault's notion of counter-power (*counter dispositif*). For Foucault, resistance as counter-power to both biopower and disciplinary power is always already caught in and shaped by networks of power (Foucault 1997, 167–68, 292). This way of framing resistance also means that strategies of resistance always reshape previously existing power networks. Foucault's account of resistance is pluralistic, that is, resistance inherently consists of multiple practices and struggles that are context dependent and local, challenging predominant discourses of power/knowledge in multiple ways (Oksala 2012, 49; cf. Foucault 1982, 780–81). This type of pluralistic conception of resistance has been called for also by trans feminist philosophers, such as Talia Bettcher, according to whom we need to rethink both trans oppression and resistance by recognizing the "multiplicity of trans worlds in relation to a multiplicity of dominant ones" (Bettcher 2014, 390). Hence, there are multiple "resistant gender practices," whereby the superficial questions of what counts as properly authentic trans experience, what is considered subversive and what is taken to be conformist, loses its meaning (Bettcher 2014, 403).

As Matthew Chin points out through an analysis of the queer and trans of color-community-accessibility activism, shared representations of struggle always shape the ways in which community and the future are imagined (Chin 2018). Research on community-based, activist initiatives complicate the simplistic, queer-theoretical logic of community as based *either* on identity-politics and recognition, *or* subversive anti-utopianism. In light of a plurality of imagined notions of the future, it is my contention that collective identity can be understood as a rhetorical, political, and context-dependent strategy of resistance to pathologizing regimes of truth.

Community building, organizing for social and economic justice, educating society, and pushing for policy reform can thus be seen as strategies of resistance—forms of counter-power—that takes momentum from the present moment without succumbing to an unrealistic utopianism or pessimism that is detached from the day-to-day lives of those persons most affected by interlocking forms of oppression. Kafer's and Clare's theorizations of community and the future provide not only an important correction to academic, queer-theoretical discussions of shame, but also constitute rich contributions for understanding how to resist shame without having to overcome one's disability, transgressive identity, or gender nonconformity.

NOTES

1. I follow here trans historian and feminist Susan Stryker's (2006) characterization of transgender studies as a Foucaultian critique of knowledge and power. In the introduction to the first volume of *The Transgender Studies Reader* (2006), Stryker writes that a central element of academic transgender studies is a Foucaultian questioning of knowledge and power, and a scholarly and rigorous inquiry into what Foucault, in *Society Must be Defended*, calls "subjugated knowledges" (Stryker 2006; Foucault 2004). Subjugated knowledges are historical contents that have been erased, and knowledges that have been disqualified, but which nevertheless form the prerequisite for critique. Transgender studies both critiques and re-narrates past truths and norms about gender. In this way, trans historians engage in the production of (de)subjugated knowledges.

2. In the early 1980s, HIV/AIDS was thought to be an immunodeficiency disease affecting only homosexual men. In 1981 The Center for Disease Control (CDC) reported of young gay men dying from Kaposi's sarcoma, a rare type of cancer normally found in elderly men. The symptoms of this cancer are highly visible lesions and blotches on the skin and the mouth. AIDS soon became termed the "gay plague" and "homosexual cancer" in mass media (Epstein 1996, 45–59). In a 1982 article, "Homosexual Plague Strikes New Victims," *Newsweek* warned that the "'homosexual plague' has started spilling over to the general population," that is, heterosexual persons (Newsweek, August 1982, 10).

3. ACT UP is the acronym for AIDS Coalition to Unleash Power. Although various AIDS activist organizations had emerged throughout the mid-1980s, ACT UP was officially established after a meeting at the New York City LGBT Center in 1987, as a radical, political response to the indifference of the U.S. government, the homophobia of the Christian right as well as the profit seeking by pharmaceutical companies. It is a queer, direct action advocacy movement fighting for the justice of

persons living with HIV. Protest strategies include theatrical die-ins, civil disobedience, disruptions and occupation of spaces. For more on the history of ACT UP, see Quimby and Freedman 1989, Epstein 1999, Gould 2002, and Bailey 2013, as well as The ACT UP/New York documents at New York Public Library, Manuscripts and Archives division: http://archives.nypl.org/mss/6148.

4. The "sinthomosexual" is a concept that Edelman uses to describe "those who reject the Child as the materialized emblem of the social relation and with it the concomitant mapping of the political in the space of reproductive futurism" (2007, 471).

5. Gay Shame is also the name of a direct action activist organization founded in NYC in 1998. The organization protests the commercialization and consumerism of Pride parades and calls for a social justice approach to tackle oppression of queer persons (Weiss 2008).

6. The National Coalition of Anti-Violence Programs (NCAVP) reported that 27 trans persons were killed in the United States during 2016. In 2017 the number was 26. By November 2018, the amount of reported unlawful deaths of trans persons was 369 (not including unreported deaths and deaths by suicide). The majority of the persons killed are trans women of color. In addition, due to discrimination, transgender people are at a heightened risk of unemployment, homelessness, and chronic illness in comparison to the general population.

7. In this context, it is also important to draw attention to the queer and trans theories that are influenced by anti-utopian queer theory and queer-negativity. Scholars in the fields of queer of color critique and critical race theory, such as Achille Mmbembe for instance, have termed the unequal distribution of life chances related to structural racism and colonialism as a form of "necropolitics" rather than biopolitics. The anthology *Queer Necropolitics* (2014) defines necropolitics as the power over who deserves to live and how certain lives must die (Haritaworn et al. 2014). In this context, queer temporality is centered on a normative conception of anti-utopianism. Another important critique of the whiteness of queer studies, which takes place in the context of "Afro-pessimism," is defined by Frank Wilderson III in the following way:

> The Afro-pessimists are theorists of Black positionality who share [Franz] Fanon's insistence that, though Blacks are indeed sentient beings, the structure of the entire world's semantic field—regardless of cultural and national discrepancies—'leaving' as Fanon would say, 'existence by the wayside'—is sutured by anti-Black solidarity. Unlike the solution oriented, interest-based, or hybridity-dependent scholarship so fashionable today, Afro-pessimism explores the meaning of Blackness not—in the first instance—as a variously and unconsciously interpellated identity or as a conscious social actor, but as a structural position of noncommunicability in the face of all other positions; this meaning is noncommunicable because, again, as a position, Blackness is predicated on modalities of accumulation and fungibility, not exploitation and alienation (Wildreson 2007, 58).

8. In opposition to David Valentine (2007) who theorizes the category of the "transgender community" as a social reality and a set of homogenic, shared practices similar to the idea of the concept of community inherent to the nation state, I argue that intersectional, feminist, trans, queer, and disability "community-building" become more understandable through Hannah Arendt's notion of collective action (*praxis*). As Arendt's most significant contribution to contemporary theorizations of

biopolitics is her focus on resistance and radical democratic foundings, communities as theorized in *The Origins of Totalitarianism* and *On Revolution* emerge where a plurality of unique and distinct agents act in concert to begin and found something new (Honkasalo 2018; Arendt 1958; 1990; Kalyvas 2008). Hence, the concept of community is not postulated beforehand by Arendt. Instead she asks how political communities have emerged through various, historical forms of acting-in-concert and in what ways have they attempted to create visions of alternative futures during times when none have existed.

REFERENCES

Arendt, Hannah. 1958. *The Origins of Totalitarianism*. New York, NY: Harcourt Brace Jovanovich.

———. 1990. *On Revolution*. London, England: Penguin.

Bailey, Marlon M. 2013. *Butch Queens in Pumps: Gender, Performance, and Ballroom Culture in Detroit*. Ann Arbor, MI: University of Michigan Press.

Bersani, Leo. 1989. *Is the Rectum a Grave? And Other Essays*. Chicago, IL: Chicago University Press.

———. 1996. *Homos*. Cambridge, MA: Harvard University Press.

Butler, Judith. 2004. *Undoing Gender*. London, England/New York, NY: Routledge.

Camminga, B. 2019. *Transgender Refugees and the Imagined South Africa. Bodies Over Borders and Borders over Bodies*. London, England: Palgrave MacMillan.

Chin, Matthew. 2018. "Making Queer and Trans of Color Counterpublics: Disability, Accessibility, and the Politics of Inclusion." *Affilia: Journal of Women and Social Work* 33, no. 1: 8–23.

Clare, Eli. 2015. *Exile and Pride. Disability, Queerness and Liberation*. 2nd edition. Durham, NC: Duke University Press.

———. 2010. "Resisting Shame: Making Our Bodies Home." *Seattle Journal for Social Justice* 8, no. 2: 456–65.

———. 2017. *Brilliant Imperfection. Grappling With Cure*. Durham, NC: Duke University Press.

Edelman, Lee. 2004. *No Future. Queer Theory and the Death Drive*. Durham, NC: Duke University Press.

———. 2007. "Ever After. History, Negativity and the Social." In *After Sex: On Writing Since Queer Theory*, edited by Janet Halley and Andrew Parker, 110–21. Durham, NC: Duke University Press, 2011.

Ellison, Treva, Kai M. Green, Matt Richardson, and C. Riley Snorton. 2017. "We Got Issues: Toward a Black Trans*/Studies." *TSQ* 4, no. 2: 162–69.

Epstein, Steven. 1998. *Impure Science—AIDS, Activism, and the Politics of Knowledge*. Berkley, CA: University of California Press.

Feinberg, Leslie. 1992. *Transgender Liberation: A Movement Whose Time has Come*. New York, NY: World View.

Gossett, Reina, Eric A. Stanley, and Johanna Burton. 2017. *Trap Door. Trans Cultural Production and the Politics of Visibility*. Cambridge, MA: MIT Press.

Gould, Deborah B. 2002. "Life During Wartime: Emotions and the Development of ACT UP." *Mobilizations: An International Journal* 7, no. 2: 177–200.

Halberstam, Judith [Jack]. 2005. "Shame and White Gay Masculinity." *Social Text 84–85* 23, no. 3–4: 219–33.

Hall, Kim Q., ed. 2011. *Feminist Disability Studies*. Bloomington, IN: Indiana University Press.

Haritaworn, Jin, ed. 2014. *Queer Necropolitics*. London, England/New York, NY: Routledge.

Honkasalo, Julian. 2018. "Superfluous Lives: An Arendtian Critique of Biopolitics." PhD diss., The New School for Social Research. Ann Arbor, MI: ProQuest.

Kalyvas, Adreas. 2008. *Democracy and the Politics of the Extraordinary. Max Weber, Carl Schmitt, and Hannah Arendt*. New York, NY: Cambridge University Press.

Kafer, Alison. 2013. *Feminist, Queer, Crip*. Bloomington, IN: Indiana University Press.

Kosofsky-Sedgwick, Eve. 2003. *Touching Feeling: Affect, Pedagogy, Performativity*. Durham, NC: Duke University Press.

Kramer, Larry. 1995. *Reports from the Holocaust: The Making of an AIDS Activist*. New York, NY: St. Martin's Press.

Lev, Arlene Istar. 2007. "Transgender Communities: Developing Identity Through Connection." In *Handbook of Counseling and Psychotherapy With Lesbian, Gay, Bisexual, and Transgender Clients*, 2nd edition, edited by Kathleen J. Biesche, Ruperto M. Perez, and Kurt A. DeBord, 147–75. Washington, DC: American Psychological Association.

McRuer, Robert. 2006. *Crip Theory: Cultural Signs of Queerness and Disability*. New York, NY: NYU Press.

———. 2017. "No Future for Crips: Disorderly Conduct in the New World Order, or, Disability Studies on the Verge of a Nervous Breakdown." In *Culture—Theory—Disability: Encounters Between Disability Studies and Cultural Studies*, edited by Anne Waldschmidt, Hanjo Berressem, and Moritz Ingwersen, 63–77. Bielefeld, Germany: Transcript-Verlag.

Mitchell, David and Sharon L. Snyder. 2006. *Cultural Locations of Disability*. Chicago, IL: University of Chicago Press.

———. 2015. *The Biopolitics of Disability: Neoliberalism, Ablenationalism, and Peripheral Embodiment*. Ann Arbor, MI: University of Michigan Press.

Muños, José Esteban. 2009. *Cruising Utopia: The Then and There of Queer Futurity*. New York, NY: NYU Press.

Nirta, Caterina. 2017. "Actualized Utopias: The Here and Now of Transgender." *Politics and Gender* 13: 181–208.

Prosser, Jay. 1998. *Second Skins: The Body Narratives of Transsexuality*. New York, NY: Columbia University Press.

Quimby, Ernest and Samuel R. Freedman. 1989. "Dynamics of Black Mobilization Against AIDS in New York, NY." *Social Problems* 36, no. 4: 403–15.

Salamon, Gayle. 2010. *Assuming a Body—Transgender and the Rhetoric of Materiality*. New York, NY: Columbia University Press.

Spade, Dean. 2013. "Intersectional Resistance and Law Reform." *Signs: Journal of Women in Culture and Society* 38, no. 4: 1031–55.

————. 2014. *Normal Life—Administrative Violence, Critical Trans Politics and the Limits of Law*. 2nd edition. Durham, NC: Duke University Press.

Stone, Sandy. 1991. "The Empire Strikes Back: A Post-Transsexual Manifesto." In *Body Guards: The Cultural Politics of Gender Ambiguity*, edited by Julia Epstein and Kristina Straub, 280–304. London/New York, NY: Routledge.

Stryker, Susan. 2017. *Transgender History: The Roots of Today's Revolution*. 2nd revised edition. New York, NY: Seal Press.

Stryker, Susan, Paisley Currah, and Lisa Jean Moore. 2008. "Introduction: Trans-, Trans, or Transgender?" *Women's Studies Quarterly* 36, no. 3/4: 11–22.

Stryker, Susan and Stephen Whittle. 2006. *The Transgender Studies Reader* 1st edition. London, England/New York, NY: Routledge.

Taylor, Keeanga-Yamahtta, ed. 2017. *How We Get Free. Black Feminism and The Combahee River Collective*. Chicago, IL: Haymark Books.

TCRCS. "The Combahee River Collective Statement." In *How We Get Free. Black Feminism and The Combahee River Collective*, edited by Keeanga-Yamahtta Taylor. Chicago, IL: Haymark Books.

Valentine, David. 2007. *Imagining Transgender: An Ethnography of a Category*. Durham, NC: Duke University Press.

Warner, Michael. 1999. *The Trouble With Normal. Sex, Politics and the Ethics of Queer Life*. Cambridge, MA: Harvard University Press.

Wildreson, Frank III. 2010. *Red, White and Black: Cinema and the Structure of U. S. Antagonisms*. Durham, NC: Duke University Press.

Index

About the Editor

Cecilea Mun (editor and author) is a Korean-American, disabled philosopher, and she is currently on the academic job market for a tenure-track research and teaching position. She was conferred in 2014 with a PhD in philosophy from Arizona State University, and was recently a visiting scholar at Cambridge University, England, the University of Edinburgh, Scotland, and the University of Sheffield, England. She is also the founding director of the Society for Philosophy of Emotion, and the founding editor-in-chief of the *Journal of Philosophy of Emotion*. She specializes in the philosophy of mind and emotion, epistemology, philosophy of science, and feminist philosophy. Her publications include, "Natural Kinds, Social Construction, and Ordinary Language: Clarifying the Crisis in the Science of Emotion" (2016), and "The Rationalities of Emotion" (2016), "Rationality through the Eyes of Shame: Oppression and Liberation via Emotion" (2019), "How Emotions Know" (2019), and she is currently completing her forthcoming monograph, *Interdisciplinary Foundations for the Science of Emotion: Unification without Consilience*. She has also presented her work in the United States and internationally, and you can read more about her in her interview by philosopher Shelley L. Tremain in *Dialogues on Disability*.

About the Contributors

Laura Candiotto (author) is an Italian philosopher, and an Alexander von Humboldt Foundation Senior Research Fellow at the Free University of Berlin, Institute of Philosophy. She is developing her project "Bond: Positive Emotions for Group Cognition." Her research merges her interests in the history of philosophy, especially Ancient Greek philosophy, and contemporary epistemology and philosophy of mind, especially the philosophy of emotions, and also discusses the social implications and the educative outcomes of the embodied, embedded, enactive, and extended model of cognition. Her publications include, "Purification through Emotions: The Role of Shame in Plato's *Sophist* 230b4-e5" (2018), "Boosting Cooperation: The Beneficial Function of Positive Emotions in Dialogical Inquiry" (2017), and two forthcoming edited volumes, *The Value of Emotions for Knowledge* and *Emotions in Plato.*

Lisa Cassidy (author) is an American philosopher and an associate professor of philosophy with the School of Humanities and Global Studies at Ramapo College of New Jersey, Mahwah, NJ. Her areas of specialization are ethics and feminism. Her publications include, "Thoughts on the Bioethics of Estranged Biological Kin" (2013) and "Reflections on Women Shopping and Women Sweatshopping: Consumerism as a Moral Dilemma" (2011).

Nancy Elsamanoudi (artist) is a Brooklyn-based artist and art critic for *The Villager* newspaper. She has an MFA in Painting and Drawing from the Pratt Institute. She has shown her work in New York, at various venues such as the Spring Break Art Show, the SFA Projects, and the Amos Eno Gallery. Her work was also recently featured in *Harper's Bazaar*, in the article "The Best Female Art Exhibitions to See this Fall" (2018). You can also read more about her in her *Artcritical* interview by the painter Natasha Wright, titled "A Space for Humor and Awkwardness: Nancy Elsamanoudi Discusses Her Work with Natasha Wright" (2018).

Daniel R. Herbert (author) is a British philosopher, an honorary research fellow at the University of Sheffield, England, and most recently a Visiting Humanities Fellow at the Universidad Popular Autonóma del Estado de Puebla, Mexico. His previous publications address the works of several figures from the history of philosophy, including Kant, Peirce, Bradley, and Sartre. He has delivered conference presentations on topics from the history of philosophy at international conferences in the United Kingdom, Germany, the Republic of Ireland, Mexico, and the United States.

Julian Honkasalo (author) is a Finnish doctor of gender studies and political scientist, and a postdoctoral scholar in gender studies at the University of Helsinki, Finland. Honkasalo received a PhD in gender studies from the University of Helsinki in 2016, and a second PhD in political science from The New School for Social Research in 2018, with a dissertation on Hannah Arendt as a critic of biopolitics. Honkasalo's current research project deals with the history of eugenics and transgender sterilization legislation, as well as the history of transgender activism.

Mariko Kikutani (author) is a Japanese psychologist and an assistant professor of cognitive psychology with the Department of Social Psychology at Tokyo University, Japan. She was awarded her PhD in 2009 from the University of Essex, England. Her research has focused on face perception, emotion recognition, psychology of language, and cross-cultural psychology. She is particularly interested in comparing emotion concepts across cultures.

Dolichan Kollareth (author) is an Indian psychologist and an assistant professor of social psychology with the Department of Social Sciences at Jnana-Deepa Vidyapeeth, Pune, India. He was awarded his PhD in 2017 from Boston College, Boston, MA. Kollareth also holds a BA in psychology, a BPh in Philosophy, a BTh in Theology, and an MA in Organizational Psychology. His publications include, "The English Word Disgust Has No Exact Translation in Hindi or Malayalam" (Kollareth and Russell 2016), and "Are Sacred Violations Disgusting?" (Kollareth and Russell 2018).

Alba Montes Sánchez (author) is a Spanish philosopher and an independent scholar. Recently, she completed a philosophy postdoctoral fellowship with the Department of Media, Cognition, and Communication at the Center for Subjectivity Research, University of Copenhagen, Denmark. She specializes in the philosophy of emotion and ethics, with an emphasis on the emotion of shame. Her publications include, "Unraveling the Meaning of Survivor Shame" (2018), "Feeling Ashamed of Myself Because of You" (2017), and "Pride, Shame, and Group Identification" (2016).

Matthew Rukgaber (author) is an American philosopher, an instructor and a visiting scholar at Eastern Connecticut State University, in Windham, CT, and an instructor at Gateway Community College, in New Haven, CT. His area of expertise is in the history of philosophy with a particular focus on the philosophy of Kant, Hegel, Nietzsche, phenomenology, and philosophical anthropology. He has written on a variety of topics, including the nature of space and time, the philosophy of religion, film philosophy, embodiment, and ethics. Some of his most recent publications are "Guns as Lies: A Kantian Criticism of the Supposed Right to Bear Arms" (2018), "Philosophical Anthropology and the Interpersonal Theory of the Affect of Shame" (2018), "Social Phenomenology, Mass-Society, and the Individual in Hegel and Heidegger" (2017), "Phenomenological Film Theory and Max Scheler's Personalist Aesthetics" (2016), and "The Asymmetry of Space: Kant's Absolute Theory of Space in 1768" (2016).

James A. Russell (author) is a Canadian-American psychologist and professor of psychology with the Department of Psychology, at Boston College, MA. His area of specialization is the psychology of emotions. He has worked on the nature of emotion concepts, the structure of self-reported emotions, children's developing understanding of emotion, and the perception of emotion from facial expression. He has developed a circumplex model of affect and a psychological constructionist account of emotion. A seminal article is "Core Affect and the Psychological Construction of Emotion" (2003).

Mikko Salmela (author) is a Finnish philosopher, and a senior researcher and adjunct professor of practical philosophy with the Center for the Philosophy of the Social Sciences, Faculty of Social Sciences, at the University of Helsinki, Finland. He is a philosopher who specializes in empirically oriented and interdisciplinary emotion research, with recent focus on collective emotions and their functions in social groups, emotions in disciplinary and interdisciplinary interaction, and the role of emotions in populist political movements. His recent publications include "Emotional Roots of Right-Wing Political Populism" (2017) and "Emotional Dynamics of Right- and Left-Wing Political Populism" (2018), both coauthored with Christian von Scheve, and an edited volume "Collective Emotions: Perspectives from Philosophy, Psychology, and Sociology" (2014), also with von Scheve.